Front Porch Stories

Front Porch Stories

Tales of the Hendry Family—Pioneers in
Florida's Peace River Basin

To Carole—

*Save a "spot" for me on your
front porch!*

Ella Kathryn Hendry

With sketches by the author and other
family members, historical photographs,
and stories written by F. A. Hendry

*Kathryn Sandige
(neé Ella Kathryn Hendry)*

Jonathan Wilson Sandige Publications

Manufactured in the United States of America

Library of Congress Catalog Card Number: 99-75769
ISBN: 1-881539-23-7
Book design and production by Tabby House
Cover design: Osprey Design Systems
Cover photos, courtesy Florida Archives: (top) F. A. Hendry and his wife, Ardeline, and (bottom), F. A. Hendry's home in Fort Thompson.

Permission has been granted by:
The Unity School of Christianity to print the "Prayer of Faith" by Hannah More Kohaus; The University Press of Florida for use of excerpts from James LaFayette Glenn's *My Work Among the Seminoles*; The Florida Bureau of Archives and Records Management for use of photographs on pages 24, 25, 81, 98, 104, 128, 169, 177; The Sebring Historical Society for material in Appendix A; The Southwest Florida Historical Society for permission to quote from Karl Grismer's, *The Story of Fort Myers;* The Englewood Historical Society and artist Patti Middleton for use of two previously published sketches; Hubert "Hugh" Hendry, for use of sketches; Sara Nell Gran, for use of family photographs and material from Hendry family reunion booklet; The *Fort Myers News-Press,* and the *Pensacola NewsJournal* for use of quoted material; and *Power and Motoryacht* magazine, for use reprinting of "The Reef Doctor" in "Harold Hudson—Marine Scientist"; the National Geographic Society; *Gulfwatch;* Florida Department of Education for material from *Florida: A Guide to the Southernmost State;* Alberta Barnes, *Yesterday's Fort Myers;* Jean Allin, Genie Plus, Inc., *John and William, sons of Robert Hendry,* compiled by Spessard Stone; Michele Wehrwein Albion, curator, Edison-Ford Winter Estates; University of Miami Press, *Unknown Florida;* Alex Shounatoff, *Florida Ramble;* World Book Publishing, "Thomas Edison."

Jonathan Wilson Sandige Publications
P.O. Box 2594
Port Charlotte, FL 33949

Dedication

I dedicate this book to my brother, Harry F. Hendry, Jr., who was born October 2, 1923. Harry was an unusually mature young man, full of ideals and promise. As a hobby, he designed and made model airplanes and along with our younger brother, Bill, spent many hours flying models and designing new ones to fit their engines. After graduation from Fort Myers High School, he worked all summer to help with his college tuition. He attended the Citadel until World War II was declared. Being very patriotic, he volunteered. He had hoped to become a pilot because of his intense interest in flying. However, Harry's eyesight was too poor to become a pilot—he had a fifty-foot blind spot in the middle of his vision—and so he went into the artillery.

Harry Hendry

Shortly before his death in the Battle of the Bulge, this article appeared in the *Stars and Stripes:*

> **AA Gun Without Sights Knocks Out Nazi Plane With the Third Army**
>
> The sights on the 40mm Bofors gun in Btry C had just been removed during the daily maintenance period when 12 FW190s swept in for a strafing run.
>
> As the battery's other guns opened fire, Cpl. Harry F. Hendry, of Gainesville, Florida, and Cpl. Alvin E. Pinkard of Center, Miss., leaped into the seats of their guns and firing without forward area sights or fire-direction equipment, scored a direct hit. The men explained that they watched the tracers and made necessary corrections.

His death was especially tragic because his entire regiment was placed in the infantry in order to stop the Nazi troops.

Had Harry lived, he would have done far more than write a book like this, but I humbly submit this book as a token of my love and gratitude to him for having given his life so that our country could continue to be the land of the free and the home of the brave.

Acknowledgments

Larry Wiggins

The three people whose pictures appear on this page are entitled to special mention for providing me with material and support beyond the call of duty. They are Sara Nell Gran, Larry Wiggins and Lloyd Hendry. Not only have they helped me, but they have done everything possible to preserve and carry on the Hendry name and traditions. Lloyd established family reunions, which have kept the Hendrys together.

I want to thank my team of helpers who have worked so hard to help me produce this book: Charlie Briggs, Juanita Beresford-Redman, Dora Smith, the Bob Lefebvre family, and Linda and Jim Salisbury. It is important that they know how very much I appreciate their special help.

Then there was my son, Jon, who was a source of strength and cheer in troubled times. His belief in me never wavered, but his unexpected death has left a void that cannot be filled.

Sara Nell Gran

I am especially grateful to the staffs of the Elsie Quirk Public Library: Jane Feldmann, Mary Berryhill, and Helen Burns. At the Englewood Public Library: Janus Chambers, Lane Bigelow, and Reggie Young. At the Murdock Public Library: Linda Johnson, Angie Patteson, Candice Petterson, Lois Harasek, Pat Martin, Patty Raisch, and Bill McDonald. At the Port Charlotte Public Library: Sharon Martin, Bob Kelly and Marrlysse Silcox, Patty Della Donna, and Joan Siemonski. And at the Punta Gorda Public Library: Jay Carter, Kate Korder, Judy Ruple, Judee Shoemaker, Sylvia Kennedy and Dorothy Wanrow.

There are my always loyal and dear friends who have supported me by listening to my stories, offering suggestions, and helping me in a million ways too numerous to mention. Among those whom I cherish are Jean Dean, Peggy Albrecht, and Mary Hanson (now deceased).

Other helpful persons are Spessard Stone, Barbara Cummings, Jean Allin, and Patti Middleton. These people, in

Lloyd Gould Hendry
Photo courtesy of Spessard Stone.

spite of their heavy schedules took time to offer help and encouragement.

I would especially like to thank the *Fort Myers News-Press* for opening up its files and allowing me to use many wonderful stories as resources. I feel fortunate in having been assisted by Carolyn Talcott, the librarian, who is devoted to preserving the newspaper's historical documents.

I thank the Fort Myers Historical Society, the Sebring Historical Society, and the Charlotte County Historical Society for their cooperation and interest.

I am proud to include stories of my cousins, and their ideas and suggestions: Charles Hudson, Harold Hudson, Hubert Hendry, Herbert Rosser, Helen Laidlaw, William W. Hendry, Jr., and Julia Pate.

A special thanks to Larry Wiggins who has spent many years searching out old records and microfilm for stories written by our great-grandfather. Almost all of F. A. Hendry's stories and records used in this book have been due to his resourcefulness and diligence. His service to the family is greatly appreciated.

Contents

Preface

What a pleasure it is to remember the old-timers rocking on the front porch on an afternoon or evening, fanning to keep cool and enjoying each other's tales. Each person tried to top the last tale told until a subject was exhausted, then they'd invent a new topic to discuss. As a little girl I was called "little pitcher ears," because I avidly listened and began to repeat the stories.

Florida was a true wilderness to be conquered, and, at the same time, to be enjoyed by the pioneers who settled here many years ago. My family—the Hendrys—were among them and left their mark on Southwest Florida. Hendry County was named in honor of my great-grandfather, Capt. Francis Asbury "Berry" Hendry. The city of LaBelle was named for his daughters, and he was instrumental in giving Lee County its name in 1887, after helping separate it from Monroe County to the south and east. Captain Hendry also was known as an honest, fair man and won the confidence of the Seminoles.

Members of the Hendry family knew Thomas Edison and other notable early residents of Fort Myers, and even some notorious ones, such as the remnants of Jesse James's gang.

The Hendrys were ranchers, owners of large tracts of land (great portions of present-day Cape Coral), teachers, school superintendents, state senators and representatives. We could wear out rocking chairs with storytelling about the pioneers and ancestors.

But there are other tales to be told, even though most houses now lack front porches. These are the stories of Florida during the early part of this century, when I was a child growing up, before the Fort Myers area became "tamed" by developers and before mosquito control and air conditioning.

I take upon myself the mantle of being "one of the aged" to pass along what it was like to live in this area more than sixty years ago. Like those who have preceded me, my memories are rich, almost as rich as the Florida muck ground that nourished us. It is this richness that I want to preserve for those who come after me—before Florida is changed forever. I feel that a time will come when others will seek information about how the early implants lived and coped in this special environment in the Peace River basin and Gulf Coast.

My stories share what daily life was like many years ago, including history and lore. In the late 1800s settlers lived in palm-thatched houses alongside rivers. The houses had no windows and only one open door. The residents sat upon stumps. They cooked over open fires and drew water from the nearby river with buckets. It would appear that they were dumped off some riverboat and took root right where they landed.

Many of the pioneers were well-educated, some were outlaws, but almost all of them had the call for adventure and felt fortunate to have this opportunity a new beginning afforded them. Among them were world travelers, military personnel, farmers, and teachers.

What knowledge they possessed was shared just as eagerly as the food and the offer of a helping hand. Everyone seemed to be a part of something wonderful and participated enthusiastically toward making it a success. The pioneer spirit was just as contagious as any disease. It permeated the air.

There was plenty of room for all, enough food, and a feeling of security in knowing that if one should need help, it was there for the asking. Most of the people were self-reliant and their children were rugged individuals who became the backbone of our state. Only a few were wealthy or had more than was needed to survive.

Tolerance was practiced by most folks so there was no great need for strict law enforcement. However, hate and greed were present. Sometimes houses were burned in order to run undesirables out. What little law there was seemed to be obeyed by the vast majority. There were times, however, when the settlers would take the law into their own hands if enough concerned citizens came forward to protest. In such cases a vigilante type of law was administered with or without the blessing of a sheriff.

Life moved at a slower pace, but things did move, as they do today, because of the movers and shakers. There was always a cohesiveness of purpose to get necessary things accomplished (in spite of little money or investment). Such things included bringing a railroad southward and digging canals to free up more land for the ever-arriving newcomers.

I have included some Hendry family history, stories my parents told, and my recollections of growing up on Pine Island and coastal Lee County. Through the years I have collected an extensive library of clippings, books, and pamphlets on the Hendry family. The *Fort Myers News-Press* has been a particularly valuable source of information through its stories and photographs. I will be happy to share my research with you and will always appreciate new contributions.

My great-grandfather's words are very timely. In 1907 he wrote in a letter to the editor that he enjoyed reading the writings of old-timers: "It is hard for the present generation to realize the vicissitudes, trials, and inconveniences through which the old-timers have passed. It is those old-timers who can fully realize the marvelous changes during the long period of a half century."

Almost another century has passed since he reflected on his "Fifty-seven Years in Grand Old Florida." And just as he wanted to share stories from those times so that those to come after him would understand the draining of the Everglades, the revolutionary new method of transportation—trains—and what it was like for Florida Confederates to be "penned in" by Federal blockade, so am I compelled to share stories from the early part of this century.

In relating these tales, I hope no one will take offense should they still be living, and I mean no disrespect to the dead, who can neither condemn or condone. Folklore sometimes clashes with reality; however, much of it is housed with truth.

I invite you to pull up a rocking chair.

ELLA KATHRYN HENDRY

Section One

Front porch stories of the Hendry
family and girlhood memories of
Southwest Florida

Hendry Family Tree, as related to names found in Front Porch Stories

Robert Hendry, Sr. ⊤⊤ (married Ann Lee, 9 children)
1752-1830 | 1752-1834

    William Hendry ⊤⊤ (m. Nancy McFail, 11 children)
     1783-1840 | 1786-1840

       James Edward Hendry ⊤⊤ (m. Lydia Carlton, 11 children)
        1808-1852 | 1812-1898

          Francis Asbury Hendry ⊤⊤ (m. Ardeline Ross Lanier, 11 children)
           1833-1917 | 1835-1917

           Louis Asbury Hendry —⊤— (m. Ella Frierson: 9 children)
             1856-1928 | 1862-1904

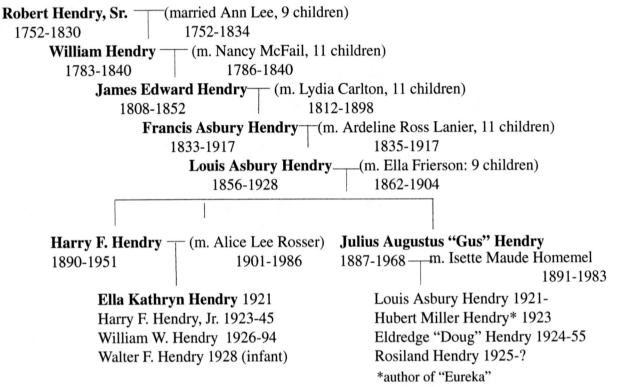

Harry F. Hendry ⊤⊤ (m. Alice Lee Rosser)   **Julius Augustus "Gus" Hendry**
1890-1951 | 1901-1986   1887-1968 ⊤⊤ m. Isette Maude Homemel
                                                                        1891-1983

Ella Kathryn Hendry 1921   Louis Asbury Hendry 1921-
Harry F. Hendry, Jr. 1923-45   Hubert Miller Hendry* 1923
William W. Hendry 1926-94   Eldredge "Doug" Hendry 1924-55
Walter F. Hendry 1928 (infant)   Rosiland Hendry 1925-?
                                             *author of "Eureka"

"The Reef Doctor" was written by Charles Hudson, brother of Harold Hudson, who are cousins of Ella Kathryn Hendry on her mother's side of the family.

"Christmas in Southwest Florida" was written by Julia Pate, a daughter of Julia Isabel Hendry and Arthur William Kelly, Sr.

From Scotland to Scout

The Hendry family history can be traced to a clan in Scotland. Three Hendry brothers came to America about 1770, but we can only document one of the brothers. The family genealogy, *John and William, Sons of Robert Hendry*, by Spessard Stone, traces two brothers, John and William, the sons of Robert Hendry (1752-1830) and his wife, Ann Lee Hendry. Robert and Ann had nine children. My family traces its lineage to William.

One family account states that after John and William were defeated at Culloden Moor in 1746, the McFail clan was punished by deportation to North Carolina, where members were given land grants. Their Scottish heritage was always important to them.

It is here that we pick up the Hendrys in 1770. The Bible lists "begets after begets," but I think I'll simply state that ten generations back, our forefathers attacked the wilderness with gusto.

The Hendry clan provided seven men for service during the Revolutionary War. My great-great-great-great-grandfather, Robert Hendry, proudly fought under Lt. Col. Henry "Light-Horse Harry" Lee, father of Robert E. Lee. Light-Horse Harry was a key figure in George Washington's army, and commanded "Lee's Legions" during the Revolutionary War, and was present at the surrender of the British at Yorktown on October 19, 1781. In 1794 Light Horse Harry's troops were sent by President George Washington to end the Whiskey Rebellion. Robert Hendry went on this excursion.

Following the Revolutionary War, records indicate that the Robert Hendry family migrated from North Carolina to South Carolina, then to Georgia. While in North Carolina, William was born to Robert and Ann Hendry in 1783. He married Nancy McFail and she gave birth to James Edward Hendry (my great-great-grandfather), in 1808, in Liberty, Georgia. In 1851 James and his wife, Lydia Carlton, migrated to the Upper Peace River Territory, about twenty-two miles east of Tampa, in an ox-drawn covered wagon.

James Hendry returned to Georgia to pick up his cattle, but contracted diphtheria along the way and died January 3, 1852, at Taylors Creek in Thomasville, Georgia. He was buried in the Hendry Cemetery, about three miles east of Southeast Ochlocknee, Thomas County, Georgia.

My great-grandfather, Francis Asbury Hendry (called both "Scout" and "Berry"), was born in 1833 in Thomas County. He was a scout, a senator, a congressman, mayor, cattleman, and Indian protector. He lived in various places in Florida, including Fort Meade, and Hendry County was named for him.

My grandfather, Louis A. Hendry, was born in 1856 in Fort Meade. During his career he owned a resort hotel, was a lawyer, a mayor, and a congressman. His home was Fort Myers. He married Ella Frierson, and they were the parents of my father, Harry F. Hendry (1890–1951), and Julius Augustus "Gus" Hendry (1887–1983). Harry married Alice Lee Rosser (1901–1986). He was a teacher on Marco Island, a school superintendent of Lee County, and college professor at Stetson University. I, Ella Kathryn, was the firstborn, followed by Harry F. Hendry, Jr., William W. Hendry, and Walter F. Hendry.

Uncle Gus was a political advisor, a special government investigator, and a great storyteller. He and his wife, Maude, were the parents of four children, including Louis A. Hendry, a renowned California caterer, Hubert Miller Hendry, an artist and author of "Eureka," Eldredge "Doug" Hendry, sheriff of Collier County in the fifties, sixties, and seventies, and Rosiland Hendry.

The Lord must have cooperated when he told his people to go forth and multiply. Back when I was a child, I could proudly boast that almost everyone in the state of Florida was related to the Hendry family in some way. The Lord rewarded one of our members in a special way.

According to Spessard Stone:

> The old Hendry plantation is now a part of the U.S. Army Fort Stewart. The old tombstones were removed from the Plantation cemetery in 1944 to the Methodist Cemetery at Taylors Creek. The church and town of Taylors Creek were razed. When the work of removing the tombstones began, it was found that the marker of Robert Hendry's grave had been gently picked up by the limbs of a growing oak, which over the years had elevated the stone to a distance of about fifteen feet above the ground.

We have always thought the Lord did what he could to help him on the journey to Heaven.

* * *

At bedtime, when my siblings and I were little, my father, Harry F. Hendry, would sit on our bedside and tell us stories about our family and other events. We always looked forward to these stories. The anecdotes he told about the family were usually true; however, we realized he could have elaborated on them to make them more interesting.

Francis Asbury Hendry

Francis "Berry" Asbury Hendry, also often called "Scout," was named for Francis Asbury, a pioneer Methodist preacher. When the Methodist Episcopal Church was organized at the Christmas Conference in Baltimore in 1784, Reverend Asbury and Thomas Coke were elected as the church's first bishops. The Methodist Episcopal Church is still the church of family choice.

F. A. "Berry" Hendry

F. A. Hendry became a scout during the Third Seminole War. Berry was unhappy about the way he had to fight the Indians. He felt that he should be allowed to combat them the way they did him. He resented losing any of his troops and went to great lengths to protect them. The Indians already knew about his bravery and admired him for it. The following family story is an example of how he endeared himself to the Seminoles even more.

The Seminoles were excellent ambush fighters. They seemed to attack without warning and were constantly a threat to Captain Hendry's men.

Berry "Scout" Hendry had an idea. He mulled the idea over and over in his head. How could it go wrong? He was going to fight fire with fire. He might end up in trouble, but it was worth it to save his men. So after much agonizing, he made plans to carry out his decision. He did not share it with anyone, but began to plan his strategy.

He called in several dependable soldiers and explained what he wanted them to help him do. They were to take work details out into the woods and using crosscut saws, cut down as many trees as would be needed. The trees were to be brought to a designated spot by oxen. There the logs would be stacked end on end and secured so that they resembled a giant haystack or a small pyramid.

The men sawed down the trees. Oxen dragged them to the selected site. Then the soldiers began to build an enormous pyramid-like structure.

Berry knew that the Indians were watching and keeping tabs on what was going on. But he kept his own counsel and proceeded with his plans.

When the structure was large enough and his instructions were carried out as to its density and height, he had the men gather limbs and underbrush. They were to place them in sheltered spots where his men could stay in ambush.

Finally, when everything was ready, he called his men together. Just before the sunset they were to hide in ambush until he gave them the signal to shoot.

At sunset, his men took their assigned places. He had one of his lieutenants accompany him over to the tower. They threw kerosene around its base and set the brush afire. The pine was full of pitch so it burned quickly and brightly from the brush. His men were far enough away that they did not feel the heat, but the fire began to light up the woods. The smoke was thick, but there was enough wind to carry it upward.

Berry and his lieutenant joined ranks with their men and waited.

Author's sketch of the block house of old Fort Myers.

It was very quiet for some time, but soon the curiosity of the Indians got the better of them. They came out in the night to see the fire and wonder at its purpose. They did not have long to wait. The men in ambush opened fire and several Indians were killed. Quite a few were captured. Captain Hendry's plan had accomplished his goal. The band of Indians he had been fighting were subdued—beaten by their own method of fighting.

The Seminoles respected him for the cunning way he fought. He did not expose his men if at all possible. He offered the Indians protection and provided them with an opportunity to win fairly and squarely.

It was rumored that Captain Hendry was nearly court-martialed for his unorthodox tactics, but he was able to walk away from that skirmish with pride and the mantle of honor bestowed on him by the Indians.

Later on, when the South entered the Civil War, Capt. Berry Hendry had his own company, Company A, First Battalion, Florida Special Cavalry, which was attached to Charles J. Munnerlyn's Battalion. This was a special unit established for the purpose of protecting the settlers, and also for herding cattle for the Confederate military.

The fort at Fort Myers fell into Union hands, and he clashed with their troops on more than one occasion. He was trying to round up cattle for the Confederacy, while the troops at Fort Myers were attempting to do the same thing for the Union. The Yankees would ship the cattle to Key West, another Union stronghold. Captain Hendry served with honor throughout the Civil War.

Hendry Becomes First Cattle King

After he married Ardeline Lanier in 1852, Captain Hendry moved from his family's home in Hillsborough County, near Tampa, to Fort Meade on the Peace River, where he established his herd. In 1870, Captain Hendry moved more than 12,000 head of cattle to pasture in prairies along the Caloosahatchee River. Ten years later Hendry purchased property, which was the site of Fort Thompson, and moved his cattle there to pasture them on the prairies of the old fort. Fort Thompson was located on the Caloosahatchee River east of Lake Okeechobee, about halfway across the state of Florida. There were a series of forts along the Peace and Caloosahatchee rivers and in the Everglades.

With the land at Fort Thompson came the old fort compound, which had been abandoned before 1856. The fort had been damaged by a flood, and its structures, made of softwood and with thatched roofs, was considered a fire hazard. The Indians had targeted it for burning and had attempted to set it on fire several times. The Hendry home became the Goodno Hotel (also known as the Thompson Park Hotel) when Captain Hendry began to sell off some of his extensive holdings.

A sketch by the author of the Hendry home at Fort Thompson.

Captain Hendry discovered the Fort Myers area in 1854 when he carried dispatches there for the Army. After moving his cattle to Fort Thompson, he shipped cattle from Punta Rassa, south of Fort Myers near the present causeway to Sanibel Island, to Cuba. The settlers bought food and merchandise that came on the ships. Once the cargo was sold, the ships were reloaded with cattle. The cattlemen were paid in gold coins, and rumor had it that gold coins were so plentiful then that children were allowed to play with them.

By 1880 Captain Hendry's herd numbered 50,000. As a result he is considered by many to be Florida's "First Cattle King." He

moved his family to Fort Myers in 1870, but kept and maintained the Fort Thompson ranch. In 1889 he sold his home in Fort Myers and moved back to the ranch in Fort Thompson.

Fort Thompson

The family and ranch staff were housed in the Hendry House. The family lived upstairs; the cowhands, downstairs. Everyone ate in the large dining room downstairs and because the family owned cattle, steak was always on the breakfast menu. There was plenty of room to entertain and the captain became known for his hospitality. The Hendrys kept their doors open to all and entertained hundreds of guests.

Meanwhile, F. A. sold his Fort Myers home to my grandfather, Louis A. Hendry, who converted it into a hotel by adding fourteen rooms. Louis's next house was built at Lee and Second streets. Eventually, Louis built a house on the Caloosahatchee River. That house seemed very large when I visited it as a seven-year-old child.

The F. A. Hendry family lived in the Fort Thompson home until F. A. Hendry built a new home in LaBelle—considered to be one of the finest in southwest Florida. Family pictures of the old house were taken just before it was demolished. These pictures show the abandoned house in a state of neglect and ruin. Evidently it was too far gone to consider repairing it. With his cattle business thriving, he devoted himself to serving the state. He served in both the Florida Senate and House.

There were two very interesting places along the upper Caloosahatchee River about which little has been written. Both places

Above: An early photo of the Fort Thompson house showing family members gathered on the front porch.

Below: The Hendry home in La Belle showing F. A. Hendry standing on the porch. Photos courtesy of State Bureau of Archives and Records Management.

were destroyed when the Hamilton Disston drainage operations cut a canal from Lake Flirt through Lake Bennett and Lake Hicpochee. This diverted the water from the falls and eliminated "Rope Bend." Lake Flirt was left high and dry. This is now the location of Port LaBelle.

The first was Rope Bend. There the river made a complete **S**. According to historian Karl H. Grismer, "The pilots had to tie their steamers to a tree before the turn could be made because such warping was required at this tricky place in the river. It became known as Rope Bend."

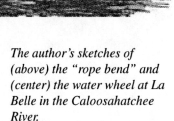

The author's sketches of (above) the "rope bend" and (center) the water wheel at La Belle in the Caloosahatchee River.

Before the dredgers began to correct this, the upper Caloosahatchee River was considered one of the world's most beautiful rivers. There were great live oaks, willows, hickories, and magnolias growing along side it. Their branches of-

ten extended out and over the river. Sabal palms grew among these trees and often extended over the banks. The custard apple trees bore delicious fruits and the moon flowers bloomed profusely among the trees.

Much of this was destroyed when the channel was widened and deepened. The beautiful trees were cut down and removed from the banks so that there was no longer any overhang.

When the channel was deepened, the river could handle more water and soon the humus from the Everglades darkened it. It was no longer clear, but had a light-colored sandy bottom.

The cutting of the channel and clearing the river for easy navigation caused the destruction of both "Rope Bend" and the water wheel.

The second site was a grist mill at Berry Hendry's ranch. It was located at a spot where there was a drop of

Photo of F. A. Hendry on horse. Courtesy of State Bureau of Archives and Record Management.

The Louis Asbury Hendry family. Left to right, back row, standing: Daisy Hendry Mayer, Gus Hendry, Ruby Hendry Parnell, Harry F. Hendry, John Hendry and Harry R. Knight. Middle row: Richard Knight, Bernard Mayer, "Miss Mary" Apthorp Hendry, Louis A. Hendry, Paul Hendry, Mildred Hendry Wells Crotteau, Josephine "Josie" Hendry Knight. Front, seated: Thelma Mayer, Ann Hendry Demasters (baby) and Josephine Knight.
Photo courtesy of Sara Nell Gran

about eight or nine feet in the river flowing through the property. This made it possible for a water-ground mill to be operated. The mill served the Indians and the settlers. The Indians were especially grateful to Captain Hendry because he always treated them kindly and helped them in any way he could. In 1878 he decided to employ a tutor for his settlement and to educate an Indian boy as well as the white children. That boy was Billy Cornapatchee, or Billy Corn Patch. He was the first Seminole to attend school. (See Appendix A.)

In 1891 Captain Hendry began to dispose of his stock and extensive holdings. It was then that the fort property fell into the hands of the Ford Foundation. In 1895 Captain Hendry donated some of his land for platting the city of LaBelle, which he named after his two daughters, Laura and Belle.

Captain Hendry died February 12, 1917 of chronic interstitial nephritis.

Seventy years later, the family still celebrated the annual Christmas Picnic tradition started by F. A. Hendry. The tradition was carried on by my grandfather, Louis, his second son.

A Christmas event that took place in Fort Myers until World War I was something out of Merry Old England. Christmas Eve 1885 began with fireworks, followed by a beef-shoot the next morning. All marksmen were hopeful of winning the prize of a fine, young steer.

The day after Christmas there was a cowboy tournament, resembling the knightly jousting held during the Middle Ages. In *The Story of Fort Myers,* Grismer noted that the contestants "tilted their lances at three rings suspended ten feet off the ground from horizontal bars. Each rider had three tries and if he was a good horseman and had a hawklike eye and nerves of steel he could get nine rings."

Each knight was given a whimsical name to identify himself from the others, for example, "the Knight of the Lost Cause." The tournament winner could choose the "Queen of Love and Beauty."

I can remember my father telling us about taking part in the activities. He told of his trying to climb a greased pole. Others were attempting to chase and catch greased pigs. Everyone could participate in some game or activity.

Our family usually went on a Christmas picnic, but its members could and did attend the big tournament on the day after Christmas.

My father was one of eight children whose lives were deeply affected by the death of their mother in 1904 after she gave birth to a baby girl. Eventually, my grandfather married again, a woman we called "Miss Mary."

Harry F. Hendry

"Come on in and sit over here. Your room is around the corner there. Ma'll get you some of her biscuits and sorgum syrup." Mr. Smallwood, a resident of Chockoluskee on Marco Island, was welcoming my father, Harry F. Hendry, to his first job as a teacher.

Harry was hungry after his trip down the Gulf from Fort Myers to Marco Island. The smell of fried salt pork hung heavy in the large room that served as a dining room, an old-fashioned store, and Indian trading post. The smell of food had whetted his appetite.

When the biscuits were placed in front of him, he stared in disbelief. Each biscuit was almost as large as a saucer. The syrup was in an unlabeled tin can with a wire handle. There was no butter. He had heard that the island people lived primitively, but he was not prepared for the bare simplicity of the food or the ease of its preparation. Next came the salt pork, a greasy slab with a streak of lean as it was called by the islanders, and four sunny-side up eggs. Never had he been served so much food or expected to eat so much. He looked at the Smallwoods and chuckled. *More like Stoutwoods,* he thought. He knew why they were so well-proportioned. This type of simple food was considered healthy.

Later, after he was shown his room, Mr. Smallwood walked with him down to the school.

It was the typical one-room cypress clapboard structure of the islands. The large, iron school bell was housed much like the bells hung in churches. In fact, it did serve for some church functions and was rung to summon the islanders for other events as well.

All the window panes were broken, old-fashioned desks were off their tracks. Dry ink from inkwells stained the floor. The slate chalkboards were filled with writing that turned his stomach. There was no chalk, no erasers, and no books. There were Sunday hymnals that were used whenever there was a funeral. The graveyard was across the street from the school.

Harry Frierson Hendry

Harry thought the situation was hopeless, but before he walked away, he decided to at least try. Within himself he felt the need to succeed. He had to succeed; he needed the job. Besides Alice, his wife, was pregnant and they had to borrow money to pay the boat fare down. *She's counting on me. I can't let her down!* he thought.

"We'll have to fix the place up," Mr. Smallwood said. "I'll get in touch with some of the folks and we'll get it in shape. Here come some of them now."

Harry looked through the open door and saw several burly men coming toward them.

"Heard you were here. We came to tidy things up."

They looked like good, hard-working stock, not gangsters or outlaws. They were skilled workmen and eager to do what was required. All the men were larger than Harry and he soon discovered that they all were younger than they looked.

"How did the school get in this shape?" Harry asked.

No one seemed to know, but as the day wore on, it was being repaired. Later in the day women came with brooms and mops. By nightfall the building was ready for school the next morning. Whatever was needed was provided by Mr. Smallwood, even the pencils and paper. Someone had thoughtfully provided a Sears, Roebuck catalog for the little outhouse with the half moon cut out on the door.

The next day dawned. Harry filled himself with Mrs. Smallwood's hearty breakfast. He walked rapidly down the two-rut oyster-shell road as though he were approaching a fate worse than death. When he reached the school, he unlocked the door and began to pull the rope that rang the school bell. He was sure that it could be heard all over the island.

It wasn't long until some of the helpers from the day before came inside. By nine o'clock there were three young boys and eight grown men. Not a single girl in the lot!

Harry assigned each to a desk. He knew most of their names from the day before; however, Pete and Seth were newcomers.

Harry was beginning to feel elated. It wasn't going to be the ordeal he anticipated after all.

"Are you going to stay while I teach the boys?" There was a big laugh.

"Yes, of course. Our pa's want us to larn to read and write along with these here young'uns."

Harry looked bewildered. Some of the students were over twenty. The youngest was only six.

He decided to begin school by reading from the Bible, followed by reciting the Lord's Prayer. Everything went well until it was time for the Pledge of Allegiance to a nonexistent flag.

The older students did not stand up, but remained in their seats. Harry thought about letting the matter pass without event, but decided that he had to establish his control now or all would be lost. He knew it was difficult for such big fellows to sit in the small desk seats and even more difficult to get up.

Harry again said it was time to say the Pledge of Allegiance. Still no one stood up.

"Everyone *stands* when we salute the flag, even though we have no flag to salute," he said. "Tom, you and Seth come up to the front of the room and stand with me."

"Who says? Want to make us?"

"I say so. Now, stand up! Place your hands over your hearts."

Reluctantly Tom and Seth came to the front of the room and the Pledge of Allegiance was completed.

After the morning exercises came the time to find out what his students knew and at what level to begin their lessons.

"How many of you can read?"

No one spoke a word. No hands went up.

"Can any of you write?"

"That's why we're here. We came to larn to read and write."

"How many of you know your ABC's?"

Again there was no response.

"Is it true that none of you know your ABC's?"

Stunned by the continued silence, Harry needed time out, so he called, "Time for recess. We'll begin work when you come back in."

Harry knew that he was in unknown territory. He was going to need wisdom and experience that he did not have. He blew his nose as though he were blowing away his problems and chose his plan of action.

After recess, when everyone was seated, he announced that everyone was going to say their ABC's. Afterwards they would make them on paper as they said them. The three young boys could make theirs on the chalk board.

His students all repeated the ABC's the first time, but the older ones decided they wouldn't write them. They began to mimic Harry in high-pitched voices.

"This is 'A'. It is made like this."

Harry was getting nowhere with the men.

"You children practice on the chalkboard while we write at our desks."

Pete mimicked Harry by saying the same thing in baby talk.

"We ain't no babies. Larn us how to read," yelled Seth.

Harry turned to lay his chalk down, and when he did Tom pulled out a plug of tobacco. He plopped some in his mouth and then passed it around to the others. He chewed it for awhile and then spit. The plug landed right on target—at Harry's feet!

Before he could recover, another well-aimed mouthful hit his shoe. Harry was unprepared for this. He quietly walked to the back of the room and locked the door. Walking back to the front of the room, he confronted Tom. "Tom, go to the open window [there were no screens] nearest you and spit out your tobacco. The rest of you spit yours out, too."

Another masticated projectile landed in front of Harry's feet. Seth and the others all followed Tom's example. "I'm waiting, fellows."

Harry's army training had taught him that maintaining control was important, even if he felt that he wasn't in control. His posture or body language showed that he expected compliance. The maneuver worked. Slowly they all went to the windows and disposed of their tobacco. He thought they had settled down, but as the morning wore on they became more defiant and belligerent.

Harry decided to try once more. "This is an 'A'. 'A' makes two important sounds. It says its name and it says 'ah' as in bat."

Someone said in a high-pitched voice, "Ah, ah, ah."

"Eh, what's that you say?" said Pete, pretending he couldn't hear. His hand cupped his ear. Everyone snickered. Just then Harry felt something sting him on the neck.

"These mosquitoes are bad here, ain't they?" said Harry, using slang to try to open communication, divert their attention. He swatted his neck with his hand and laughed with the group.

Again there was laughter. Even the little boys at the front chalkboard were roaring in laughter.

"Yessirre, them mosquitoes are real bad," Harry said as he slowly walked back where Jim was. Harry saw him hide something quickly, but Harry knew what was going on. Suddenly something pelted him on the cheek.

"I think I've just been bitten by a great big one, and I'm going to swat him right now."

Before Jim knew what had happened, Harry had knocked the bamboo bean shooter out of his hands. It rolled on the floor. Jim was stunned and he winced as though he expected to be clobbered.

Harry returned to the front of the room to continue his teaching. "All right, fellows, we've had our fun. Now, let's get to work."

No one picked up a pencil. All the eight men sat. They pretended to be deaf.

Harry looked at Seth. He seemed to be the ringleader. "Seth, come up here to my desk."

"Wanna make me?"

"I said come here."

"I said come here," mimicked Seth. Then the others followed. For a moment, Harry decided to ignore them. He had to do something, but what? In desperation he turned his attention to the younger pupils who needed help at the moment.

That minute's time was what he needed. Now he knew what he had to do. He turned around and told the grown men that they could not go home until they had copied ABC's from the chalkboard.

The troublemakers just laughed.

"You gonna make us?"

"Yes, I'm the teacher here. I'm not going to leave this island, and you are not going to leave this school until you do as I say!"

"Oh, yeah?"

"Yeah."

Harry stood his ground.

"If I have to, I'll take every one of you on to prove that I'm boss here."

Seth laughed. He clumsily got out of his seat and slowly sauntered to the front of the room. He lunged toward Harry and threw him to the floor.

Seth was surprised when Harry didn't buckle under. His army training again enabled him to hold his own against the heavier man. Soon it was Seth who was yelling uncle.

Harry didn't know it, but he was going to have to take on each of the men, sometimes fighting and sometimes wrestling them until they were overpowered. Fortunately for Harry, they did not jump him all at once. Each waited his turn as though each of them wanted to be the one who had made Harry admit defeat. The thought occurred to Harry that these men may be undisciplined and backward, but they were fair.

However, when it was Tom's turn, Tom pulled out a knife that he had tucked under his belt. Harry saw the flashing blade come at his throat and ducked the first thrust. He stepped backward and lunged for Tom's legs. When Tom fell, Harry jumped on top and grabbed hold of his arm that held the knife. He held it to the floor and soon the knife fell out of his hand.

He was the last of the troublemakers. Harry had tackled and subdued eight grown men, one after another.

To each man, he handed a sheet of paper. "Now, write your ABC's on this sheet. You will not go home until you do."

Eight reluctant men sat. Eight reluctant men continued to sit.

"Just wait until my Pa hears about this," pouted Seth.

"You'll be on the steamer in the morning like the rest of 'em that we got shed of."

Suddenly Harry's eyes caught sight of a stream of water slowly coming from under the desks. He knew what had happened. In the excitement, one of the children needed to go outside, but the door was locked. He walked to the door, unlocked it, and returned as though nothing was amiss.

At three o'clock the young boys finished their assignments. They were allowed to go home.

Four o'clock came. Then five o'clock came. For three hours not a sound was heard. The room was as quiet as a morgue. No one moved. By six o'clock the sun was beginning to set. While it was still twilight, Harry lit the lantern he had found in the supply cabinet. Once again he stated his terms.

Another hour passed. Harry could see swinging lights coming up the road made of crushed-shell [also called "marl"] in the dark. He girded himself for trouble. He didn't know what was next, but he was in this fight to the finish.

There was a knock at the door. As Harry walked toward the door, he thought of those boys who reminded him of Texas outlaws and wondered how he was going to cope. His hand went into his pocket and felt his rabbit foot.

When he unlocked the door, Seth's father asked in an angry voice, "Why are you keeping our young'uns here after dark?"

"The students must learn to do as I say. When they have finished their assignment, they may leave. If you want them to learn to read and write, they have to know that I'm boss here."

Down came a rifle butt hard on the floor. It shook the school's foundation.

Three other men stood behind Seth's father. They stood with rifles in their hands. Another had a pistol in his holster. They thundered into the room. They were rough, disgruntled men. They sat down on top of the desks where the younger pupils had been sitting. They leaned their rifles against the seats. They all huddled together, silently, each folding his arms in disgust, and acting as though he were waiting for something. Their silence was threatening. Even the older students picked up the tension in the room. The smell of the kerosene lantern filled the room and a rattling of papers could be heard. Then one of the armed men said, "All right. You boys get movin'. You heard the man. Do what he told you."

Harry's heart stopped pounding. He stood tall and pretended he was in complete control. These men were not criminals. They could be led. Again he detected a sense of fair play.

There was a flurry of compliance. Soon Seth handed his paper to Harry. On his way out, his pa grabbed him by the collar and pushed him down the steps.

One by one the students finished. As each did so, he was released to a parent or ushered out into the dark. Finally only one student remained. Harry pulled out his watch and looked at the time. It was midnight. When the remaining one finished, Harry closed the windows, blew out the lantern, and locked the door.

He felt tried, but unbeaten. He sighed and said to himself, "Round one. I won."

His thoughts then turned to his wife, Alice. *Honey, I think we won the first battle hands down, but we have yet to win the war.*

Then his thoughts wandered toward the type of men with whom he was dealing. They seemed to be the same type of frontiersmen that made our nation great. They had the brawn and the will to tackle anything. He no longer feared his future on the island. He was eager for tomorrow to come. His taste of victory was going to be sweet.

My Mother's Family

Alice L. Hendry, my mother, was born into a family of wealth and distinction. Her grandfather, Llewellyn John, came to the United States from Wales after he was graduated from Oxford University at age sixteen, with a degree in mining engineering. Because of his young age, he spent another year studying in the British Isles before embarking on his dream of coming to the United States. He arrived shortly after the beginning of the Civil War. To expedite his citizenship in his new country, he enlisted in the Union Army. During the Civil War, the Union needed soldiers and many newcomers gained citizenship this way. Llewellyn was immediately made a captain and was sent to Fredricksburg where the Union and Confederate forces were engaged in battle.

Llewellyn was a proud man coming from a family that traced its ancestry to the early days of Welsh history. The Johns honored their tribal affiliation (de Glamorgan), claiming never to have been conquered. Among his ancestors and family members were knighted artists, musicians, and poets. His brother, Willie, was knighted by King George V for his fine work in art. He could rightly be proud of his heritage.

I have not been able to verify the details of my grandmother's account of why Llewellyn emigrated. Grandmother was not the type to misrepresent things, however, so I'll include it as part of our family history. The dates do not seem to indicate that it happened during Napoleon's reign as emperor. It is more likely to have occurred during the reign of Napoleon III.

Llewellyn's immediate family had been merchants with a fleet of ships based in Pontypridd, Wales. One day when my great-grandfather went down to the wharves to attend to business, he struck up conversation with a sailor. He told the sailor about the expected arrival of several ships from the Orient but he was unaware that the sailor was a spy for Napoleon. As a consequence, the ships were attacked and destroyed. The family's fortune was in question. He felt responsible causing such trouble, so he decided to leave Wales and make his fortune in the United States.

After the Civil War, the then-Capt. Llewellyn John went to Pennsylvania and then out west to Nevada where he worked in a mine. According to his great-grandson, after an explosion, Llewellyn and a companion were trapped far beneath the ground and assumed dead. But they were very much alive and began digging their way out. They quenched their thirst by collecting droplets of water seeping from the inside walls. They even caught and ate rats. Amazingly, after three weeks, they were clear of the debris and exited the mine.

After that incident, through his Pennsylvania connections, Llewellyn accepted a position with De Bardeleban Coal Company in Birmingham, Alabama. He was hired to be the superintendent of all of the company's mining operations and opened Margaret Mine, which is still in operation. He surveyed and platted all the coal lands for the company, but he amassed his great wealth from his patents on coking processes.

Alice
L. Hendry

In the meantime he had married and had a family. Being financially secure, he proceeded to see that his children received the best education he could give them. And because most people called him Johns, he formally added the "s" to change his name.

My grandmother, Katie C., was one of Llewellyn Johns's children. He had great plans for her. At first he insisted that she become a concert pianist. He would bring home important people from all over the world and wake her in the middle of the night to play for them. Then he decided that she should go to medical school. Katie C. knew the only way to escape his preoccupation with her career and to have a life of her own was to get married, which she did to Charlie Rosser.

Oftentimes Katie C. wondered whether or not her marriage was a mistake, but all she had to do was think of her Charlie and she was happy again. Her recollections were particularly happy of when they met and their courtship. He was the handsome conductor of the newest train running in and out of Birmingham. It was on one of his trips that they eloped. She knew it would break her father's heart, but she, like her father, was strong-willed. So she put an end to her schooling in no uncertain terms.

Shortly thereafter she became pregnant and for awhile that seemed to end his dreams and aspirations for her. It was also the beginning of many years of tension and disagreements between father and daughter; he still wanted her to pursue her talents.

My Mother's Birth

Upon the birth of Katie C.'s second child, the situation became critical. Llewellyn gave her notice that if she had any more children, she would be disinherited and receive none of the fortune he had accumulated. Katie C. defied her father and so my mother, Alice Lee, was the third child to be born. The night of Alice's birth was stormy. It was Halloween and there had been another big argument between Llewellyn and his daughter. Because of the tension and unhappiness, the delivery had been hard. Finally Alice arrived and turned out to be the only black-haired child in Katie C.'s family. The other children had red hair or were brown-headed. She always jokingly claimed that she was living inside a pumpkin and on Halloween night, the night of her birth, a rat gnawed her out.

Llewellyn W. Johns

Alice had to endure the painful knowledge that her birth might keep her mother from becoming rich. Great-grandfather eventually relented and Katie C., along with her brothers, did inherit some money, but everything was lost when the stock market crashed.

On the Christmas shortly after she was two years old, presents arrived from Llewellyn. Alice's gift was a little toy iron cook-stove that actually worked.

One day when the maid was not looking, little Alice Lee decided to start a fire in her stove. She found some kindling and the kerosene can that was used in the kitchen. She poured the kerosene all over the stove and lit a match. There was an explosion and little Alice Lee was burned severely. She had to be carried around on a pillow for at least two months. The doctor filled the deep burns with Fuller's Earth, a type of white clay that easily absorbs impurities from oil and fat. Like other clays used by natives, it enhanced the healing process. Friends and family all prayed that she would recover. No one expected her to live, but she did. And

Jenny Scott Johns

39

for the rest of her life, that Fuller's Earth kept working up and out of her scars.

Alice Lee was a very bright little girl, but she had great difficulty in reading. It was thought to have been caused by her difficult birth and prebirth traumas brought on by her mother's stress. In all other intellectual areas, however, she was very advanced. But because of reading problems, school was difficult. In desperation, Katie C. sent Alice to a convent boarding school where the nuns were supposed to do exceptional things with children. Unfortunately, the nuns were unable to work their usual miracles with Alice. Soon Alice Lee was back at home helping her mother care for the family and her younger brothers and sisters.

Alice was skillful in covering up her difficulty. No one knew outside the family that she could barely read and write. For her to do so was a trial of extreme endurance. No one understood why she could not pronounce certain words. Later on, the mystery was solved; she was unable to hear certain sounds. What is not heard cannot be said. Alice's reading disability is today called mirror vision. She saw words as if they were images in a mirror, then had to convert them, and her inclination was to read words from right to left. On her own she discovered her difficulty and finally mastered transposing the letters so that she could read. Her hearing never did improve, but it was not a problem because she chose to use words that she knew she could pronounce.

Alice Lee married Harry F. Hendry after he came home from the first World War. She did not disclose her disability before they wed. Although though it was a shock to him, Harry proceeded to try to help her, but only she could do what had to be done. Many times she did not know how to correct the problems caused by her learning disabilities. However, she continued to improve until she had mastered what she was working on to her satisfaction. Although she never returned to school, with my father's help she was able to take and pass her examinations. She secured teaching credentials, but she never taught. Instead she settled on marriage.

Their marriage produced three children. I was the first and named in the Southern tradition of two names after my grandmothers: Ella Kathryn. My brother, Harry, Jr., was next, and finally came William Warwick. My mother was an excellent wife, and she never forgot what it was like to be afflicted. She spent years helping needy children, those who were deformed and those who were too poor to get the proper medical care. She was constantly taking some needy child to St. Petersburg for help—a very long drive in those days.

Quite often, in her mellow moods, Alice would speak about how Katie C. purchased a railroad car to move their belongings to Florida from Alabama. They went by train to Jacksonville and then boarded a paddle-wheel steamer to go on southward down the St. Johns' River. She would elaborate on the beauty of the large, old yellow pines, the mossy oaks, and the flowers that overhung the banks. There were thousands of birds and all kinds of wild animals. The thing that impressed her most was the size of the large trees. Even in her young days, their size dazzled her. Several decades later on a return trip, she was saddened to learn that the trees were almost gone.

Alice's family brought with them two black servants. Upon their arrival in Florida, Katie C. bought an orange grove with an old farm house on it. That old farm house was built on stilts on high land, about a mile east of Yellowfever Creek, across the Caloosahatchee River in North Fort Myers. Most older houses were built on stilts so that when the floods came, the family and possessions were out of danger. One could usually find a skiff stored under the house to be used in a flood.

The roof was high and steep and was covered with cypress shingles. There was a porch that extended around   *Alice Hendry*
the house on all four sides. It shaded them from the fierce summer sun, and provided ventilation. Because of the porch overhang, the windows could be opened twenty-four hours a day. The windows were covered with screens but they did not keep the sandflies (now called no-see-'ems) out. Every night someone had to paint screens with kerosene and tend the smudge pots, which were made by burning B-Brand Insect Powder. The smudge pots were to control flying insects, including palmetto bugs. All beds had mosquito nets on them because a mosquito bite could mean death. Mosquitoes carried malaria, typhoid fever, and yellow fever. Dengue fever was thought to have been spread by human contact. Later on it was learned that dengue fever was caused by anthropods, such as cockroaches, beetles, bees, and crustaceans. Almost everyone in the early years of Florida settlement had bouts with these fevers.

About 1910, Katie C. had an opportunity to sell her orange grove, and moved closer to the Caloosahatchee River where she and her husband, Charlie, built a large two-story frame house.

Grandmother Scott's Fruit Cake

2 pounds of raisins
2 pounds of currants
1 pound of almonds
1 pound of citron
1 pound of figs
1 pound of dates
1 pound of brown sugar
1 pound of butter—no substitutes
1 pound of flour (4 cups All Purpose)

1 dozen eggs
1 medium glass of currant jelly
1 tumbler of wine (1 1/2 cups)
1 tablespoon mace
1 tablespoon cloves
1 tablespoon cinnamon
1 pound of candied cherries
1 pound of candied pineapple

Blanch almonds and leave whole—dredge fruit with flour after having been hand-cut into small pieces.

Important: *Line pans with three layers of brown paper, sides and bottom. Also, place three layers of brown paper on top of each cake.*

Cook in slow oven at 300 degrees.

Makes three cakes. Bake from one to one and one-half hours.

That old house had an inside stairway that always frightened me. At the landing was a door that led to her library. There were shelves after shelves loaded with books. One of those books was an old Welsh Bible, with English printed on the opposite pages from the Welsh. Unfortunately, that old Bible disappeared. It contained much of the history that I have been trying to remember.

Jenny Scott's   Fruit Cake

My grandmother was another wonderful storyteller in the family. She told us about trips to Wales and England where her mother, Jenny Scott, had lived before marrying Llewellyn John.

Evidently the Scotts lived quite well. I was told that Sir Walter Scott was a member of her family. She always spoke of the lavish parties and wonderful meals that were prepared. Katie C. carried down the tradition and to eat at her home and be served one of her meals was a special treat. She was considered a marvelous cook, and until they died, my grandparents always dressed for dinner, even in hard times when money was scarce.

We do have one recipe that has come down through the years. It was for a dark fruit cake that was prepared every year and delivered to the king and queen. On my mother's copy of the old recipe, it states that it has been in the family since 1750. To the original recipe candied cherries and candied pineapple seems to have been added sometime later on.

Boys Will Be Boys

After the death of Louis A. Hendry's first wife, Ella Hester, my grandmother, on August 1, 1904, he had a difficult time caring for their eight motherless children. Ella had died in childbirth. With the help of Aunt Mamie Jane, who suckled the baby girl, he tried to maintain the lovely home he had built for his bride on Lee and Second streets in Fort Myers. (Aunt Mamie had been one of my great-grandfather's slaves who chose to remain a part of the family.)

It proved to be impossible, though, even with the additional help from Aunt Julia, who was Ella Hester's sister. The two sisters, Ella Hester and Julia had married brothers, so Julia considered Ella Hester's, as her own. The baby fared quite well, but the boys were a concern for Louis. Aunt Mamie Jane, cooked and cleaned for them, but their home life was changed forever. And though Aunt Julia did what she could to help, she had her own family to rear. The boys were left on their own, but Aunt Julia did mother the girls as best she could.

The boys, whose ages ranged from sixteen down to eight were more than a handful for the beloved Aunt Mamie Jane. Louis, a state representative, was in Tallahassee much of the time attending to state business. He left instructions for the boys to be kept busy tending the orange trees, keeping the grass down, and doing general grove work as was needed. Julius Augustus, known as Gus, was sixteen and hardly old enough to be responsible for so many younger brothers.

There was an old house out on the grove, situated in the area of Palmona Park, on the north side of the Caloosahatchee River. It was built high above the ground, as were many of the houses at that time to protect it from high water that came up over creek banks. This was before the era of canal digging, which carried away excessive water and freed up more land from the encroaching swamps. The house was part of the vast estate of F. A. "Scout" Hendry, which had been divided among his nine children when my great-grandfather died. On this section (forty acres) was an old house built with cypress wood, as were almost all the older homes. The house originally served as a residence for a foreman who cared for and supervised those who tended the orange groves.

Since all the men in the family were hunters, the family always had hounds trained as deer dogs. The dogs usually slept under the houses where it was cool in the summer and warm and sheltered in the winter.

With the dogs came a constant companion—fleas. The boys were used to city living. The mosquitoes and sandflies were bad enough, but when the fleas began to invade the house and their living quarters, they began to think of ways to cope. Without adult guidance, they devised a surefire way to get rid of the pests.

They went into the barn and began to rake up the hay that was stored for the milk cows. Load after load of hay was piled under the house until it was at least a foot deep. The house was a good five feet off the ground, so the hay was soon spread. Now for the riddance of those varmits!

The four boys each lit a lighterknot, a heart of pine tapered splinter, and proceeded to set the hay on fire. It went well at first, but soon the fire began to burn with a very hot blaze. They had to quickly change their tactics and try to save the house before it burned.

Their only water came from a hand-pumped well. Pete, the youngest boy, had to pump the "artesian" water, while bucket after bucket was thrown under the smoking floor boards. Finally, the fire was out and the house was saved, and their unorthodox efforts were rewarded. The fleas were gone for good; the house spared.

There were still the sandflies and mosquitoes, though. But everyone in the territory learned to live with them. (When I was a young girl, we used dried manure in the smudge pots if we were out of B-Brand Insect Powders.)

With the flea episode behind them, they continued the grove work until it was time for the cattle roundup. At that time, it was open range; the cattle were allowed to range wherever there was food. All kinds of brands could be seen in a herd, but at roundup time, only a rancher's brand would be selected or cut out from the herd.

Many of the cattle had interbred with the wild Spanish stock. Their horns were long, wide, and sharp. The offspring, when interbred with domestic stock, had much shorter horns but seemed to retain the sharp, pointed horn tips of the original wild Spanish cattle.

On one such roundup, the boys ran into trouble with one of the offspring of the wild herd. A heifer, in an attempt to avoid capture, ran directly into a bog where she became trapped in mud. Being wild, frightened, and completely immobilized, she began to bellow and fight to keep from sinking. The more she tossed about and became increasingly agitated, the deeper she sank.

At that time, the boys were alone and away from the cowhands. Gus had the boys cut palmetto fronds and young saplings, and gather charred logs from the underbrush. Finally they had enough debris to provide a stable foothold, which was placed in front of the cow so that when she was pulled up from the bog, she could put her feet down on something solid. Gus and Harry threw lassos out over the bog and over the cow's head. Then they proceeded to use their horses to pull. They pulled and pulled. Finally they freed the heifer, and as she walked onto the debris and out of the water, she lowered her head. She was ready to charge the two boys who had just dismounted. Bellowing like a banshee, she proceeded to attack. Soon she had all four boys treed, and there they stayed until the cowhands rescued them. That crazy cow headed back into the bog, but escaped the mud and never was captured.

The roundup continued and the cattle were driven to Punta Rassa. There they were loaded on a steamship headed for Galveston, Texas, or sometimes to Cuba.

Later that same year, there was a bad drought. The water in the well was running low, so the boys decided to drill another well and make it deeper. They, like most of the early settlers, did their own work; however, there was always someone willing to help out or show them how to accomplish what they wanted to do. It wasn't long until they had built a scaffold. Someone had loaned them a pulley. They found several very large, heavy rocks and placed them near the site. Then came the casing and well liners.

The four boys hoisted those heavy rocks up with the pulley. Then they dug a hole for the casing until it was deep enough for it to stay upright without support. With a shout of "timber," the big rocks were hoisted and then let fall with great force. The rocks pounded the pipes downward. The brothers continued the process until they found a good flow of artesian water, which flows upward freely due to underground pressure. It wasn't perfect—it smells awful and stains objects around it. When the well was capped, the boys had all the water they could use for the grove as well as for other uses. Then they dug a small pond around the overflow valve where the water accumulated and turned into a slimy, white substance after a time.

Making Wine

It was in the good-old summertime when the wild scuppernong and muscadine grapes were ready to eat. These wild grapes climbed trees and then let their vines trail to the ground. This particular year there was an abundant supply as was often the case after a mild winter.

A group of neighborhood men who lived on adjoining plats of land decided to make wine. So one day a neighbor came knocking on the door to ask for help gathering the grapes and pressing out the juices. All four boys were delighted to be asked. When they had gathered enough grapes and the wagon was full, they headed back toward Yellowfever Creek, where one neighbor had his log house. There they washed the grapes in the creek, sorted them out and began to stomp on them barefoot in large tempered steel wash tubs. As they poured the juice off, they loaded the trampled grape hulls onto the wagon and took them over to the man's fenced-in pigpen. The pigs were happy to get such a treat, but as the day progressed the grapes began to ferment as the late afternoon sun poured down on the hulls.

The men had just loaded the juice into barrels to begin the fermenting stage of winemaking, when they heard all kinds of wild squealing and squalling coming from the pigpen. Everyone rushed over to it and there they saw a sight to behold. The pen was full of drunken animals. Some were running wildly about mounting each other, some were lying on their backs with their feet extended upward and wallowing in ecstasy, others were rooting up the ground in a maddened frenzy, and all were disoriented.

The men had never seen anything like the show that was being staged. For hours they watched and many swore that they had the best time of their lives.

During the summer, there were all-day singings at the church. Food was plentiful and everyone enjoyed the communal get-togethers. There were other types of activities such as quilting bees for the ladies, raffles for money-making purposes, and box lunches for the younger set.

It was at one of these activities that Harry, my father, met Alice, the girl he was to later marry. His younger brother, Paul, liked her as well, but her heart was won by Harry. Some say to this day that because he did not get her hand, Paul remained a bachelor.

Courting was difficult and earning money was even worse. Harry needed a new shirt to wear. He had no idea how he was going to earn enough money to get one, but after a lot of thought he came up with an idea.

There were a lot of wild boars, hogs, or pigs running loose on the range like the cattle. They, too, were left behind by the Spanish, but there was no domestic stock to interbreed with so they reverted to a wild state. This meant that they were wiry, had tusks, and were for the most part, too tough to eat.

Harry took out his rifle, not knowing that these animals were different from the domesticated ones, and shot one. He proceeded to dress it and get it ready for market. After it was cut and its entrails were drawn, he built a big fire under a black iron wash pot. When the water was boiling, he dipped the meat into the pot. He was trying to take off the fur that was wiry and hard to remove. He had seen this done to chickens to remove their feathers. To his amazement the bristles would not come out. He tried pulling them out one by one, but that was too big a task. Then he had another idea. He went into the house, found his razor strap, and went quickly to work. Soon that old boar was as cleanly shaved as his face. He then butchered the meat and packed it into flour sacks. He was going to take it to the local butcher, whose shop was over in Fort Myers. He quickly bathed in a wash tub, dressed and loaded the flour sacks into the wagon. He drove his mule and wagon down to the creek. There he tied the mule to a shade tree, and proceeded to load his precious cargo into a skiff. He rowed down Yellowfever Creek and on down to the Caloosahatchee River. The river was about a mile wide, but he rowed on until he reached the wharf, where there was a landing site.

Harry then headed toward the butcher shop. The butcher was delighted to have some fresh pork to sell so Harry was able to get his new courting shirt.

This is not the end of this story, however. The next time Harry went to town, the butcher sought him out. He wanted to know why he had sold him meat that was so tough it couldn't be eaten and so full of bristles that all who purchased it had to throw it out.

A Storm to Remember

When Harry finished his business in town, he headed back toward the wharf, and as he approached the boat, he noted that the black warning flag was flying high above the wharf. This meant that a hurricane was approaching or soon would be; all fishermen, ships, and citizens were advised to be prepared. They needed to take whatever steps that were necessary for their safety, the safety of others and to secure their belongings.

The sky was clear and the winds were calm, so Harry decided go back into town to visit his Aunt Julia. Maybe there would be more news coming by telegraph if he waited a couple of hours.

Harry walked up the unpaved streets, swinging his arms and whistling. His Aunt Julia was happy to see him, but as usual, she began to pressure him to continue his education. In the course of their conversation, she finally convinced him to return and get his diploma. None of his brothers had pursued an education with the tenacity he had demonstrated and had dropped out of school; thus, Harry was the only male pupil left.

After a few hours, Harry headed back to the wharf. He checked the telegraph office on his way to the dock, but no more news had come in. The sky was still clear, but the sun was beginning to set. He knew he had stayed longer than he should have considering the approaching storm. He would have to cross the river and travel a couple of miles inland.

It was dark by the time he reached the middle of the river. He could see the moon rising. It was going to be a full moon, so he relaxed and began to whistle. As the oars touched the water, he noticed that there was phosphorus in it. Every bit of movement in the water seemed to reflect light. He laid down his oars to appreciate the beauty of the night. Stars sparkled in the heavens, the moon was laying down a path of gold across the river, and all movement in the water was aglow. Even little fish and crabs lit up as they darted back and forth. A large mullet passed by the bow of the boat. Its reflected light made phosphorescence a spectacle to behold.

In the distance, he could hear alligators bellowing out their mating calls, and as he neared shore thousands of fireflies danced about.

Suddenly the wind picked up. The calm night had been invaded by rippling waves. As his oars dipped, the splashing noises brought him back to reality.

Finally he reached his landing spot on the creek bank. His mule was waiting. With the full moon shining down, he had no trouble finding his way through the palmettos and on to the much-travelled cattle trail that led to the grove.

When he reached home, he was happy to see the lights of the kerosene lamps shining through the windows. His brothers had already heard about the approaching hurricane and were beginning to worry about his safety since it was so late.

The next morning brought rain that descended in slanting sheets as the hurricane approached. Finally the winds pushed the torrential rains even harder. Trees bowed near the ground. The old weathered house stood. When the center arrived, all was calm until a neighbor rode up on horseback.

"You had better get down to the river if you want to see it completely dry. All the water is gone. You can walk across it."

Without another word, he was off to spread the word.

It didn't take the boys long to saddle up the horses and head for the river. Sure enough, it was completely dry. The murky water was gone. In its place, cream-colored sand extended a mile or more to the other side.

Harry had expected to see a muddy bottom, but there was no trace of silt or decaying matter there. He got off his horse, tied it to a stout limb, and started to walk across the sandy river bottom. The other boys joined him, thinking that this was something they might not see again. Everything had been carried out with the water when it was blown out into the gulf. There were no dead fish, turtles, or crabs left behind.

They returned home before the winds started to blow from the other direction. Again the storm spent its fury and swept the skies clean. It left in its wake downed trees, broken limbs, and water everywhere. The lakes were full. Streams flowed with fury and washed away bank after bank to birth new inlets. One such stream created a new waterway and left the old section dry.

At the end of the summer, each boy sought to go his own way. Harry returned to high school to be the only man in his graduating class. Gus headed out Texas way. He was gone for seven years and no one knew where he was. John was in and out of school, but finally ended up in Cuba. Pete, the youngest, stayed on to become a fisherman.

The four girls grew up under the care and supervision of Aunt Julia. The eldest, Josie, married an engineer. Next in line was Daisy, who married a banker from Brazil. Ruby married a doctor and moved to Miami. The baby, Mildred, married a wealthy business-man and moved to Tallahassee.

Little Wild Rabbit Eyes

I often wonder if all children were like I was when I was young. I wonder if they were fascinated by changing light patterns, or if they experienced the range of emotions I did when I heard different sounds or was affected by different smells. How intensely these sensations colored my experiences!

I think I had an affinity for everything that lived. Somewhere in my childhood, I became civilized, but I still yearn to return to the past where I was at one with all, and did not live as a separate entity.

My mother stated that when she first saw me, I looked up into her eyes like a small wild rabbit. She always thought I could see from the day I was born. Her descriptive experience moved me to write a poem that I call "Little Wild Rabbit Eyes."

After I was born my family lived in one of my grandfather's tenant's houses on an orange grove. The owner of *National Geographic* magazine purchased the grove, and built a home in the same area.

Soon after, my parents built their first home, working alongside each other. Their tract of land was part of a section deeded to them by Louis A. Hendry. My grandfather subdivided his land and gave each of son, Harry F. and Augustus "Gus," forty acres as a wedding gift.

This rural setting was the perfect place for children to play and learn about nature. "Little Rabbit Eyes" was too young to explore on her own as a toddler, but she didn't know that.

When I was about one year old, my mother and father were sitting on the back steps one late afternoon watching the sunset. Mother had let me down to play on the grass while she and my father discussed some pressing problem. Before long they noticed that I was not with them. They began

> ## Little Wild
> ## Rabbit Eyes
> Like a little wild rabbit
> You stare.
> Dark eyes.
> Mysterious.
> Round, full dark eyes
> Frozen in awe.
> Birth's terror behind you now,
> All round you shines.
> Breathe softly.
> Air caresses what water bathes.
> The ark of life cradles
> Your fear
> And wraps it in swaddling love.
> Little wild rabbit eyes,
> My life lives in you
> And dies.

to call out and hunt for me. It seemed to them that I had vanished into thin air. Soon, the sun had sent its colors to rest, but it was still twilight. As they continued to look for me, they became alarmed.

By chance, my mother spotted a crack in the wire door of the chicken pen. She pulled it open and walked into the pen and on toward the henhouse, where the chickens had gone to roost. She looked up on the rack where the chickens were sleeping and there I was. I had climbed up on one of the lower timbers and found my place, roosting, sound asleep, among the hens. Evidently, the hens had just moved over and made room for me.

My sensitivity for living creatures made another childhood experience rather frightening. My folks had taken me over to my uncle's farm so that my father could help him with the "hog killing." All I can recall now was the terrible pain I *felt* when I heard one of the hogs screaming. I'll always remember the animals' screams and the sense of impending death.

Alice Hendry and the author as a baby

No one had anticipated my hysteria. I actually seemed to be experiencing the hog's pain. Both the hog and I screamed. This behavior may seem irrational, but it was the way I reacted to violence. This experience was so vivid that I never forgot it.

Another tale of those early years, as told to me by Mother, was one that demonstrates how undaunted I was by certain things. I was two or three years old and Mother had placed me on a quilt on the floor next to the old treadle sewing machine so she could sew while I slept. Although it was supposed to be my naptime, I was wide awake. When she began to sew, I slipped out the front door. I didn't know where I was going, but I was on my way to a big adventure. As I look back, I'm sure that the Lord was with me every step of the way.

I walked out in the front yard and climbed through an open space in the wooden gate. I crossed the white marl paved road and found the canal. There was a felled yellow pine lying across it. I managed to cross the dead pine in spite of its stubs and broken-off branches. Its bark was rough and its footing was dangerous. Below the pine tree ran a sluggish stream of water. It was full of gars, alligator turtles, and snakes.

After I crossed the canal I walked into a pine thicket, where I spotted some blueberries and sat down to eat. Since it was past naptime, I was tired, so I crawled up near a big palmetto boot and went to sleep.

In the meantime, Mother discovered I was missing. She searched everywhere, but could not find me. Finally in desperation and anguish, she walked the half-mile up the road to my uncle's house for help. Luckily, he was at home.

My mother, my aunt, and my uncle came back and began to search further. They feared that an alligator might have caught me and dragged me under the extended canal bank. But being practical people, they didn't give up searching. No one initially thought that I had made it across the dead pine tree until my uncle wondered if I might have done it. So he began the task of getting to the other side of the canal. He had to shimmy a couple of times, holding on for dear life, and ride it like a steer once, but cross it he did.

He searched among the saplings, flycatcher bushes, pitcher plants, pawpaws, and other subtropical plants that grew in this partly cleared land.

In passing, he remembered the blueberry patch and wondered if I could be there. Across the underbrush and toward the patch, he loped like some wild thing. There near a big palmetto clump's root I lay asleep. My mouth and my little hands were stained with blueberry juice. I awakened suddenly when my uncle called my name and grabbed me. Nearby was a large, black gopher snake slowly crawling away, in search of a mouse or a rat in the cool, shaded undergrowth.

Huckleberry Pie

I still love blueberries to this day, but I like huckleberries better, as the following story will tell:

While Mother was in the garden picking spinach one day when I was about six or seven, I decided to surprise her by baking a huckleberry pie. Luckily she came back in time to save the house from burning down.

I made up a batter of various things and placed it in a skillet. The skillet went into the oven after I lit the kerosene stove. Knowing that the pie needed time to bake, I went out to play, forgetting all about the delicious pie. Soon I smelled smoke and I think Mother smelled it, too, because she came running into the house.

Author's sketch.

Such patience my mother had! I can't remember whether or not I was punished, but I suspect not. Her way was to explain to me that my idea was good, but I should have asked her to help me.

With her help I would not have wasted food or made such a mess. As a result, I nearly burned the house down.

When asked what I was baking, I told her it was a huckleberry pie. I showed her the recipe I had written out in her cookbook.

"Can you bake a huckleberry pie without huckleberries?" she asked.

"No, Ma'am," I replied.

"Let's go pick the huckleberries first the next time you make a huckleberry pie. I think it'll taste a lot better. What do you think?"

I nodded my head in agreement. It had not occurred to me that huckleberries were necessary for a huckleberry pie.

Some years later I found the recipe I had written out in Mother's cookbook and used to bake that ingenuous pie. She had added, "About six or seven years old, 1926 or 1927."

At that age I thought I could do anything. I did not seem to have any fear. I do not remember having any limitations placed upon me. I felt as big as an adult, but my body couldn't do some of the things I wanted it to do.

I am inclined to believe that old saying, ignorance is bliss. I long for the days of bliss or that age of innocence when life sparkled with its own childlike splendor. The older I become, I find that there's little difference between the beginning and the end. From birth we begin to die before we really live, but after having lived a full life, we revel in the knowledge that life is sum and substance of all its parts.

When we are ready to complete the circle, I believe that we will find that life sparkles with that same childlike splendor as it once did. In addition it will be crowned with grace and reverence—the reward for experiencing life at its fullest. Then we'll experience our own Gestalt, and ultimately the Infinite Gestalt—GOD.

A Creative Childhood

My mother used to tell me stories about when she lived in Alabama before moving to Florida. Her description of frosty windows was so vivid that I experienced both a visual and a sensory experience even though I had never lived in the North. I saw the ferns arranged in beautiful designs and felt the tingle of winter's chill going up my spine. I could be on that Alabama mountaintop watching the clouds roll down it, as she explained the approach of a storm. Her imagination stimulated mine and kept us both entertained. She helped me learn to enjoy the bountiful world around me.

When Mother and I looked up into the sky exploding with diamonds and one big silky pearl of a moon watching everything, I thrilled with the pleasure of its beauty and vastness.

When we watched clouds in the sky, the clouds weren't clouds. They were animals, men, buildings, trees, or a make-believe combination of things.

There was joy in allowing a sunset to consume you. Smells, colors, textures, and sounds were experienced as enhancements to living. It was frosting on the cake.

Nature's Messages

When I was growing up, the world sparkled with excitement. Our surroundings were very important to our development.

The wind sang us lullabies, the bird songs came as epiphany sounds in a symphony. Bees buzzed in their perfect harmony, and the leaves of the trees seemed to sweep away tensions caused by irritants, like mosquitoes and wasps.

Nature had its special message and my own presence was its sounding board.

All creatures, big and small, played a role in the harmony of life. I think it is difficult for children to accept the boundaries of their own skins when they are absorbed in life's perfect peace.

Mother told of her trip down the Saint Johns River when she was a little girl, shortly after 1900. Trees were tall, large, and she felt enveloped by jungle-like ambiance. Wild cranes, swans, egrets, and spoonbills abounded along the banks as the boat churned southward into this beautiful new land of Florida. Most children of this period could communicate with nature easily. There was little to distract them and so many new and exciting natural adventures were waiting for them to see, hear, smell, touch, and even taste.

Southwest Florida foliage, as photographed by Leonard Vanderwulp.

There seemed to be fewer barriers between age groups than there are now. Older children accepted the care and responsibility of the younger ones, whether cousins, neighbors, or even strangers.

It was such fun to take walks into the woods with a group of neighborhood children. The smells were almost intoxicating at times. I still love the smell of fresh pine rosin. The pine needles after a rain smell crisp, pungent, and slightly acrid. Nothing smells better than freshly dug sweet soil as it ripens for spring. I have often wondered if animals who wallow in the dust or dirt experience another dimension of life that we've missed. Surely it must be more meaningful than merely a way to cope with insects.

I often think of the hands-on experience I gained from those walks. We learned about leaves, plants, flowers, trees, and everything in the forest. The older children always were full of knowledge. They shared information about poison ivy, milkweed plants, or even white sumac's poison (red is not poisonous).

We learned about bird nests, eggs, and animal tracks. Usually we had a yard dog with us. He'd sniff and hunt. Sometimes he would run into a covey of quail, or find a rabbit to chase. Near the rivers, often we'd see an osprey nest.

If we came to a creek and the water looked clean, we'd consider swimming in it if we could see the bottom and if it flowed swiftly enough to keep from collecting moss and algae.

If the day was hot, we might take a dip. We didn't know about skinny dipping and I doubt if we would have done it if we were aware. Girls were taught to be quite prudish and very protective of their bodies. However, we didn't mind pulling our outer garments off and running like mad for that wonderful first big splash.

We would often play leapfrog in the water. If it was deep enough, we'd swim under each other's legs. Sometimes we'd go to a regular swimming hole. Most of them had a rope tied high up on a tree limb, which fell freely almost to the water. We'd climb onto a tire tied to the end of the rope and swing out over the water. When we were far enough out, we'd jump off with a big splash.

Bog Treasures

There were times when we were in danger, but even this was a learning experience for us. We learned about snakes—both bad and good. It was particularly dangerous along the ponds because of moccasins. We also learned about bogs, quicksand, and alligators, and searched for carnivorous plants. The pitcher plants caught flies, bees, or ants. Some folded up rapidly while others closed ever so slowly. We also spotted the flycatcher plants and small Venus's-flytraps. We loved to watch the pretty sundew.

Other times we'd walk along the edge of a pond. There were always pollywogs, frogs, and minnows. Sometimes we'd bring along a fruit jar to catch specimens, such as speckled trout minnows, and baby sunfish with colorful fins. They were placed in the glass fruit jar along with duckweed and moss. Once in a while we'd catch a salamander or a baby turtle. Occasionally, we would find a small skink. Sometimes we'd try to catch baby pollywogs to see if we could keep them until they turned into frogs. They never did. They either died or disappeared.

In the fall, many of the lakes had black-eyed Susans growing in them. If so, we'd always take home a bouquet. Should we come to a canal, we'd look for alligator turtles, gars, or other types of murky-water-loving animals. There were times when we went out into the fields where vegetables were growing. We'd take along a salt shaker and eat our fill of tomatoes. In those days, pesticides were seldom used. The soil was so rich from the humus that plants were vigorous and able to resist insect attacks.

And then there were snacks that we had at nature's invitation. Wild pawpaws, blueberries and blackberries, as well as huckleberries. We pulled up the palmetto fronds from the plant and ate their soft white tips. We tasted wild grapes, which Mother loved for jelly, and spit them out because they were too sour. We also ate watercress from the swampy creek banks and wild plump rose hips. Have you ever slurped the juice up from the cup of the wild honeysuckle?

You should have seen us when we found some scuppernong or muscadine grapes! We'd plop them into our mouths with wild abandon. They squirted out their juices in our mouths, but we rolled them about before it was our turn to spit them out, seeds and pulp at the same time. Then we could hardly wait to plop another one in and let its tangy sweetness stain and run down our chins.

We'd climb trees and sometimes just sit up there in them like a bunch of monkeys.

On a hot summer day, we headed for a watermelon patch and ate like porkers! We enjoyed the red slushy-like fruit just as much as if it had been manna from heaven. We broke the melon open and placed our teeth right into the firm mush. It tasted so cool and sweet. Sometimes we'd have a seed-spitting fight, but not too often. With juice dropping from our faces and sticky hands, we'd try to find a place to wash off. Sometimes we'd find only a flowing well of artesian water.

Childhood Games

By late afternoon, we had another delightful thing to do. If we were not helping our parents mow, clean the yard, or rake, we'd play games.

Sometimes they would sit on the front porch and supervise our games such Mother, May I?, Hail Over, Drop the Handkerchief, Blind Man's Buff, Hide and Seek, and sometimes even rougher games like Red Rover. On our own we'd play tag, or Red Light.

We'd play until the bullbats came swooping down and the whippoorwills began to call. Then my father might even treat us by answering the whippoorwills. They'd respond to his calls, and creep closer, but they would never come near enough so that we could see them. It was as if they had discovered they had been tricked.

We loved to play games in the woods. Our favorite was to ride a pine sapling. The older children would work together to pull an eight- or ten-foot sapling down to the ground. They would hold it down for one of us to sit on its top branches, and we were told to hold on tight. We clutched a stout limb in each hand, then they let go. Off into the wild blue yonder we would sail! As soon as the tree had returned to normal, we would climb down and eagerly await the next trip upward. Some small children had to be helped down, and then the sapling was lowered enough for the little one to get down without being afraid.

Even Hurricanes Were Fun for Children

We never minded when a wind storm came, even if it was due to a hurricane. Our parents made it a fun experience for us, even when a window blew out or part of the roof was blown away. There were always pots and pans available to catch the dripping water or an old tarp ready to be put to use. Our bathtub was filled with water in case we needed water after the storm and mother had all kinds of goodies baked up ahead of time. Before we had a radio, my father learned about coming storms from neighbors or friends whose transportation was by boat. On one of the city docks, a hurricane warning flag would be flying, alerting us that news had come in by the telegraph.

We would watch the fury of the storm with wonder and feel awed by what damage the winds could do. Wash tubs, still filled with water, were capable of flying by a window. Once we saw a four-by-four piece of lumber, carried by the wind, ram into the trunk of a tree. It could not be pulled out.

During the calm, we would go outside to see how things had weathered these terrible blasts. Usually things were in pretty good shape. My father always watched for rising water. He had a skiff available for us to get into should it rise too high. He had taken care to build on higher ground to prevent such a thing, but he was always prepared, just in case disaster struck.

We could hardly wait for the storm to pass. In front of our house was a canal, built originally for drainage. After a hurricane, the water would be high, and when it was, we had wonderful times. The water would run in swift currents in the canal down to the river. After it calmed down enough so that the danger of being swept away had passed, we were allowed to get out the wash tubs. With two sticks of wood to use as paddles, each of us jumped into our own tub and were on our way. Down the canal we would go, but we could not go beyond the house that was nearest to the river. This was our safety zone; beyond that was trouble.

Mother always worried about us running into a nest of moccasins. Hundreds of them would gather, and as a unit, be carried down waterways. She made us promise that if we saw a nest of them, we would head for the canal bank in a hurry. I never did see any, though.

Creating Toys

We had only a few store-bought toys, but mostly we made whatever we played with. One of our favorite games was playing store. We gathered field crates and apple boxes for our display tables. There were always empty tin cans that the grown-ups disposed of by burying, so we would raid the "holding pens" for our store goods.

We made play money and colored the bills green. Sometimes we'd use marbles or rocks for change. We learned how to buy and sell, as well as count money.

Sometimes we'd build a stand and sell juice. Our mulberry trees would produce a bumper crop. We'd squeeze out the juice, including seeds and pulp, and serve it to paying customers. We were the customers. We'd play like we were patrons.

My brothers always had a hammer and saw available. They could not play "Cowboy and Indians" without guns and bows and arrows, so they made them. The guns were cut from a board and had inner tube bands of rubber attached so that they could shoot. For bows, they found willow branches and tied string to both ends. They found enough lighterknot splinters for arrows.

During their transition from boys to men, my brothers were always involved in either doing something adventurous or making something, and I often participated.

One quiet day when things were rather dull, we looked out our front porch door to see a most remarkable thing. The Ewton boys who lived nearby had opened our front gate and were walking toward the house on stilts. Neither my brothers nor myself had ever seen such a thing; so out the door we ran to welcome these larger-than-life creatures.

The older boys jumped down and asked us if we wanted to walk on the stilts. Naturally, we did. It was such fun, but it took a while to learn just how to do it. After several good tumbles, we finally mastered the skill and could walk a short distance on them without toppling over.

Then they offered to help us make some for our very own. First, we had to find some empty lard cans. We raided the trash, just as we did whenever we played store. While we did this, the Ewton boys went through the lumber pile in the back of the garage. There they found six two-by-twos just the right length. Each stilt had to be the same size as its partner.

Soon one lard can was nailed to the first two-by-two with shingle nails. Another lard can was nailed to the matching two-by-two. Both were nailed high enough up so that the can and the board were level with the ground. Eventually, the cans were removed. In their place were nailed scraps of wood. The scraps were nailed up as high as we dared, sometimes as high as two feet.

My youngest brother, Bill, was given the first set. He immediately stepped up on the cans nailed inside the poles. He grabbed the boards about where his arms touched and held on tightly. Two of the Ewton boys walked him as he steadied himself. Soon he was able to hold on and walk by himself.

My other brother was next. Finally, it was my turn. Soon all of us were walking down that white marl road like kings of the walk!

We headed up toward my Uncle Gus's house to show off to my cousins. They were just as excited as we were and soon we had them up on stilts and walking down the road like professionals. To this day, I still thrill whenever I think of what fun it was!

The girls had some activities, such as making paper dolls, that did not appeal to boys. Hours would be spent drawing women figures. Everything had to be right. The women wore underwear, but paper dresses were cut out with two flaps on the shoulders. These flaps could be bent down, with the dress hanging down over the doll's body, covering her underwear.

I think that we played with paper dolls more than we did with real dolls because my doll's china head had been smashed. I didn't seem to think that made a bit of difference, though. She was still my doll, head or no head. She was a very special person named Gertrude. In fact, all my dolls were called Gertrude. I've often wondered if that had some hidden psychological meaning. Even the heifer my grandfather gave me years later was called Gertrude. I think I liked the feel of certain sounds in my mouth just as I liked the feel of certain foods.

There is one thing I can say with assurance—we were never bored. We didn't like what we had to do sometimes, but as I look back, I had a good time.

I smile with a wistful memory of complete and total childhood fulfillment.

Frosty Reflections
A Late-1920s Freeze

About two years before the Great Depression landed on the rest of the country, hard times had already begun in Florida. Mother had just turned on the radio for the latest weather report one day. From the speaker horn of one of the early models of radio came this ominous message:

"A cold north wind will bring freezing temperatures to the state of Florida tonight. We have received a call from the farmer's association. They need all the help they can get to save the crops. There will be a hard freeze tonight when the wind dies down."

I watched her turn the radio off and walk quickly back into the kitchen where she was boiling coffee on the kerosene stove. I should have been in school that day, but I had a cold. There wasn't enough money to buy me a sweater. Mother had me try on her old frayed one—it was too large even with the sleeves rolled up. I was small for my eight years. I shivered as I thought about how cold it was. I slowly edged toward the fireplace where a pine log was spitting. The fire blazed warmly and the heat felt good on my bare arms. My feed-sack dress smelled freshly ironed from the heat.

Oh, how I hated being so poor! I was tired of eating peanut butter on biscuits. All of the pupils at school, the little one-story school house about halfway between Weaver's Corner and the Caloosahatchee River on the north side of the river, carried lunches in empty lard cans. Nell and I traded lunches the day before. That cold fried-potato biscuit she gave me was awfully good!

"Times are hard," the grown-ups said. From where I stood I could see my father's old Ford truck with its bed packed with men, women, and children who had arrived to pick the produce before the anticipated freeze. Some were dressed no warmer than myself. Men were unloading crates. Old Moss, our hired man, had built a big bonfire at the edge of the field. He was warming himself as he leaned on a shovel. It looked as though he has just about dug all the ditches needed for the artesian water to cover the fields. Later that day he would unplug the packed earth and let the water flow down the rows. He said it helped keep the crops from freezing.

Something is wrong, I whispered, as I saw everyone scurrying about like ants. Through the sweaty window, I saw children my age helping the hands pick. The men dug, hauled, and loaded; women picked with the children.

There was Tommy. He wasn't in school either. He was trying to tote a whole sackload of potatoes, just like a man. I wanted to help, too, but Mother said my cold might get worse. She said I needed warmer clothes to be outside when it was this cold.

I smelled the strong coffee. Soon father would come in for a refill for the hired help. Mother had biscuits in the oven for lunch. We would have cane syrup on them.

UGH! I was tired of eating the same things all the time.

Mother paced back and forth like she always did when she felt upset. I dared not talk for fear of having her yell at me and say things she didn't mean or throw things again. Once she even told the preacher that the Lord didn't care how bad things were. She told him she would not come to church until the Lord showed her He cared about all the hungry people and how terrible things were for the poor.

Back in the kitchen, Mother turned the radio on again. The same warning: A hard freeze tonight.

I thought about the days when Mother was laughing and smiling all the time. They seemed so long ago. Mother always wanted pretty things. She had worked hard to help my father. It seemed to her that ever since the boom burst, no matter what they did, they stayed poor. Once she exploded after someone came to take the cows away because we couldn't pay the feed bill. She said, "I refuse to live this way," and burned all our ragged clothes. I think my sweater was one of the things she threw in the fire.

The boom was a time when everyone seemed to be rich. There was money for everything. Suddenly, in a short time, everyone was poor and there was no money for anything. People were hungry. There were no jobs and everyone was hurting in some way. It was as if a big balloon had suddenly burst.

All through the day the field hands worked. I looked through the steamy window and could tell that it wouldn't be long before sunset. The last load of produce was being taken to the packing house. This made the third I counted that day.

The last crates had been wired and trucked away. Moss was digging again, preparing to let the water flow between the rows to keep the plants from freezing. Sometimes it worked and sometimes it didn't. Everyone gathered around the fire except Moss. He was busy unplugging the small dams at the beginning of each row. Soon the water came! It gushed down the ditches like a gully washer and after awhile the fields looked like a lake.

Beyond the field and over on the other side of the big ditch, I saw smudge pots bellowing up their puffy smoke to keep the citrus trees from freezing. Cold wind was circulating freely among the orange and grapefruit trees. Sometimes the wind seemed to make smoke patterns as it swished in and out, up and down, and across the newly made lake. The last truckload carried the workers away. Father and Moss put out the big bonfire. It was none too soon because the sun was setting.

When Father came in the kitchen door, he was so tired he could hardly talk. It seems to me that he would have done even more if he had thought it would have done any good. As it was, he had done all he could do. He shivered. I wondered if he was that cold or if he was afraid that the freeze would ruin him.

"Can you stop now for supper?" Mother asked, "Beans and cornbread tonight, but if we are lucky, by this time next week, we'll be eating high off the hog."

"Can't say that's so," he answered as he rubbed his stiff red hands before the fire. "Got to wait and see what prices we'll get."

Just then a commotion was heard outside. Rover was barking wildly, the hens squawking.

"Get the lantern. I don't know when I've seen it so dark. It is so dark it is thick." He looked out over the yard as he raised the lantern. "Something's after those chickens. Feathers are everywhere."

He slammed the back door and yelled to my mother, "Sally, we've got to get them hens back in the hen house soon or they're gonna be goners. Sis, take Rover in the house with you."

"Whew. Here, boy. There, that's a good boy." Rover's tail fell between his legs as he crawled inside the door. I took hold of his collar and pulled him down beside me.

Mother put on her old frayed sweater and almost tripped over Rover as she hurried outside to help. I listened as they tried desperately to round up the disturbed hens, a task that proved to be impossible. Rover didn't like being inside. His head was between his paws and his eyes were downcast. Soon I heard my father say, "Come on in, Sally. We'll never get them back in the hen house tonight."

As he came through the door, he said, "There's no wind. The cold will settle down fast."

* * *

When morning dawned, I was amazed—the frost had created a winter wonderland, something rare in South Florida.

"Come on out, Rover. Out you go," Father said as soon as he was out of bed.

I watched Rover as he hurried out the door. It was funny to see how he reacted to the thick white frost. His tail went up as he caught a whiff of something. Off he went in pursuit, stopping now and then to lift each paw. Suddenly he yelped. He raced back to the door with something in his mouth and pawed on it.

"Open the door, Sis, but don't let any of that cold air in. I've got a good start on the fire in the fireplace. I don't want the draft to blow it out." Mother cupped the small blaze in her hands. I opened the door to see Rover with a frozen hen in his mouth. Father made Rover put the hen down and come back inside.

After we had eaten our eggs and biscuits, my father stepped outside to assess the damage. I think he was afraid of what he was going to find. Rover walked slowly ahead of him, sniffing every step of the way.

The sun was beginning to peep over the pines. Everything glistened as icicles began to shed droplets of water.

There on the ground beside the back door were six frozen chickens huddled together. Under the water tank were two more. Frozen feathers lay mounded together as though an owl had feasted and left the trimmings when he had eaten his fill. There were no footprints. Nothing moved in the morning silence.

From the door, I could see my father's shoulders sag. With his hands on his hips, he seemed to stand frozen along with everything else. His head seemed even lower as he walked toward the grove. I knew he was going to examine the smudge pots—burned out by morning, but he would know if they had done any good during the cold night. I watched him as he walked back towards the house with his shoulders bent, his hands in his pockets. The brim of his hat was turned down. He hurried as if he were anxious to get out of the cold. Rover followed closely behind, head down, tail drooping.

I opened the door. After what seemed to be an eternity, he finally said, "Maybe the fruit trees will live, but everything else is gone."

My father was discouraged because after all the hard work, there would be little in return. The cows had been sold to pay the feed bill debt. The chickens were dead. The fruit trees were vulnerable to the freeze. There would be no second crop to pick now. A second picking would have been a real bonanza to the family.

Mama was not ranting and raving as she sometimes did when things went wrong. She was strangely silent. She just reached out and pulled the three of us together. Her eyes were full of tears as she softly said, "All is not lost. The crops are in the packing house. They didn't freeze. We are together. We are warm and all our needs are met. Aren't we lucky?"

She bent her head and purred like a happy kitten, "Thank you, Lord. I'll be in church Sunday, just as I promised I would if you showed you cared!"

Despite my father's discouragement, Mother was happy that the Lord had helped us get at least one crop to the packing house.

Swamp, Bog, and Native Flowers

When Ponce de Leon landed in Florida on Easter Sunday, 1513, he saw "the land full of flowers," expressed in his native tongue of Spanish in one word—Florida. The name is fitting because Florida really is blessed with an abundance of flowers.

Ponce de Leon was seeking the fountain of youth, but he found an earthly paradise, in spite of its many biting insects. Since that time, settlers have imported flowers, bulbs, shrubs, and trees thinking they were adding to the state's beauty. There are so many varieties that it is sometimes difficult to determine which plants are indigenous. Many of the imported varieties have escaped into the wild to become naturalized in their environs; so it is with many of the swamp and bog flowers, such as the beautiful water hyacinths. When in bloom, their blue-violet blossoms are a sight to behold. And sometimes you need to get off the beaten path to see them.

One day when I was about two years old, my mother was rowing a skiff back from Pondella, now called Cape Coral, where we had been visiting my grandmother. In those days traveling by boat was one of the best ways of getting where we wanted to go. Even so, the Caloosahatchee river was often rough. Her little boat would bounce up and down upon the waves and water splashed in on us. As we neared Yellowfever Creek we were confronted by a sudden storm. Mother rowed frantically to get to shelter before the storm became worse. I was too young to help. Lightning flashed near the boat. I was terrified. I probably added to Mother's anxiety by screaming "Dis boat eeks!" as the heavy rain collected in the bottom. Mother kept rowing until she came to the mouth of the creek. There, near an area where the creek was nearly clogged with water hyacinths, she seemed to finally relax. On that day, they were not only beautiful, they provided Mother with a buffer to the waves. The weight of the matted, tangled life support system of the hyacinths tamed the waves and calmed the water enough so that it allowed the boat to stop bouncing. The surface plants were so thick that we could not pass through them even if we had wanted to. We would have had to chop our way through, or find a way around them.

She poled her way around them and entered the safety of the creek. There the winds were less fierce, even though lightning crashed about and rain pelted us savagely. We stayed in the water, rather than seeking shelter on the land, because Mother knew the tall yellow pines attracted lightning.

As soon as it was possible for her to do so, she gathered me up in her arms and soothed my fears. Then together we began to bail out the boat. Mother handed me my drinking cup. She used a tin lard can. Between the rain and the splashing waves, the skiff was about half filled. When the storm finally subsided, we continued our journey home, which was about one-half mile from the creek.

She never let me forget my cute saying "Dis boat eeks!" In fact, it became part of the family's stories.

As for me, I never forgot the water hyacinths—breathtaking beauty in the midst of a storm! They smelled heavenly and when they were not bent over with rain, their green leaves and petioles glistened in the effusive light. It was my first recollection of ever seeing them.

Water hyacinths serve mankind in several ways, but they also can be one of his cruelest environmental enemies. The leaves and petioles offer shade and protection for some of the smaller river or pond inhabitants. They prevent oxygen loss and keep the water cool, and they purify the water and provide shelter for small fish. The fish in turn trim excessive growth by eating the algae, the mosquito larvae and other insects.

I was interested to read the following in *Gulfwatch* magazine, a publication of the Environmental Protection Agency, and quote with permission:

"When he [Dr. Bill Wolverton] started at NASA's Stennis Space Center in Mississippi in 1971, the agency was under pressure to make its waste lagoon comply with the Clean Water Act. Wolverton suggested planting water hyacinths to purify the water. Many people at the agency thought he was crazy, and he quickly became known as 'the man with the weeds.' The center's director, however, decided to let Wolverton plant his 'weeds.' To almost everyone's surprise, it worked, and still does, sixteen years later.

"To many of Wolverton's detractors, the whole idea of plants removing contaminants like benzene, acetone, toulene and formaldehyde from water seemed too simple to be possible. But, in actuality, it is a complex precess that science has begun to understand only recently, according to [Fredrico] Marques [of Miles, Inc.].

"The key is the symbiotic relationship between plants and microbes. Microbes are part of plants immune system. They live among the roots of the plants, and when a toxic compound comes into contact with the plant roots, the microbes break them down into substances the plant can use for food The plant then absorbs these usable substances as nutrients. The microbes thrive, the plant thrives, and the water is purified. 'This is the way nature has always done it,' Marques said."

When the Everglades absorbed too much of the commercial fertilizers used for crops, the canals and waterways became inundated with water-growing plants. They were crowding out native plants, especially saw grass, and taking over. The fertilizer increased plant life and created an imbalance in the ecological system. It affected snails, frogs, and the native fishes by taking away their natural supply of oxygen. Native grasses and sedges were smothered out.

To control the spread of the water hyacinths, tilapia were imported from Africa. They are bronze-green to brassy red in color and resemble sunfish. They primarily eat vegetation and are voracious eaters.

From what history I have read, the water hyacinths were imported from South America and escaped into the wild like so many of Florida's imported plants. They were used by the early Mexicans for fertilizer. When they cleaned out the canals that carried irrigation water to their crops, they piled them up on the canal banks to decompose and make compost.

I have heard that Disney World uses water hyacinths to purify some of its reclaimed water. In some places water hyacinths are used for cattle feed. It could be considered as a food source for people in the future if the food supply runs low.

Water lilies serve much the same purpose as the hyacinths, except that I have not heard of their being a problem. It seems to me that all the water lilies that I have seen are on sluggish streams or still inland ponds or quiet, calm pools that act as their own ecosystem, complete unto themselves, with their myriad varieties of plant and animal life that are symbiotic in their relationships.

The water lily is usually anchored to a muddy bottom, but its large rounded leaves float. Although there are many varieties, the one that I have seen most in Florida swamps has white flowers that are six to eight inches across and extend upward for not more than twelve inches. They open during the day and close during the night.

When I was a child I heard much about the lotus lily that grew in Egypt. It was supposed to be related to our water lily. Our native lotus (*Nelumbo lutea*) is found in Florida in quiet pools or ponds. Its bloom stands about forty inches above the water surface. Its leaves are light green. A cultivated variety that has escaped into the wild and is sometimes seen is the pink lotus (*Nelumbo nucifers*). I am fascinated by the many varieties of swamp and bog plants—cow lily, pickerel weed, bladderworts, and purple butterwort. Then there is the trumpet, an insect-eating plant, the white-top pitcher plant. Other water-loving varieties are the sky-flower, the watershield, the burt-reed, the glades lobelia, venus looking-glass, the primrose willow, yellowtop, green eyes, and floating hearts.

Wild butterfly orchid. Courtesy of Larry Evans.

I have personally located two kinds of iris in Southwest Florida. The prairie (*Iris hexaqona*, variety *savannarum*) blooms in the spring; however, the wetter it is, the more blooms. It is located on the low pinelands, prairies, and cypress swamps. I've also found the rooster tail or walking iris, so called because new plants are produced from the stalk of the root.

Many of the above-mentioned flowers grow there because the Everglades is a haven for all kinds of flora. What will not grow in one place will be happy growing in a nearby spot. Its diverseness of marshes, pinelands, cypress heads, mangrove swamps, and prairies allows for its abundance of unique species. In these hammocks, trees help to provide the proper environment for lush growth.

One might find a grove of pondapples (*Annon glabra linnaeus*) sometimes called *custard apples.* They may be submerged in water or dry as the season dictates, but what a beautiful display. There are still places where the moon vine (*Ipomoea alba linnaeus*) stretches across an area of twenty feet to provide shade to the forest floor beneath. The blooms can produce a canopy across the entire grove in the moonlight. Imagine what it is like when the moon is full! During the day the blooms fold up and look like white candles.

While there is daylight, the rugged tree trunks and rambling branches display bromeliads, called quill-leaf (*Tillandsia fasciculata swartz*) that light up the dreary, dismal, steamy swamp with bright orange and red flashes of color. On the branches of these trees and many other kinds of trees hang Spanish moss (*Tillandsia sneoides*), on wiry, dangling stems. When in bloom its flowers are small and fragrant, with yellow blossoms so small they are hard to see. To some people the moss resembles a man's long gray beard.

This moss once was gathered for stuffing mattresses and pillows. It was worn by early Indians as clothing. We were always taught never to pick this moss, because chiggers and red bugs thrived in it.

And the family has quite a story about the use of Spanish moss. After my maternal grandmother Katie C.'s death, my aunt Ruth came back from Hawaii to help clear out her house. It was decided that since she wanted the cut glass, the crystal, and china, she could have them. Others in the family were allowed to choose what they wanted. Aunt Ruth, being practical, thought she could pack her portion rather than have the movers do it. She went out in the woods and gathered all the Spanish moss she could find. Piece by piece her treasures were carefully wrapped in the moss (in spite of the red bugs). After it was all packed away and crated, it was shipped to her home. To her amazement and chagrin, when she unpacked the crates some years later, she discovered that the moss had dried out during the move and had provided no padding for the heirlooms. Every piece of the beautiful family glass and china was broken to bits. Moral of the story: Always find out all you can about wild plants before using or eating them!

Swamp and bog areas are only part of the wondrous Everglades that border on the area of Lee County where I grew up. The terrain is changeable from pine flats to salt marshes, from hammocks to barrens, and so on.

The barrens are places where the undergrowth is scant due to the few nutrients in the soil. Often surrounding them are the flat pinelands. They were once blessed with large pines that were cut down by the logging industry. To replace them, an "inferior" pine (the slash pine) was planted to provide wood products like pulp and turpentine.

Swampy area near author's childhood home in Southwest Florida. Photo by Leonard Vanderwulp.

It was in the pine flatlands that I tasted my first ground pawpaw, saw pitcher plants, and orange milkweed plants that butterflies like so much. Sometimes creeks run through these pinelands. Along side them in shady areas there are wild blueberry bushes.

Further away under shaded trees, where it is partially wet, there will be huckleberry bushes. They lay close to the ground and provide food for animals as well as shelter for snakes. When picking huckleberries, one always has to be on the lookout for rattlers.

Beyond the flatlands lay stretches of marshland where fresh water and salt water mingle. Here one finds the mangrove forests. Nearby are the salt flats. Then saw grass savannas pop up and seem to stretch on as far as the eye can see. This is the reason why the Everglades is called the "river of grass." The saw grass thrives on the moisture of the underground river that flows beneath, consequently the soil remains wet and mucky.

Scattered throughout the grassland are cypress heads or islands. There one finds the bald cypress and a swampy area of unique beauty. The knees protrude from the water and stand from one to three feet tall. They look much like someone has placed stakes or stobs throughout the cypress islands. The water is alive with alligators, water turtles, frogs, snakes, and birds—not to mention other animals such as opossums, raccoons, a few panthers (that are left) and an occasional black bear or otter. The cypress knees are well-known by lamp and furniture makers, who cut them down and polish them.

Few of the large pine forests remain, but the animals stake out their territories from one area to another wherever food is plentiful. During the dry season many shallow water ponds begin to dry up. When this happens, there is an easy fish-catch for the animals that travel from one region to another.

The area that supports beautiful flowers are the hammocks. They are higher lands usually based upon a limerock ridge. There one will find what is termed tropical hardwoods. The water does not cover the land all the time, and in some spots it remains dry the year around. The land drains after a rain but remains moist and promotes excellent growing conditions.

These hardwoods include live oaks, red maple, gumbo limbo, pigeon plums, and wild tamarinds to mention a few. Once in a while one might even see a coontie palm, which has a root that, when cut up and ground, makes a starch. Years ago there were many coontie plants. The Indians first used the plants' starch to make bread and they showed the white man how it was done. In time, the white man used this knowledge to make money. The enterprising men began to dig the plants up to make starch. Since it was similar to corn starch and was an excellent thickener, much of it was sold. In time, their source dried up and the coontie almost became extinct. In recent years the plants are making a comeback, however.

In this lush hammock environment ferns also thrive on the forest floor. They are one of the many kinds of plant life that is enriched by cooler temperatures and high degree of humidity, and constantly fighting for the flickering light that filters from above.

One will find blackstem spleen wort ferns, netted chain ferns, Boston ferns, bracken, and cinnamon ferns and others like the climbing fern, the royal fern, and the resurrection fern. The resurrection seems to die back when it doesn't get enough moisture, but when it rains, it comes back to life.

Most of the trees will have mistletoe, as well as Spanish moss on them. Some will have slimy, green algae and lichens on their trunks and exposed roots.

True mistletoe (*Phoraddendron serotinum*) is a parasite. Its roots dig into the host tree and suck out the nutrition they need. It usually grows high up in the tree to hog the sunshine as well. The stems are brittle. During the Christmas season mistletoe produces white berries. An old custom is to tie a sprig of it over a door and anyone who stands under it gets kissed, coming and going.

On the tree trunks under the branches supporting the Spanish moss and the mistletoe, one will find wild orchids. Some orchids like dry ground, some prairies, some barrens, some swamps, and others prefer bogs. Those ground-loving orchids are as different in their demands as other species.

I can remember my grandfather talking about the numerous varieties of orchids he would see on his hunting trips into the Everglades. He told us about orchids so beautiful it was hard to believe.

My father often took northern friends of his on hunting trips. All came back with bags of orchids to take home. In those days it was not against the law to pluck them off the trees.

In our own back yard under the mango and guava trees we had an orchid garden. Most of them did not do too well, but the butterfly orchid always bloomed for us. It seemed to say to me, *See how beautiful I am.* Its thin stalk was crowded with lovely yellow ocher-colored petals with a dab of purple on one.

When it became unusually hot, many succumbed. It was impossible to keep them alive out of their element—they thrived on a moist, well-protected area.

It was then that my father began to discourage the picking of wild orchids. All natives have a respect for wildlife beauty and want to protect and preserve it for posterity. Others joined the ranks and after many years it became unlawful to remove them from the swamps. Even so, these rare orchids are seldom if ever seen; they may have perished, for all we know. The loss is tremendous.

Willow Pond at Sunset

Summer had faded into crisp orange autumn days. Shadows fell long and lavender. Soft winds kissed each tree and tugged at their branches.

On such a day I saw Willow Pond—a lake of black-eyed Susans as far as my eyes could see. Winter would soon mow the dancing daisies down and the pond water would no longer reflect their beauty like a mirror. But that day belonged to the willows, the daisies, and me.

I was about five when I first saw the tall green willows that circled the pond. Soon they would be bare, but that day they stood as guardsmen enjoying the daisies as much as I.

We were friends, the willow trees and I. We shared that autumn day. We breathed air full-blown with an herblike smell. We watched as fire clouds slowly swallowed the sun. The willows spied on me as I plucked a cattail to release its seeds into the wind—so like a dandelion did they twirl! Then I felt the black-eyed Susan's smooth velvet petals and stepped back in awe. The willows saw me shudder. They seemed to know that I could not pick a single flower!

Bullbats (nighthawks) hummed as they swooped. A whippoorwill called. From a distance I heard the echo of his mate.

Slowly the fire clouds burned to ash. Twilight muted all but the frogs and owls. Choruses of tree frogs filled the dampening air. A symphony began when the bullfrogs played bass fiddle. An alligator bellowed French horn calls. Fireflies frolicked in a staccato frenzy.

I bowed my head in reverence and bid the daisies farewell. Twinkling stars saluted the black cloak of night as it covered the daisies, the willows, and me. It remains in my memory just as it did when I followed the path home.

Encountering Seminoles

Early in the morning, just before sunrise, I was out of bed ready to begin the day. As usual I stepped out on our screened front porch, the place where even though I was only about five or six years old, I usually cared for my younger brothers, at least until my parents woke up.

On this day I was playing alone with my paper dolls and looked up to see a Seminole Indian woman coming into our yard. She went directly over to the faucet on the side of the porch, turned on the water and began to wash something. I was spellbound; I couldn't keep my eyes off her. She wrung out a piece of clothing she had washed and proceeded over to our rose garden where Mother had planted a dozen Red Radiance roses.

She carefully laid out the garment, which looked like a full skirt, over one of the rose bushes. Evidently, she intended for it to stay there until it had dried. Then she headed back to the faucet. I then saw her very carefully slip off a second underskirt, leaving the top skirts untouched. She proceeded to rub it out under the water with her hands, then rinsed it, and hung it on the rose bush next to the first one. She must have taken off, washed, and placed to dry at least six skirts. Then she washed a blouse, rinsed it, and found another rose bush on which to hang it.

She ended up washing all her clothes except for one remaining blouse and skirt, which she wore.

Then, without saying a word, she quietly left our yard and returned to the Seminole Village that had been put on display for the winter tourists. In the late or middle 1920s, the Chamber of Commerce created Indian villages as tourist attractions. The Indians lived in these villages as they lived in the Everglades. None of them spoke English, and even if they did, they would not carry on a conversation.

My little brothers and Mother soon joined me on the porch, and I told her about the woman.

Author's sketch of Seminole woman.

Later, Mother and I went to examine the drying clothes. Neither of us had ever seen anything like them. The garments were put together with tiny quilt pieces. Each piece was beautifully sewn—no raw edges and no unfinished seams. The pattern she had created in each outfit was different, but they were all colorful masterpieces of design.

All day we watched for her to return. When she finally came for her clothes toward supper time, I could see her in her beauty. Her raven black hair was pulled up and over something like a fan. Mother said she did this to make a sun screen to shade her eyes. She was barefoot, but around her neck were rows and rows of colored beads. We later learned that each string of beads meant an honor, and were added one at a time. The first was given at her marriage. If her husband died before she did, she had to give up all beads except the original string. She also had to cut her hair at his death and mourn until it grew back.

After checking to see if her clothes were dry, she gathered them up and then went to the faucet again. This time she took one of the clean, dried skirts and placed it over the skirt she had on. Off came the under skirt onto the ground. She washed it, then placed another blouse over the blouse she was wearing. She pulled the under one off and washed it, also. When she was through, all her clothes were clean. She carried her clothing with her and if we hadn't seen her, no one would ever have known she had been there. We did not try to speak to her because we knew she would not respond.

This was my introduction to the Seminole Indians. My second encounter came when some neighborhood children and I went to see the tourist display that was on the highway about a quarter of a mile from our house.

The display consisted of a thatched-roof shelter out in the middle of a wooded area. There was a platform about three feet off the ground on which a woman, two children, and her husband sat. The woman was sewing on her little hand-cranked machine. How cleverly she handled the small scraps and how beautifully she put each together, row upon row.

I saw cabbage palm posts onto which the thatched roof was attached, and sleeping hammocks alongside the hut. They looked much like the mosquito nets we slept under when we camped out on Sanibel Island.

There was a campfire near another shack. The burning logs were put together like spokes of a wheel. As the fire burned in the

Top: Members of Seminoles in Naples, Florida, circa 1920s. Photo Courtesy of State Bureau of Archives and Records Management.

Center: F. A. Hendry among the Seminoles. Photo courtesy Sebring Historical Society.

Bottom: Seminole chickees on Pine Island. Date unknown. Courtesy of State Bureau of Archives and Records Management.

*Author sketches of Seminoles:
Top, Seminole Indian family in
traditional dress worn until the
early 1920s.*

*Center: Seminole Indian women
grinding corn into sofkee (grits).*

*Bottom: Seminole man crossing
creek in dugout canoe.*

center, the husband would push an unburned part toward the fire to keep it burning. On the fire was an iron pot full of grits. There was no water where the huts were placed. They must have had to walk quite a distance to get water.

We could not communicate with the Indians and they did not act as though they wanted to talk to us.

When I returned home later that day, Mother told me that the hut was called a *chickee*. The grits were called *sofkee*.

The third time I was exposed to Seminoles was when we traveled over the Tamiami Trail for the first time, to Miami. The Tamiami Trail's name comes from the cities at either end—Tampa on the west coast and Miami on the southeast coast of the state. Also known as U.S. 41, Tamiami Trail was built through the Everglades when I was six or seven years old. Canals were built on each side of the highway as it went across the southern tip of the state.

As we proceeded into the wilderness where the cypress trees were citadels, we came to higher ground—still marshy, but dryer. Suddenly we came upon a field of tiger lilies. If Cezanne or Renoir had glimpsed fields of red-orange tiger lilies that grew near my childhood home each would have painted another masterpiece. Words cannot convey the ecstasy I felt when I saw those lilies for the first time. Those wild orange-petaled lilies with spots jumping all over them were as beautiful a sight as I ever expected to see. My father stopped the car to allow us to pick a bouquet and behold their beauty. For the first time I could understand what the Bible alludes to in Luke: 12:27: *Consider the lilies how they grow: They toil not, they spin not; and yet I say unto you, that Solomon in all his glory was not arrayed like one of these.*

I was allowed to cross a dried-up ditch and gather a bouquet of the orange flowers. I didn't realize that they would soon wilt as the warmth of my hand crushed them together. How sad I was when their heads began to topple as I held them tightly.

Those wild tiger lilies will always be in my treasure chest of memories.

For the next hour or so, all of us were captivated with the egrets and other kinds of birds feeding along the canal beds. The gray herons, some called them blue herons, the ducks, the mallards, teals, the loons, and the snake birds or anhingas, were as thick as fleas. We wondered how so many birds found enough to eat. Later on, we saw the ospreys and their nests high up in the dead pine trees. They seemed to prefer a dead tree to build their mammoth nests.

As we drove through the Everglades, there were miles and miles of sawgrass, and clouds of ever-changing flights of birds.

They seemed to fill the air with flapping wings and screeching sounds, but the beauty of them in flight was like turning a page of a big book and letting each page flap down.

We spotted some Seminole men in their dugouts, poling their way along the canal. My father told us how they would burn the trees and chisel out the splinters to make those special low-cut canoes. The men used the long poles to pull or push the canoes as was needed through the swamps, creeks and marshy areas.

Soon we came to Seminole villages. We stopped our car and "pretended" to be tourists because my folks wanted us to learn all about these wonderful people.

We were interrupted by a little Indian boy whose pet otter was running between the visitors. When he finally caught it, he pulled it close to his chest in a warm embrace and soon disappeared.

Monday Morning Washdays

"Grandma, what am I to do with the grease from the fatback?" my mother, then ten years old, asked.

"Pour it in the grease jar on the back of the stove, Alice." It was washday in Southwest Florida in 1910. The Rosser women were preparing supper early in the morning. On washdays they always had lima beans. After the beans had been washed, the fatback was fried and added to them. They would cook all day over a slow fire in a wood-burning stove, and be ready to eat when the wash was done.

Alice's mother called from the backyard, "Get me another bar of soap. I'll rub the colored things first. Then I'll boil them later." Alice hurried to get the soap for her.

"Ma, this is the last bar of lye soap."

"Maybe you and Granny can make more soap tomorrow," she answered.

My mother began to rub the soap on her blue, flour-sack dress that was already folded over the scrub board. In those days, flour and sugar were sold in cloth sacks that were printed in all types of designs and colors. When the sacks were emptied, the fabric was used for clothing.

"Ma, can I do it?"

Her mother moved back and Alice began to rub her dress on the metal ridges of the board. "Watch your fingers! They can get skinned."

Her grandma came out to see how things were going. She, too, wanted to help in any way she could.

It was then that Alice noticed the water in the last rinse tub had not been emptied. She stopped rubbing and began to drain the tub, one bucketful at a time. A white residue clung to the tub bottom after the water was softened with lye; it had to be wiped out. Then the tub was refilled with the buckets of water she had just removed. It was now soft, but not as soft as rainwater.

Her mother took over with the scrub board. All day long she would rub, douse, rub and rub again. Then she would rinse the clothes twice. Deciding Alice could help with that as well, she said, "You can begin to rinse now, Sis."

Then her grandmother brought a bag of clothespins and a clothes hamper. "It looks like you'll be needing these pretty soon."

The clothes pins were made of wood and had small metal springs to hold the clothes on the line, even during heavy winds.

Alice's mother built a fire under the iron cauldron. When the water boiled hard for a few minutes, she placed the white clothes in and poked them down. When they had "boiled up good," they were lifted out into a big dishpan. From there the clothes would go into rinse water to be sloshed up and down until they were rinsed thoroughly.

"I need some more water, Sis."

Alice went over to the pump stand and began pumping "artesian" water into a bucket. When it was full, she toted it over to her.

The three generations worked as a team all day long. When the colored clothes had been washed and rinsed, they were hung on the line. On a good washday, the wind flapped them dry pretty fast. Her mother always tested the wind direction before building the

Sketch by author of typical wash day in the early 1900s.

fire. She made sure that the wind did not blow smoke on the clothes. They needed the air to help whip them dry. The more wind there was, the quicker they dried and the fewer wrinkles there were.

When the colored clothes were dry, Alice's mother would wipe her hands on her apron and begin to take them down. So that she would have enough clothes line wire, she placed the rinsed white clothes on the line where the colored clothes had been. She then folded the colored clothes and placed them in a basket. She had another basket for the clothing that was to be ironed the next day. Meanwhile, Alice placed the empty tubs on a table so that if a rain came, they could collect rainwater. It was used to wash their hair.

Alice's mother would not let Grandma help carry the baskets because they were too heavy, but Grandma always found something she could do to help.

"I'll make the cornbread," Alice's mother said. "Sis, you set the table. Granny, you can peel the onions. Beans are done and the hot-pepper sauce is on the table," she said.

"Now supper'll be ready for Pa when he comes in from the field."

Pa was tired when he came in, but he washed up.

Alice's mother served the beans in soup bowls and they all sat down.

Pa said grace and when he finished, Grandma, Ma, and Alice said a loud amen because they knew that the day was about to end as well.

Alice saw her mother reach down to rub her aching back. It hurt but her mother never complained.

"Tomorrow I'll iron. Sis, you and Granny can make soap."

My mother and grandmother used to do the following to make soap: They first purchased one can of Red Devil lye, which they emptied into a large enamel container. The contents were heated slowly without boiling. Next they poured five cups of water into the container and stirred until the lye was thoroughly mixed. Then, five pounds of bacon fat or grease were added a little at a time. They mixed until it began to thicken. Before it got too thick, they poured it into a baking pan. It stayed in the pan until it was thick and cool. By then it had firmed up and hardened. When hard, they cut the soap into squares.

Eatin' Possum

Eatin' possum is not akin to eatin' crow. However, after *not* tasting possum some folks do eat crow. As for me, I've never tasted it, but I always felt a tinge of guilt because of my behavior as a child when possum was served up to our family on the equivalent of a silver platter.

I was a child during the period of segregation in the South. Our family had several black people who helped with various chores, and we considered them part of our family. In fact, "Old Moss," our handyman, was one of the reasons I have so much respect and admiration for black people today.

Old Moss reported to my mother that an opossum had found his way into the hen house. He recognized the tracks and found numerous feathers strewn about. Of course, he knew what to do about the situation—kill the critter. But he apparently considered possum meat a delicacy and wanted to know if mother had ever eaten some. When she replied in the negative, he offered to dress the opossum and cook it for our family. He was so enthusiastic and excited about sharing that mother could not turn him down.

He must have killed the opossum later that night, because the next day when his chores were done, he appeared at the back door with his prize. Mother turned the kitchen over to him and he went to work. He walked out in the field and dug up sweet potatoes. He seemed to be as at ease in the kitchen as in the field.

Hours later, when it was time for dinner, Old Moss appeared in his Sunday best. When we were seated at the table and after grace was said, Moss emerged from the kitchen with a white dish towel folded across his arm like a waiter in a fancy restaurant, asking if we were ready for the 'possum.

Mother nodded her approval. Soon he returned with the 'possum on a cookie sheet—an improvised silver platter. The meat smelled like a bit of heaven and his eyes sparkled like heaven's midnight stars.

He placed the cookie sheet on the table in front of Mother, perhaps at her suggestion. She may have been concerned about my father's acceptance of this surprise gourmet treat.

Moss then left the room as one who had bestowed a pot of gold upon his queen. There on the table was a wonderful smelling food swimming in fat. It was not only swimming in fat, but it was glistening in fatty paradise. The rest of the meal included mother's homemade sliced bread, milk, and additional baked sweet potatoes.

I'm sure that he could hear from the kitchen the tones of our voices and what we had to say about his culinary delight. It was total rejection by all except my mother.

My father was the first to reject the meat. My brothers and I were quick to refuse to even taste it.

A few minutes later Moss came back into the room with pickles and jelly for the table.

Gone was his jubilant countenance. He looked expectantly at Mother. I'll never forget the look on her face when she looked up at him and asked him to serve her the part of the meat he thought she would like best.

Old Moss cut her a chunk of the carcass oozing with fat. Next he served her a sweet potato browned to a turn.

"Thank you, Moss," she said.

Moss was quick to note that no one else asked to be served. He waited a moment. Mother (bless her heart) picked up her fork and took a bite. "Why, this is delicious!" she replied. "Won't some of you at least try it? Please. Really, it is very good."

No one else ate 'possum that day, but Old Moss's efforts were not in vain. He had shared something special with my mother, and she had accepted it with grace. Thus was born a bond of one human being to another—a type that existed for many years in the deep South. It is hard to define, but it was understood by all who chose to give and receive with respect.

He Otter Know Better

Mother had just waved good-bye to us. My two brothers and I were riding to the rodeo at the Fort Myers fairgrounds with my father in his Model-T. It was Mother's idea that we go so that she could color the eggs for the Easter Bunny. This year she planned to hide the eggs after sundown because she hated to get up so early on Easter Sunday to hide them.

As she started to fill a large cook pot with water, she heard a knock at the door. "Aunt Alice, have you seen Willie?"

Willie was my cousin Louis's pet otter. While hunting, my uncle Gus, his father, had found the creature abandoned in a cypress head one day. Uncle Gus assumed that something had happened to its mother so he decided to bring the orphan home.

"No, I haven't, Louis. If the boys had seen him, I think they would have said something," said my mother.

"Yeah, I passed them on the road. They hadn't seen him either. I'm afraid I've lost him."

"Go ahead and call him and look around. I don't think that you'll find Willie here, though."

"He's never taken off like this before. Once he slipped away, but we found him out teasing the cats and chasing them."

"Go around back and talk with Old Moss. He knows a lot about animals, and he was especially fond of Willie."

Mother went back to work. She filled the pot, put the two dozen eggs into the cold water, then started to cook them. "I wonder what's happened to Willie," she said as she reached for the food coloring.

All afternoon she worked on the eggs. Some were colored red, some blue, and some green. Others were spotted, checkered, and some were even decorated with flowers. When she was all through, she hid them in the pantry, way up on the top shelf where no one could see.

She prepared dinner and waited for us to return. In we came in a mad rush, hungry as bears. The rodeo had been fun out in the open air, but when the excitement was over, we were left drained, hungry, and ready to go home.

After dinner, it was play time. Since it was a holiday weekend, we had no yard work to do so we played games on the front lawn. It was always great fun when our parents sat on the front steps and directed our activities. We played tag and hiding games and did somersaults and cartwheels. A good romp on the grass usually tired us out and we slept soundly after our baths.

When bedtime finally came, water for the bath came from cool artesian well water. But the walls turned black from the sulphur in the water when the water splashed them. Our baths were a nightly ritual.

When the weather turned cold, Mother heated water and bathed us in front of an open fire in the living room, which was the only heat we had for the entire house. Mother always hated to entertain during those times that the walls looked terrible.

After our baths, we all kneeled down beside her big bed and said the "Prayer of Faith."

> **Prayer of Faith**
> God is my help in every need.
> He does my every hunger feed;
> God walks beside me, guides my way
> Through every moment of the day.
>
> I now am wise, I now am true,
> Patient, kind, and loving, too.
> All things I am, can do, and be,
> Through Christ, the truth that is in me.
>
> God is my health, I can't be sick;
> God is my strength, unfailing, quick;
> God is my all, I know no fear,
> Since God and love and truth are here.
> *Hannah More Kohaus*

Sometimes Dad would come in and tell us a story after our prayers, but not the night before Easter. We were tired and Mother had one last chore of her own before she retired. After we climbed in our beds, Dad blew out the kerosene lamp and we soon were in slumberland. When all was quiet, Mother and Daddy set about doing what they hoped would be the solution to a problem every Easter morning. It was hard to have an egg hunt and still make it to Sunday school on time.

Carrying a flashlight, they hid the eggs around the yard, under rose bushes, in flower beds, and beneath the sago palms. When the job was done, they were happy to fall into their beds for a much-needed night's rest.

The next morning, just after the sun was up, my brothers and I ran out into the yard. We noticed the empty basket on the front steps, but where were the eggs? We couldn't find a single one!

We searched and searched. My little brother began to cry. He just knew that the Easter Bunny hadn't come. My other brother and I wondered what had happened.

We marched in straight line like soldiers into my parents' bedroom. I led the pack. "Mamma, the Easter Bunny didn't come," I said.

"Of course he came. I thought I saw him last evening before I went to bed. He had a large basket full of eggs."

"He must have taken them up to Uncle Gus's house. We can't find a single egg," my brother said.

With that Mother and Dad hopped out of bed. They hurried out into the front yard. They looked and looked.

"I'm sure that the bunny came last night," she said.

"Something or someone must have stolen them," added my father.

We all began to speculate. "Willie is missing! Do you suppose he could have taken the eggs?" asked my brother.

"I bet that's what happened," said Billy, my baby brother.

My father shook his head and said, "I think it may have been a raccoon."

"Why?" we asked.

"I don't think it was Willie. If Willie is missing, he's probably dead by now."

We were all shocked at this statement and we disagreed.

"Why? He would be hungry, wouldn't he?"

"Probably, but he would go back home to get food where he usually ate."

"I still think he ate the eggs," said Billy.

"Whatever stole those eggs had to have good night vision and be able to have a good sense of smell to steal them all. There's not a single one left."

"Do you really think Willie is dead?" asked my mother.

"I think he's dead," said my father. "Most animals that are tame cannot go back into the wild."

Mother shook her head, "Otters are different."

"How's that?" he asked.

"Otters are social animals. They can go back to the wild," said Mother.

"I'll admit that they are good fighters and they can run fast," said Father.

"I think Willie is alive and will make it whether or not he comes home."

Father admitted that he could be wrong about Willie and hoped that the little fellow would survive. Then he added, "I feel confident that Mamma Raccoon and her family had a nice Easter dinner."

"I don't understand why you think raccoons took the eggs," Mother said.

"Of course, I don't know for sure, but raccoons like to wash off their food before they eat it. I don't see any egg shells lying around. The eggs were carried away to be eaten later."

Just then, Old Moss came limping up. He was awakened by the excitement. He just stood there and chuckled.

"They's sho nuff gone!" he said.

Mother knew breakfast had to be cooked and she was going to make sure that we made Sunday school. "Come on in and eat. We'll try another hunt this afternoon after dinner."

We ate, and then went to Sunday school and church. On the way home, my father stopped at Weaver's Corner. Soon he came out with bottles of Delaware Punch (a carbonated grape drink) and two dozen eggs. Delaware Punch was always a special treat that we seldom ever had.

"We're lucky. These eggs are the last eggs he has," Father said.

After a hasty Sunday dinner, Mother cooked the eggs and all of us decorated them together. What a fun time it was for us all. Usually Dad was too busy to spend so much time with us. He wrote "I love you" on all the eggs he colored.

Finally, the eggs were ready. Mother and Dad went outside to hide them.

It was my job to see that no one peeked. "No, Billy. You can't watch them," I said.

My other brother, Harry, took his little brother's hand and pulled him gently to the floor where we all sat until they finished.

"You can come out, now!" yelled Mother.

We raced outside to search for the eggs. As we gathered them, we placed them in the empty basket on the steps. It was the same basket that was placed there last night and again earlier today.

It didn't take us long to find the eggs. Mother had me count them to see if all twenty-four were there.

"There's only twenty-three," I said.

"They're all there except one," said Harry.

Again we searched and searched. We couldn't find the missing egg.

Suddenly, Little Billy yelled, "I found it."

It was placed inside a clump of rose blossoms. He had looked there by chance. We all laughed.

"I wondered which one of you would find it!" said my father. It was his way of playing with us. He often presented us with puzzles to solve or problems for us to deal with and find their answers.

"Billy, you're the best egg hunter in the family!"

Just about then, Old Moss again came up limping with something hidden inside his shirt and under his arm.

As he unbuttoned the buttons on his shirt, he said, "Look what I've found!"

Everyone turned to look as he pulled open his shirt.

There was Willie, nestled closely like a kitten under his arm. His little head peeked out. Moss reached in and pulled him out for all to see. He held him so that we could see that his hair was all matted and covered with mud and blood. He looked like he had been in a fight.

"Where did you find him?" Mother asked.

"He was all curled up and sitting on the pillow of my bed," said Old Moss. Billy reached up to pet him, but he bared his teeth and let out a low growl. Billy pulled back when he heard him growl. He stood there a bit puzzled, but he didn't attempt to touch him again.

"Poor thing! We'll just have to leave him alone for awhile, won't we, Billy?" said Mother. Then she added, "Come on, kids. Let's eat our Easter eggs! Have some, Moss."

"No thanks. Ma'am. I'm gonna take Willie home. They's sho nuff gonna be happy he's back. He's one real tuckered out young'un and don't need nary a bit more trouble."

"Willie didn't eat the eggs, after all, did he?" stated Harry.

"No, he didn't, but Willie otter know better than to run away!" said Old Moss, chuckling, as he slowly ambled up the road.

The Wrong Still

Early in 1930, when I was about eight years old, my mother began to help take the U.S. census, and she allowed me to go with her as she made her rounds. Mother drove a little Model-A coupe as we wandered out on many logging roads looking for people to count. We covered much of the territory between Fort Myers and the village of Alva—a distance of about twenty miles. At that time, Tice was only a settlement, and Olga was not much larger. Crime was almost nonexistent so we weren't looking for trouble from the people who lived in our area. In fact, our biggest fear was of rattlesnakes and alligators.

One day we were looking for a turpentine still that was supposed to be located in Mother's territory. It would be a place to get census data from workers. We saw and smelled smoke some distance away. Every road we took in that direction seemed to take us anywhere but where we wanted to go. Finally, after about three attempts we found where the fire was. There were several heavily-bearded men standing around with shotguns lined up against a wall. I had never seen such rough-looking characters. Pots, kettles, and bottles lay strewn about. Nearby, was the largest copper kettle I had ever seen. A fire burned brightly beneath it. There were funny pipes and tubes, some wound in coils, running to and from it. The men didn't seem to be happy about our having found them. They refused to give Mother any information and behaved as if they wanted to be left alone.

Mother asked the way to the paved road. She was told that since she found her way here, she could find her way back. With that, we left in a hurry. She lost no time getting us in the car and we sped off down the muddy ruts that looked more like two winding water hoses. Every now and then the ruts became too muddy for her to chance driving on, so she drove out on the ground and straddled one rut. As a last resort, we always had a shovel available in the back to dig us out.

Mother appeared calm, but maybe she was afraid. The way she drove seemed to indicate that she was fearful being alone out in the woods with ruffians such as those we had just encountered. She had told me that she was supposed to find a turpentine still. Seeing the smoke she thought she had found it.

"Mother," I asked her, "Wasn't that a still?"

She replied, "Yes, but I don't think it was the kind of still we were looking for. I'm pretty sure that it was a whiskey still. I believe those men were moonshining."

"What's that?"

"Moonshining is making illegal whiskey. It is against the law." She began to realize that the still was for something other than turpentine when she got a whiff of the rotten smell.

I agreed that it smelled about as bad as any outdoor privy I had ever encountered.

Just then the road curved and right in the middle of it was a big rust-colored coachwhip snake. Mother put on the brakes. She reached for the shovel and started after the snake. In those days, anyone encountering a snake was supposed to kill it. The snake moved very fast, but Mother gave it a good swat with the shovel head. It turned on her and reared up like a horse and began to lash out at her. They were in a battle royal, but Mother won with her persistent shovel-pounding.

Turpentine distillery and workers. Photo courtesy of State Bureau of Archives and Records Management.

I do not know who was the more exhausted after that surprise encounter. I felt weak from fear. She sat in the driver's seat and put her head down on the steering wheel. In a minute or two I heard her whisper, *Thank you, Lord.* Soon we were on the one-car road headed home.

I never did get to see a real turpentine still, but while writing this story I've learned a lot about turpentine, rosin, and creosote and its by-products because they were a part of the industrial history of Southwest Florida.

* * *

As a child, the pine forests grew everywhere except where there were cabbage palms, saw grass, or cypress trees. When we drove along the highway that was wide enough for only one car, the piney woods were somewhat boring. Whenever a hammock appeared or a pond steamy with early morning mist came into view, it was sheer serendipity. It should be remembered, however, these woods helped to shape our early beginnings.

In his 1974 book, *Florida Rambles*, Alex Shoumatoff writes:

Sketch of a turpentine still by Patti Middleton. Used by permission of artist and the Englewood Historical Society.

> First the Spanish and the English harvested it for "naval stores," and the era of transoceanic commerce began with ships whose masts and spars were long-leaved and whose cracks were plugged with its gum. Then the turpentine industry came into the woods, bleeding the trees from Vs cut upon the trunk as high as a darky could reach. Special hollers and shouts were composed by the gangs of blacks as they collected the turpentine in pots and poured it into barrels. Salty old rednecks then drove the barrels out of the woods, conducting teams of mules or oxen with rawhide whips, for which they came to be known as "crackers."

> An accomplished cracker could use his whip to brush a fly from an ox's ear, silence a rattlesnake at five paces, or send a hound dog yelping through the massive colonnades of pines. But then the pulp and paper industry moved into the piney woods and wiped out the largest stand of long-leaved pines, replacing them with inferior but faster-growing slash and loblolly pine. Other industries took their toll.

> The tree, according to Harrar and Harrar's *Guide to Southern Trees* was and still is, in hot demand for the manufacture of paints, varnishes, furniture, and shoe polishes, soaps, cloth-printing, inks, pharmaceutical preparations, greases, specialty lubricants, sealing wax, roofing materials, brewer's pitch, and sweeping compounds. By the 1920s, the long-leaved, the prince of southern pines, no longer dominated the hilly uplands of central Florida and could only be found on a few islands in the scrub.

We were located in just such an area and many of the trees were slashed for their oozing sap. Pine after pine was cut and a container was attached beneath the openings to catch the tree's sap.

This collected sap became one of Florida's early industries. After many of the large pines had been cut for timber their stumps lay bare like a graveyard. Slash pine and loblolly pines were planted to replace the long-leaved pines, but the once lush forest looked like a cemetery; stump after stump could be seen. Some were partially pulled up with their roots creating strange gargoyle-looking monsters. It was these tree bottoms that were collected and taken to creosote plants—roots and all.

Sixty years later, I see that not only has the former one-car road changed, but the columns of slash pine forests have turned into row after row of houses. When I was a child, one car could not pass another. One had to pull off the road and wait for the other to pass. It was the same with bridges. Sometimes a car had to wait for another to cross the bridge before its could cross. The road, now U.S. 41, is so large that two to four cars can pass without any trouble.

Our Last Christmas Picnic

Capt. F. A. Hendry, my great-grandfather, began our family's unusual Christmas tradition in 1888 when his young family lived at Fort Thompson. He celebrated Christmas with a picnic!

The tradition continued with my grandfather, and I fondly remember one of the picnics of my childhood when I was six—Christmas 1928. No one was aware that this was going to be Grandfather's last Christmas picnic.

I can remember waking early. We had arrived the night before at my grandfather Louis Hendry's big house in Fort Myers, located on the banks of the Caloosahatchee River. I walked into the kitchen where my grandfather was hand-grinding coffee. The aroma of the freshly ground coffee beans filled the kitchen. He threw the contents of the grinder into a large pot of boiling water, the pioneer way of preparing coffee. Then he threw another piece of wood into the wood cook stove. The large iron kettle reluctantly accepted the grounds by spewing out steam over the stove top. After stirring the coffee with a wooden spoon, he moved the kettle onto the warming section of the stove. It could be kept warm there without boiling. He reached for a ladle and dipped himself a cup of hot coffee after the grounds settled at the bottom of the pot.

On the table lay the most beautiful bird I had ever seen. It was a wild, male turkey brought in from the woods where it had been shot. Its feathers were iridescent blues and greens, sparkling in the early morning light. I remember thinking it was almost as large as I was. Then there were sweet potatoes, nuts, and my step-grandmother's Rhode Island Red hen eggs littering the kitchen table and counter tops. I climbed up on my grandfather's lap and brushed a kiss near his left ear.

My grandfather was a "land poor" lawyer, and a former public servant. At seventy-eight, he still walked seven miles back and forth to his office in downtown Fort Myers. The walk was never dull.

The people he loved to help most were very poor and payment was often made by bartering. In one typical day, he might have accumulated a quart of oysters or scallops and other unique items such as scuppernong or muscadine grapes, swamp cabbage boots, or smoked mullet. These foods were available to the penniless poor just for the taking; some people called it "living off the land." Many of these foods found their way to our Christmas feast.

We heard Miss Mary, his wife, coming. I had to get off his knee because I knew that the activities of the day were about to begin.

After eating a hearty breakfast, my father and two of his brothers went outside to take care of the meat. I saw my father take my beautiful turkey bird by the legs. I'll always remember it dangling there with its crimson wattle swinging back and forth. The bird was placed in boiling water heated in an iron cauldron over a campfire and then plucked clean.

I thought of my turkey bird as he may have been in the wild. How awful it was that he had to die! I thought of the deer that was also outside waiting to be cooked. A tear fell down my cheek.

But this was the custom in our family and had been for many years. The male members of the family would go on a hunting trip down into the Everglades to get the needed meat and fowls for the coming annual holiday picnic feast. While they were gone, the women busied themselves cooking their favorite cakes, cookies, and other festive foods.

Uncle Paul dug a pit for cooking the deer that had been hanging on a scaffold. It had been hung there to bleed. After having been skinned and cleaned, the venison would be wrapped in cheesecloth and lowered into the pit filled with hot coals. More coals would be placed on top of the meat, and finally it would all be covered with dirt. Another fire was built on top of it so that the deer would cook evenly.

By the time my cousins had finished eating breakfast, they decided to take the skiff out into the Caloosahatchee River for a treasure hunt. It was fun bringing home weathered objects, wood, or whatever else the river offered as it flowed toward the Gulf.

While we were in a skiff, taking turns rowing, the women did their kitchen tasks. They had to make meals for the visitors as well as prepare food for the picnic the following afternoon.

During the day, family members would arrive. At night quilts were placed on the floor for pallets. All the beds in the house were full as well as the sleeping porch, which was not usually used at this time of the year.

When everyone was finally bedded down, no one could sleep because of the giggling, horseplay, and moving about trying to get comfortable.

Finally a big booming voice yelled, "Quiet! No more talking! Quiet!"

I can remember snuggling down on the quilt next to two of my cousins before falling asleep.

Christmas Day dawned with a rush of children's feet running down the stairs. My older cousins threw open the study door and headed for the Christmas tree. Santa always left a present for each of us there. There was much laughter and excitement. Soon wrapping paper and ribbons decorated the carpet, but no one seemed to care. We had looked forward all year long for this day. It must have been a sight for the adults to see all those youngsters in their night clothes enjoying each other and enjoying their gifts.

The commotion and general uproar continued for some time. Finally the fifteen to twenty youngsters, their parents, guests, and family members were dressed and ready to go to the picnic.

With so much help available it took no time at all for the cars to be packed. Basket after basket of food was stacked into the old-fashioned Model-T cars, the old Buicks, and a Studebaker. All of the cars were open sedans, or as they were called then, touring cars. I had never seen so many cars packed so full of people and food.

When the time arrived for us to depart, our caravan of cars began to cross the Caloosahatchee River, one behind the other. The old wooden bridge was not wide enough for one car to pass another. Should someone want to turn around, it was almost impossible. Once we had to turn, though, when we were crossing the river. Mother remembered that she had left the fire burning on the stove, and it was either turn around or risk having the house burn down. There were only two feet of bridge on which to maneuver the car. Father managed it with skill, but to this day I fear crossing bridges.

We traveled miles and miles, then turned off the highway and on to a logging road. We followed that until it disappeared in a clearing, and then my Uncle Gus, who was the best hunter of the men, directed us toward what was called Yucca Pen Cypress.

En route we crossed the grassy plains, dodged bushes, went over cross-tie bridges with no railings. We also had to help two cars pull out of the black muck, which turned into a job where everyone worked. We placed palmetto fans, bushes of all kinds and small saplings under the wheels. They stopped spinning when there was enough traction for them to pull forward. Then we were on our way again. Had it not been during the dry season, we could never have made the trek into the Cypress Head.

Soon we arrived at a place where the grass was short enough for us to set about making a picnic. Large quilts were placed down first. Then came the fine white linen tablecloths and even napkins, mind you. All the food was carefully laid out on as many as five or more cloths. It was covered with dish towels to keep flies and other insects off.

As the day went on, the men just did what the men usually did when they got together, after unloading the food. First they went off into the woods with the boys who wanted to practice shooting their new guns. Some chewed, some drank, and all told interesting stories.

About the middle of the day, a shot was fired. This was the dinner bell shot. All knew not to wander too far off because of the feast coming up. By this time the coffee water was simmering on a campfire, and the china plates were ready to be distributed. The children were served first. We were ushered over to an area where quilts had been placed on the ground for us to sit. Everything one could imagine was waiting on the white tablecloths. In addi-

Originally one of the officers' quarters of the fort, this was later the home of Francis Asbury Hendry. It was located near the banks of the Caloosahatchee River in Fort Myers. It was later torn down to make room for the Royal Palm Hotel. Photo courtesy of State Bureau of Archives and Records Management.

tion to the venison and wild turkey, there was sea-grape jelly, roasted quail, marmalades of all kinds, pickles, and always the traditional swamp cabbage, huckleberry pie, and guava jelly.

When we finished, we were allowed to wander into the swamp area or do whatever we liked while the grown-ups ate. I remember finding myself a cozy little enclosure under the cypress trees. There was a green, mossy log close by and all kinds of toadstools. I thought it was fairyland because it was so beautiful. Nearby were lily pads in a bog and ankle deep cypress leaves, which were soft and smelled something like grandmother's cedar-lined closet. Wild orchids were growing on the trees whose branches nearly touched the ground. I thought how tiny the flowers were. Upon several occasions Mother had taken some home with her to stick on the mango trees in our back yard.

Some of the children played games, but most of us wandered about exploring and hunting for animals.

When the sun was midway in the afternoon sky, it was time to go home. The trip back was bumpy and hard going, but we arrived back at my grandfather's house just after dark.

Some of the family dispersed after making plans to go out again on New Year's Day, as was our tradition. Others remained overnight. Christmas lasted all week—through New Year's Day.

Again Grandfather and several of his sons, plus some of our double-first cousins, went hunting just before the New Year's holiday. They hoped to kill another turkey and deer for the New Year's Day dinner.

The hunting party split up, several going one way and others going in the opposite direction, but all were to go home when they finished. They would not meet again until tomorrow. They left their gear where their cars and trucks were and proceeded to hunt.

My grandfather's party was composed of just two. They walked together for awhile, then my grandfather headed north and his companion, a young relative, went south. He continued to walk a mile or more in a southerly direction deeper into the woods. Suddenly his companion saw something move in a tall palmetto clump. He thought it was a deer and shot directly into the clump. He heard a loud yell, but nothing more. He ran over to the palmettos and saw my grandfather's dead body sprawled across a frond. My grandfather was a big man, too heavy for the man with him to carry or to move. The companion fired three shots into the air, the signal for trouble. No one came. Evidently, the other members of the party had returned to town or were too far away to hear. There was no one there to help him move my grandfather. The heavy hearted man found God-given strength to drag Grandfather as far as he could. Grief-stricken and at the point of collapse, the exhausted man wandered back to the car, drove it to town, and delivered the sad news. A party of eight men went into the woods with lanterns and flashlights to find his body. He was located and taken back to town.

That ended my father's hunting days, even though he was not with the party that fateful day.

No one ever mentioned going out into the woods for Christmas or New Year's Day after that. When my grandfather was buried, the Christmas tradition that brought so much happiness was buried also.

* * *

One of Francis Hendry's great grandsons and the grandnephew of my grandfather has sought in recent years to pull the family together again with a reunion. The family gathers in the woods on the banks of the Orange River, which flows through his ranch. Appropriately, it is held the Saturday after Easter each year.

From the ashes of tragedy, there has been a renewal of togetherness.

Island Odyssey in the 1920s

During the 1920s, there was a brief but exciting period of land development along Florida's Gulf Coast. The land "boom" made some people very rich as they sold residential and commercial property. But then the prosperity ended and the years following the "boom's bust"—as we referred to it—were very hard for most people in Florida. Money disappeared entirely and all the northern investment dried up. Almost everyone had to retrench from a posh lifestyle to one of abject poverty. During the boom period swamps were sold as desirable properties, but after the balloon burst, entire subdivisions were abandoned and parts of Florida became almost ghost towns. It was the first of many such times of failed development.

Jobs were at a premium. Many of the natives reverted to an earlier lifestyle of farming or other food-related activities—anything to feed hungry people.

Homeless men, often called tramps, wandered in droves from place to place seeking work or food. Life became even worse for the tramps when the Depression came a couple of years later.

Those tramps were an unusual lot. Some rode the rails by climbing aboard empty railcars when the train slowed down. Others hitched rides or walked. They had their own social structure, their own meeting places, customs, and even a sign language known only by them. They would mark houses and places of business that were good to them. Places intolerant to tramps were also marked. I never did know how it was done, but they took care of their own and tried to assist those who might follow in their footsteps.

Whenever someone knocked at our back door, nine chances out of ten, it was a tramp. Some were white and some black, but all used the back door. I have often wondered if they felt inferior because they could not get a job. Most of the men were excellent workers who were happy to do anything for a meal, a place to sleep, or even a job promise.

Mother always filled up their plates and gave them extra bread. She said the bread could be carried with them and it might last until they could get work.

Like everyone else, my father's real estate and insurance business was gone. But he was fortunate that his education always came to the rescue when times were hard and he could get a job teaching. For a while he rode his bicycle eleven miles to and from Olga to teach. Olga was a little town eleven miles up the Caloosahatchee River from where we lived in North Fort Myers.

My father would awaken at four o'clock in the morning, milk the cows, feed them and the chickens, and do what he had to do in the garden before leaving home. When he returned, if the light permitted, he'd do the hard farm work until dark.

He often told us the story about his sweet potatoes. Even though times were hard, his city friends would be happy for *him* to dig up the potatoes and deliver them to their houses. But if he told his friends to come by the house and dig some potatoes themselves, they would never come. Finally, my mother refused to let him continue this free service. She gave the extra sweet potatoes to the church. Even then, the work fell upon my parents because the church folk had no desire to dig them up either!

Soon a better opportunity opened up for my father—the job of principal of the school on Pine Island. The ten-mile-long island is parallel to Sanibel and Captiva islands, stretching from just north of Fort Myers to the mouth of Charlotte Harbor.

My father packed up his little family and moved us into a tenant-farmer's house on Pine Island, and shortly built a chicken pen and a shed for the cow. His school resembled the typical little red school house but it was painted white.

We had just settled in when we realized that we had to adjust our lifestyle in order to survive. Pine Island was almost desolate except for several homesteading families, and a few fishing houses built on stilts out in the bay. There were fishhouses where fish were sold, but the island was sparsely populated. My father and I walked daily down a crushed-oyster-shell road. When we rode in the truck the road felt more like a washboard than a road.

Mosquitoes, gnats, and sandflies were an immediate problem that had to be solved. If we went outside sometimes the air would be black with mosquitoes. I thought it was fun to rub my arms down with my hands to make them look black from smashed mosquitoes. Mother didn't like it, but "kids will be kids."

It was then that my father learned he had to kerosene down the screens every night and light smudge pots to control the insects in the house. The cow, though, was almost eaten up sandflies and, after week, had to be sold. The chickens, the dog, and cat were next. They could not tolerate the insect bites.

Inside the rough wood shack we were fairly comfortable, though cramped. Mother cooked on a kerosene cook stove, and Dad kept the kerosene lamps lit at night until bedtime. Needless to say, our house smelled of kerosene on the inside and turpentine on the outside, because of the oozing pine sap from the untreated lumber. We did have pumped ground water we called "artesian," which as usual smelled like rotten eggs. Fortunately for all, we were able to adjust to the combination of unpleasant odors. We learned to bathe in a washtub and use an outhouse.

Sometimes we went home to check on our house or to get needed supplies. On one of these occasions we found what we considered trouble. Our home in North Fort Myers had a garage where my father stored things, such as Paris Green poison that he used to kill insects that destroyed our crops. As we pulled up in front of our house, we saw our uncle's pet goat was loose in our yard. Whenever he was loose he'd eat anything on the line or anything else he took a liking to. Our garage door was open and that crazy goat had taken a liking to that bag of poison. Something about it attracted him. Maybe it was that we were persistent in keeping him away from it, and he was just as persistent in trying to get it. After we closed the garage door, my father tied a rope around the goat's neck and led him home. He found my uncle sitting on a milking stool squirting milk into the mouths of his ten cats. They were lined up in a row waiting their turns. He considered his ability to aim directly into each cat's mouth an art.

My father interrupted his act to tell him about the goat's stubborn attitude. My uncle wasn't the least bit worried. He said, "That goat's got plenty of sense. He won't eat anything that will hurt him. Don't worry about it. He'll be all right. He'd already be dead if he didn't know what to eat. He's already eaten just about everything."

With that said, he returned to his squirting. My father knew better. And sure enough, a few days later, someone failed to close the garage door. You guessed right. The goat gorged himself on the Paris Green and died.

We had not lived on Pine Island long very long before my father and my brothers developed an immunity to the mosquito bites, but I don't think my mother ever did. I was relieved that they didn't bother us as we walked to school. Along the way there were osprey nests, built high in the top of dead pine trees. It was said that the trees were killed because of the excessive salt left after a hurricane surge. When the salt water covering the land evaporated, it left behind a salt residue. The pines were also killed by infestations of pine beetles.

The nests of the osprey were very large and bulky. They stood out in the pine forest when the trees were bare. It was fun to watch the birds swoop down to their nests with a fish in their claws. It was even more fun to watch a fledgling flap his wings and try to fly.

One day as we walked we saw one of the last wild, green parrots in Florida. My father who was a native Floridian and had seen many of them when he was a boy, told me how scarce they now were. Originally, they were brought in from Mexico or Central America by high winds or a hurricane. We tried to catch it, at my insistence, but Dad did it only to please me, I think. He knew that we could not catch it or probably keep it, even if we did catch it.

There were many land tortoises on the island. The native name for them was either gophers or turtles. I was cautioned not to ever try to reach into one of the gopher holes because snakes loved to crawl into their cool underground tunnels. My brothers and I decided one day that we wanted a turtle for a pet. We rounded up three of the defenseless critters and placed them in the empty chicken pen. We played with them until we were tired and then went inside. Had we told mother of our capture, she would have informed us that they could get out of the pen, but we remained unaware. The next day, we looked for our gophers, but they were gone. They had tunneled their way out by digging under the fence. We never did try to capture any more wild creatures.

I remember a sad event from the days on Pine Island. One day, when I was playing with my beautiful china-headed doll, she fell and her head shattered into a million pieces. It saddened me that her head was gone, but she was still my beautiful Gertrude, head or no head. I embarrassed my mother when a friend of hers brought me another doll with a china head. It was a lovely, expensive gift, but I didn't warm up to it at all. She thought I would be delighted to have a new doll, especially one with a head, but the new doll was an outsider. She was placed in a chair near the visiting friend and left to fend for herself while I wandered off with my beloved headless doll.

About twice a month my father would go to Fort Myers for supplies. Since I tagged along wherever he went, I climbed up in the truck seat along side of him during these trips. As we drove, I noticed the miles and miles of slash-pine trees. There was the smell of pine sap in the air from the slashed openings cut into the trees. We saw salt marshes beyond the trees. Maybe there would be a stand of saw grass or even an area of salty white beach sand that lay uncovered when the tide was out. Usually those flats would be covered with fiddler crabs. They could be so thick, one could not put his foot down without stepping on them.

On one of our trips back to Fort Myers, we suddenly heard something that sounded like a gun going off. The truck swerved and began to bump as one wheel turned over and over. We were going slow enough so that Dad could stop without any trouble. It wasn't a gunshot—it was a flat tire. The road was so narrow he could not pull the truck off it. There was no need to do so, anyway. On the roads outside of a town there was little traffic. Days might pass before a car came by because most people in that region used boats for transportation. If there was any trouble, a person had to be prepared to take care of the problem without expecting help from anyone else.

From out of a storage box in the back of the truck, my father took a jack, a box of rubber patches, some glue, and an automobile tire wrench. Before I knew it, he had the front-end of the truck jacked up and he was using the lug wrench to unscrew the bolts that held the rim in place. I watched as he removed the tire and found the hole in the inner tube he needed to patch. Then he glued a patch over the hole. After that he returned to the toolbox for a hand pump. He screwed in the pump and began to pump air into the inner tube. When it was filled with the right amount of air, he stopped to examine the black rubber tire for damage. Fortunately there was nothing wrong with it.

He then placed the inner tube back inside the tire. The tire went back on the rim of the wheel and was secured. When everything was in place he tightened the screws and spun the tire around. After removing the jack, the wheel sat on the road just exactly like the other three.

As he was placing his tools back in the tool box, an enormous white bird flew overhead. Dad called to me and said, "Sis, look up! See that big bird. It's a whooping crane. I haven't seen one in years. They're just about extinct. Look closely and watch him. You may never see another one. The last one I saw was in a slough deep down in the Everglades."

Both of us watched as he flew down to the salt flat that lay across the road quite a distance away. We saw him reach down to eat something. We couldn't see what, but since fiddlers were so plentiful, we suspected that he was eating them. Soon he flapped his wings, hardly moving at first as though he were having trouble getting off the ground, then he flew slowly away. I noticed the black-tipped feathers on his wings and the red splotch on his head that confirmed his true identity. When he was out of sight, I knew I had experienced something very special. Several years later the whooping crane was put on the endangered species list. I am happy to report they are now making a comeback.

Dad said I could help him start the truck. I pulled out the choke, then pressed down a small lever on the stem of the steering wheel. My father took out the crank from his tool box, inserted it in the front of the truck under the radiator into the crank case. He began to crank the engine. Round and round swung his arm. Then the magneto produced fire to the spark plugs, the crank was released, and the truck started. I closed the choke and pushed the time lever up to advance the spark.

"Good job—well done!" he yelled to me.

We were then on our way.

On another day I went with him to an Indian mound. He was digging up the bones of a Calusa Indian which the university had commissioned him to do. While I collected shards and bits of broken pottery, he slowly wired the bones together and readied them for shipment. It was frowned upon then to dig in the Indian mounds, but since he was doing it for research, he felt he was not doing anything wrong. (Today it is against the law.) No one likes to disturb the bones of the dead. The university was most pleased with his work and thanked him for helping them find what they had been seeking. When I was much older, we went to see it on display at the University of Florida.

Sometimes my father and I would take a journey through our neighbors' homesteaded land since we had to cross it before reaching the Gulf. They had dug a canal through a swamp and made it just deep enough for a skiff to pole through the saw grass, reeds, and muck. Dad poled the skiff through it until he'd have to get out and dig up roots and underbrush that clogged the way. When we were finally free from the swampy mess, the water was clear and deep. It had a sand-white bottom. Soon we'd see what he had come to see. Beneath us, way down in the water, were beautiful colored bay scallops. They were sweeter to eat, too. With a long pole that had a rounded net attached, he'd reach down and scoop up the scallops, emptying them onto the bottom of the skiff. These were wonderful days full of adventure and meaningful experiences.

Sometimes our entire family would go after clams in the bay. The water was never as clean and clear there. Sometimes logs jutted up from out of the water with barnacles upon them, but underneath the brackish water there was a muddy bottom. Down in that mud the clams lay. To get us to help him, Dad would promise to play our favorite diving game with us. We would often gather a bushel or two, then it was fun time. The game was like leapfrog, only we dived beneath each other's legs to emerge at the front of the line after our dive. If we could not dive through, then we were out. Of course, we learned to swim under water as well as have a fun time.

When we went fishing, we never knew what we might catch. Many times, we caught only jack fish, which we threw away. On one fishing trip we discovered an old burned-down store at the end of the island. The loading dock remained untouched. It provided a wonderful place to fish since the water was deep there.

Mother had just finished throwing her line out when the cork went under. Whatever hit her line was so big that it almost pulled her overboard. Fortunately for her, my dad was standing by and held on to her while he took the pole away from her and began to reel in the line. When he finally had the catch within sight, we noticed something big and black. It was flapping what looked like wings. It took the strength of both Mother and Daddy to pull in the manta ray. It was the first and only live one I have ever seen. Some of the old-timers fishing there that day called it a "whip-ray" and scared all the kids who were on the dock. We expected it to come after us with its big long stick of a tail and beat us. We already knew about sting rays since my little brother had been stung by one while swimming on the beach.

We made friends with Czechoslovakian neighbors, and learned to accept their strange ways. We had been buying milk from them ever since we had to sell our cow. They seemed to have managed beautifully with a big barn to shelter their cattle. They showed us how to make and preserve butter without ice, since no one on the islands had refrigeration then. Refrigeration was used mainly for cooling the fish down and keeping them fresh to take to market at fishhouses. We didn't even have an icebox, in fact, it was years before anyone could buy a refrigerator. Their milk was unpasteurized, but it was handled as cleanly as any dairy. When the milk soured and the cream was thick, the sour cream was put in a gallon bucket. The bucket was then placed inside a wooden bucket. The bucket was lowered deep into a covered open well where the water was cool. When the sour cream was cooled, it was brought out of the well and placed in a bottle. It was shaken until the butter formed, then rinsed in the cool water until all the milk was washed out. The butter was then placed in a pan on the stove and heated. Later the curds separated from the fat and the pale, light-yellow fat rose to the surface. The yellow fat was poured off and covered so it would not spoil. We later learned that this was the way the people of India kept their butter (*ghee*) from spoiling. Fancy cooks in the United States had been doing the same thing, but they called it drawn butter.

One day before we left Pine Island, a dentist friend of ours wanted to come to see us. My father explained how primitively we lived, but he wanted to come see us anyway. We told him that we drank our milk warm and freshly-milked, but the dentist said he just couldn't drink his milk that way—he had to have it cold.

My father went to the fishhouse and bought some chopped ice so our guest could have iced milk. Naturally, we had to taste it iced down. We decided that we preferred our milk fresh, warm, and frothy. After he left, my brothers and I talked about the event and thought the dentist didn't know what a treat he missed.

Our foreign friends taught us many interesting things about living on the islands and when it came time to leave, we left with a bit of sorrow.

So ended our odyssey to Pine Island where one event after another created adventures for a little girl that Homer's *Iliad* didn't surpass!

Growing Up in Palmona Park

At Berry Hendry's death, his vast holdings were split among his ten children, my grandfather, Louis, among them. When grandfather passed away, his share of the land was practically swallowed up by debt and taxes. He was one of the unfortunate ones, who almost lost everything as a result of the 1920s' boom and the "bust" that followed. During all periods of prosperity, land prices go up. Whenever they go up, so do the taxes.

A board member of *National Geographic* magazine, a Mr. George Judd, bought up much of Louis's largest parcels, on the north side of the Caloosahatchee River, when none of Louis's family could raise enough money to save it. George Judd built a nice house for himself and his Japanese bride and that particular site soon became known as Palmona Park. It was located on the north side of the Caloosahatchee River and never did gain the social status as did some parts of Fort Myers. Little by little the property along the road to Pine Island opened up to subdivisions and small-acreage plots.

By the height of the Depression many people had settled on grandfather's former orange grove and open range land and built a school there. The school was named after one of our cousins, J. Colin English and my father became principal after holding similar positions at Olga and Pine Island.

Both my father and his brother, Gus, lived on twenty-acre plots of the original F. A. Hendry's holdings. One block to our south ran Pondella Road. From our house to the school was a good mile and a half. Most of the time my father and I walked together back and forth to school as we had done on Pine Island.

Times were very hard. Children often came to school with nothing at all to eat. Some had only a biscuit with catsup inside. Almost all children went to school barefoot. As a consequence, many acquired what we called "ground itch." The itch was really the larval stage of the hookworm as it began to bore in between their toes.

Not only did it itch, but it allowed the worm to find its way into the children's intestinal tract and they became infected. The worms sucked almost all the nutrients from their intestinal tract, scarce as those nutrients were. The children became skinny and malnourished, as evidenced by bloated bellies and listlessness. The children were always tired and dull looking. In fact, it was impossible for them to learn with empty stomachs.

Annie Mae Sykes, a friend of my father's and an agent for the Florida Extension Service, which helped farmers and people who lived in rural areas, set up a clinic and offered shots and medications to treat children. The program was free to the needy.

I remember well the treatment that we took for hookworm. We were not allowed to eat until the medicine, called calomel, passed through our intestinal tract. What a hungry lot we were! Whether or not it was true, we were told that if we ate anything at all during this period, our teeth would fall out. So my brothers and I endured the ordeal without fussing too much.

Another remedy for hookworm was to wear shoes at all times. This my father and mother insisted upon regardless of the teasing and ridicule we had to take; going barefoot was the thing to do.

At that time my father was working on his master's degree from Duke University. He decided to write his thesis on reducing the health problems and increasing the children's ability to learn by providing a school lunch program for them. With the help of the PTA, the teachers, and the local churches they began the first school lunch program in our area. Annie Mae Sykes bought a stove for the school. Grandmother donated a large aluminum cook pot. One of the churches had soup bowls to lend, and Mother baked the first loaves of bread.

The program was off and running and each child brought a vegetable to contribute each day to the lunch program. As a reward they were entitled to a bowl of soup and a slice of buttered bread. On many occasions, Mr. Weaver, at Weaver's Corner, donated the needed items to round out the soup, and milk if he had extra. He had a small store and a gasoline station. Soon the idea caught on and in spite of the hard times, everyone was generous with their time and efforts.

So began a program that was later introduced all over the United States by the government and it still exists today. Good ideas that are tried and copied are seldom credited to the person with the original thought. I believe my father is due this credit.

The activities held to make money for the lunches were fun times. There were pie suppers, box suppers, and children's plays.

I'll never forget the Halloween play when I was the witch. I had a big iron pot and a stick to stir up my magical brews. To this day, I remember the song I sang: "Oogly, Woogley wow, the soup's most ready now!" I tried to make it sound spooky by emphasizing the "ow" sound.

Christmas was another big event in our community. In addition to a decorated tree, we had a play. Someone volunteered a dance team and an ole-timey fiddler who made his fiddle talk.

I wish you could have seen the audience when he began to play "Turkey in the Straw." You have never seen such a stompin' good time in your life! Between stomping and clapping, that audience went wild. It took quite a while to move onto something else, but to those culturally deprived people, it was something special.

When Santa arrived with a pack on his back and gave out bags of candy, raisins and oranges, it was almost pitiful. Some children had never had the likes of such goodies.

That Christmas at our own house was rather special, too. Times were looking up for us. My father's career in education was becoming established (he later became superintendent of the Lee County School District) and everyone seemed to be getting along as well as could be expected.

On Christmas Eve we had gone out behind the barn to cut a long-leaved pine tree. It was hard to find a sapling that was filled out because of the drought, but we finally found one. Its long needles seemed to be very dry, but they helped to fill in the bare places.

My father nailed two cross boards to the bottom cut so that the tree would stand up straight. He placed it in the corner of the living room near the fireplace.

Mother told my brothers and me that we would decorate the tree after our nightly bath. When we were bathed and had on our night clothes, we were ready to decorate the tree. When it was cold, we'd bathe in front of the fireplace in a galvanized tin wash tub. Two iron kettles were filled with water and placed over the logs in the fireplace. When the water was warm enough, the tub was filled and placed near to the fire where it was warm. Since I was the oldest, I was last to bathe. If Mother ever ran out of Ivory soap, she'd use some P & G bar laundry soap, but we were never bathed with homemade lye soap. Mother used this for heavily soiled things.

Dad emptied the wash tub by bucketsful until he could lift it. When it was removed, we waited patiently watching the fire crackle and spit. I just knew that the spots of burned soot were Santa's fairies watching us for Santa. Needless to say, we had been very good because we didn't want Santa to leave us any switches.

Finally the moment arrived. Dad cranked up the old Victrola. Round and round he cranked until the spring was fairly tight. He then placed a thick Christmas record on the turntable. (All the old records were very thick and broke easily.) As the needle touched the record, it began to play a squeaky "Silent Night." He then blew out the kerosene lamp. In the firelight we watched with fascination as Mother opened a sack containing a dozen or more small tin candle holders. It was dramatic. They had set the stage for our entertainment.

One by one they clipped the candle holders to the tree branches, then placed white pencil-sized candles inside. Dad struck a match and began to light each candle. I had never seen a tree so beautiful. Not only did the candles shine, but the tree seemed to be drenched with a golden light.

Suddenly without any warning, one of the candles fell and began to burn. Dad tried to put out the fire, but in so doing, two other candles fell. Soon the tree was beginning to burn before our eyes. It caught fire so quickly that it was frightening. Somehow, my father was able to get the tree outside without being burned. By this time, my brothers and I were crying. Our beautiful tree was ruined. We thought Santa Claus wouldn't come because we had no tree.

Mother comforted us by taking all three of us up into her lap in a big rocking chair by the fire. She held us closely as she rocked. She assured us that Santa would come, and promised to leave a cookie and a glass of milk for him.

Dad came in after a while and placed another big log on the fire, and told us we would cut another tree tomorrow.

* * *

When the holidays were over, school resumed with its usual hectic pace. All the children had a hot bowl of soup every day and buttered bread if they wanted it. Some brought their own lunches and ate the soup as well.

Hart's Dairy also began to furnish milk at a discount rate and it wasn't too much longer after that when the ladies of the PTA took over the entire lunchroom, and complete meals were served.

By the end of the my father's study, all the school children scored higher on their tests and he was able to prove his hypothesis. What a wonderful feeling he experienced to have been the instigator of something that did so much good. However, he never would take any credit for himself, even though he earned it.

But things don't always stay wonderful when dealing with the public. I was enrolled in the third grade and word started spreading among the children that I was given special treatment, which was not the case at all. But some of the children wanted to test my father.

Beth had come to school with candy. Another student went into her desk and stole it. Whether it was Anny who stole the candy or not, she was the one who offered me a piece of candy. I didn't know the candy was stolen, but I did know that Mother wouldn't buy candy for us. I wanted it very much. Naturally, I accepted. Someone saw me eating candy and reported it to the teacher.

I was accused of both stealing and eating the candy. As a big group formed around me, the teacher led me off to my father's office. The teacher told him that I was caught eating the stolen candy, so it was thought that I was the one who stole it.

My father asked me, "Sis, did you steal the candy?"

"No, Sir," I replied.

"How is it that you were eating the candy?"

"Anny offered me some; so I took it."

"I'll ask you once more. Did you steal the candy?"

"No, Sir."

"Come into the office."

He closed the door and the teacher went on down the hall.

My father looked at me and said, "I know you didn't steal the candy, but the others think you did. You have never lied to me, and I know you aren't lying now."

I began to cry.

"Don't cry. Get across that table."

I thought I was going to get paddled for sure.

"Sis, when I hit the table, you are to cry. Cry hard. Even yell. You must pretend you are getting a paddling."

He hit the table. I yelled. I screamed. Again the paddle hit the table. Again I yelled. It hit the third time. I screamed. He said in a loud voice so if anyone were listening, they could hear, "Now, don't let me ever hear of your stealing anything again!"

As I left the office I pretended to sob. After that event, I never had any trouble in school.

* * *

Meanwhile Palmona Park continued to grow. There were no building codes then, and shacks and houses sprung up everywhere. Soon work was available.

Slater's Saw Mill hired many men. The turpentine industry soon petered out and the cattle industry was changed forever. No longer could the cattle roam about as they did in earlier years. We saw fewer and fewer cattle-roundups. Those we saw were small operations. With the building of the Edison Bridge, people could come and go much more easily across the Caloosahatchee River to Fort Myers.

Crime was almost nonexistent, but I remember one terrible event that introduced me to the "facts of life." One of the new settlers had an only daughter. She had five brothers. Those brothers were very protective of her and made it known that nothing bad had better ever happen to her. Being new in the community and of dating age, she had several interested beaus. One night she didn't come home when she was out with one of them. The next day when she came home, she was in bad shape. Not only had she been beaten, but she had been raped as well. When her brothers found out who hurt her, they formed a posse and went after the beau. When he was found several hours later by his family, he had just about bled to death. They took him to the hospital where he was treated for being castrated. Everyone talked about the incident and knew who had done it, but nothing was ever done to the brothers, possibly because no one could prove anything.

* * *

Since there was plenty of open space under the spreading live oaks on the north bank of the river, there were many picnics and political rallies held there. Once, when visiting with my mother's parents, we went to a political rally there. The candidates were all energized and selling their programs and ideas. They made promises that they wanted to keep, but sometimes that was about as far as it would go.

As the afternoon turned into evening, a big bonfire would be built. Several kinds of meat would be barbecued. There were hot dogs for the kids and barbecued pork ribs for the adults. Usually the food was served before sunset.

On this occasion, I remember the men were going out in the river to an oyster bed. As they brought oysters in, another group was ready to open them, and all could eat raw oysters for as long as they wanted or as long as the oysters were available.

Lester Fox, one of the youngsters there, was telling me how delicious they were. I decided to try one. It was more slimy than okra, but I kept on trying them until they tasted pretty good. About

Politicians

Candidates stifle stories—
Stories, hidden, or disguised—
Stories abloom with deceit and
Intrigue.
Our leaders are forged from less than gold
Precious few cannot be bought or sold.
With candor muted, or
Denied
Their beliefs lay hidden.
Lies are drafted to fool or trick.
Such garish pretense!
A pox on their persona!
In death as in life
Our honored lie,
Untruths enthroned,
Veracity unquestioned, and
Lack of integrity renowned.
Our leaders wear crowns of gold
Glorify the lie.
Glorify the cheat.
Glorify the bunglers.
Our leaders are forged from less than gold.
Precious few cannot be bought or sold.

that time my father arrived. He saw me over at the oyster table and came hurrying over. He took me by the hand and told me that I was to go with him. I had to tell Lester I was going, but I didn't want to leave.

After we were away from the table and in another area, Dad told me that I must never again eat oysters from the river. When I asked him why, he replied, "Raw sewage runs into the river. Everything in the river is not fit to eat because of this."

I thought then about the river where I swam, the river we had sailed in, and the river that had killed Volney Kantz.

Volney Kantz died before I was born, but I had heard the story all my life. It dealt with teaching children about dangers in a subtle, effective way. From this story, I learned never to call wolf when I was only teasing or trying to get attention.

It seems that Volney was a big tease. He had fun going out into the river and then pretending he was drowning. Often times several people would jump in and swim to him frantically to keep him from drowning. All the while he kept calling, "Help! Help! Help!" He was just pretending. After so many times, it wasn't funny. So people began to ignore him.

One day while swimming, he started again. "Help! Help!"

Everyone heard him. He yelled again. No one paid any attention to him. Suddenly he disappeared beneath the water. All was quiet. Then there was a mad rush into the water. He was reached, but it was too late. He was already drowned. He couldn't be revived.

* * *

As time went on Palmona Park grew and kept growing. It grew on up to Bayshore and finally to Slater itself. Soon all the classrooms were filled in the J. Colin English School and many of the residents wanted Dad to try to do for the county what he had done for North Fort Myers, so he ran for county superintendent and won.

Call to Worship

When Fort Myers was a small cow town, the cattle had about as much right to live there as humans. Cattle roamed the streets in what was then called open range. Even the settlers became concerned that Edison's plan to install electric lights might interfere with the amount of milk their cows would give if the town was all lit up.

That didn't stop the town's development, though. My great-grandfather, F. A. Hendry, was part of the group that built the First Methodist Church on First Street; he had stained-glass windows installed. Everyone had a hand in the church's construction and it became the pride of the community.

I'll never forget the church's quaint charm. It was constructed of cypress clapboard and painted white. Its structure graced a central nave and two transepts. Above the vestibule rose a tall steeple complete with its bell and spire.

I was saddened when I learned that the original building was torn down sometime in the early forties to build a much larger church. Its steeple bells for so long had been the rallying call in case of an emergency in earlier days.

I was the fourth generation of the Hendry clan to attend services at the original church and I remember that there still were old-timers in the congregation when I was a child. Some of the widowed women continued to wear their black mourning habits, complete with bonnets and high collars. My great-aunt Lulu always wore a black outfit, even when it was so hot one could fry an egg on a car fender.

Some of the congregation thought they were the pillars of society and dressed accordingly. It was awful to try to see around those wide-brimmed hats decorated with flowers. Some of us in the younger generation hid behind them to flip through the pages of the hymnals. One of us would turn the pages of a hymnal to a song title, such as "Abiding Love." We wrote or whispered "under the sheets" after the title so that it became "Abiding Love under the sheets," a naughty thought for teens or younger folks in a prudish society. Being one of the "young'uns," as we were called, we often were eyed with reproach if our giggles ever turned into squeals—if we thought that what happened "under the sheets" was sufficiently funny.

The silence was deafening after such an event and the disapproving stares were as cruel as blows. But in spite of it all, we were in church every Sunday. I even received an award for not having missed a Sunday for five years.

In our more playful moods, we'd pinch, stick out our tongues, or poke fun at one another, but it was a tension-relieving response rather than being naughty or sacrilegious. One of our group always jingled the coins when the collection plate went around. Sometimes he'd finger the coins or make change, but the look on his face was always somber and righteous—that is until the spotlight was off him.

As the years progressed, I ended up singing in the choir along with the older children. We wore purple robes with white undergowns which were always hard to put on. But with our choir caps, we presented a worshipful lot.

One Sunday we had just finished singing our anthem when there was a buzzing sound around my head. My eyes began to follow the sound. It was a horsefly. As I watched, I imagined it to be a dive bomber. It darted in and out and zeroed in on the robed members.

I tried to concentrate on the prayer the minister was giving, but to no avail. After the prayer, he began to read from the Bible: Proverbs, Chapter 30: 25–33.

My eyes continued to follow the errant fly as I heard:

25) The ants are a people not strong, yet they prepare their meat in the summer.
26) The conies are but a feeble folk, yet they make their homes in the rocks.
27) The locust have no kings, yet go they forth all of them by hands.
28) The spider taketh hold with her hands, and is in kings' palaces.
30) The lion, which is strongest among beasts, and turneth not away for any.
31) A greyhound; an he-goat also; and a king, against whom there is no rising up.
32) If thou hast done foolishly in lifting up thyself, for if thou hast thought evil, lay hand upon thy mouth.
33) Surely the churning of milk bringth forth butter so the forcing of wrath bringth forth strife.

What about horseflies? Surely they bring forth blood and pain, I muttered to myself. *There's no need to cover my mouth. I can't even yell if it stings me!*

The fly lit upon my shoulder, then began to crawl over my robe, onto my throat and then down under the heavy robe. I could not get to it without removing the garment. I froze in tormented silence as it explored my chest. Soon it crawled down in between my breasts. It seemed to be examining the folds of my bra. I could not do a thing except endure the torture. Had I reached down into my bra my actions would have been viewed by the congregation. I think that such an act would have raised many an eyebrow.

Every move the fly made tickled. Under my breath I was thinking an unChristian thought: MURDER and how to it. I moved from side to side. I would shift my body as much as possible, but it did no good.

Just as I was about ready to crawl over everyone in the choir loft and make a spectacle of myself by a hasty exit, the fly decided to crawl down to my abdomen area.

Under my breath, I kept saying, "Damn that fly!" As it crawled over my belly, I had an idea. I would try to crush it. To my satisfaction, it worked. Hallelujah!

No one saw my wicked deed. My hands quickly returned to their folded place in my lap. I tried to assume an angelic innocence and listen to the sermon with rapt attention.

I had no guilt whatsoever for having murdered one of God's creatures in His House even though it was doing what it was created to do. The deed seemed to be right, necessary, and appropriate. When it comes to judging one's guilt (or lack of it) I think I described it best in the above poem.

One Sunday morning our family went to church as usual. We knew that there was a big drive to raise money to expand the church and its activities.

Sunday's Service

I'm all dressed up in my Sunday best.
I put on a show, wear even a vest.
What you don't see is my real self.
On Sunday I lay it aside, up on the shelf.
Oh, I can pray and pay and say,
I really go all out on the Lord's Day.
I'm so clean and pure, washed, and demure.
There's not a church member any purer!
But, during the week, watch me wheel and deal,
There's not a single eyeball I won't peel.
I'll lie, I'll steal, and I'll cheat.
There's not a deal I can't beat!
You should hear my line of sale!
Jokes? They get dirtier tale after tale.
Week days are for making dough.
Sundays are for my best show.
The church wants its ten percent,
No matter if it's ill gotten or already spent.
Pay up, you fancy lady or gent.
It costs money to run this here establishment.
Sunday's service is the best show in town.
Pressed suit and newly purchased gown
Attests to its special importance to all.
More will go than attend a charity ball.
There's gossip, intrigue, and mystery, too.
I'll see you in church in plain view
Because I don't want social disdain
Should I refuse to play the game.
Sinners, all, you can be sure.
But on Sunday, everyone is pure.
We shine our halos like our shoes
And piously sit in our pews.
We welcome the message of Salvation
While we contemplate our social position.
We sing our praises and say our prayers
Oh, what a great hoard of social purveyors!

Everything went on as anticipated until it was time for the sermon. The minister entered the pulpit. Suddenly the ambience shifted. The minister looked out into the audience and picked out one of the town's leading citizens and addressed him personally. "Mr. Smith, we're trying to raise $50,000 dollars. Can we count on you for $1,000?"

Mr. Smith was so dumbfounded and embarrassed, he stood up and made his pledge as asked. Next to be addressed was another of the town's political leaders. "How about a $1,000 pledge from you, Mayor Jones?"

After a while all adults in the church were squirming. One or two others quietly slipped out the side door. When the minister had come down to the $500 level, he looked in my father's direction.

"How about you, Professor Hendry?"

My father rose to the occasion, but he never entered the church doors again. That day the church earned its planned donations, but it lost its clout and many of its strongest supporting members.

As in every church, there are a few whose religion is as sacred as their word. These are the backbone of the church. They feed the poor, they visit the sick, and tend the graveyards. They always give of their time and ask no reward for their efforts.

This type of person takes pride in keeping the church clean. On his days off he repairs something that needs attention, paints a room, or even cleans up after a church social. Such a man was Homer Powell, a stouthearted Baptist. He was known for his humanitarian deeds not only at his own church but also in the entire community. We were fortunate also to have him as school custodian. My father often spoke of him as being the best maintenance man he had ever seen. Powell was often observed counseling students with problems and offering them an opportunity to learn new skills. When school was out, he participated in social events to help finance educational causes.

It's strange how we honor these deserving people—not during their lifetime, but in memories such as mine. I wonder if this gentle, humble man ever realized what an important service he rendered?

I think not. He was just honoring his call to worship!

The Difference between Crackers and Cowboys

Early settlers had to be innovative in order to survive. Their needs had to be satisfied, and often the needs became a way of earning a living. During the Civil War, food was needed for both Union and Confederate troops, and the South and North both invaded the Everglades, rounding up cattle for shipment to the troops. After the war, the Cuban market opened up and the cattle business thrived.

I have a natural interest in the cowboys and outdoors life because this was the world I was born into. I found it interesting to compare and contrast the wetlands of the South, where I was born, to the range in the West where I lived for many years.

Southern cattlemen in Georgia and Florida were called crackers because of their skill with a whip. When it was cracked, it could be heard for over a mile. Florida cattlemen enjoyed being called "crackers" because they did not like being called cowboys or cowpunchers. I was familiar with crackers because the Hendrys had cattle and even during my childhood, the cattle were in evidence in the Peace River basin.

Besides exercising skill with a whip, many crackers also liked to demonstrate their proficiency with knives, and would throw jackknives as a form of recreation. A favorite cracker activity, however, was to set up a cockfight. Spurs were attached to the roosters' legs and a fight would last until one or the other was killed.

Some of the crackers enjoyed rounding up wild boars and driving them to market, the same as if they were cattle. In the West, this was not possible because the wild boar or Javelina is very dangerous. It was and still is often hunted for sport only, although some say the meat is delicious. Nowadays it is fashionable to hunt wild boar with bows and arrows.

When our frontiers were opened and Alabama was part of Georgia, this territory was raw with vitality. The timber of the pioneer men came from their Anglo-Saxon brawn, language, music, and customs. Backwoodsmen pushed the frontiers westward and southward. In doing so, they aroused the wrath and ire of the Indians. In the pursuit of water rights and access to good grazing land, many a cracker and cowpuncher died at the hands of Indians. In the South crackers fought the Indians to recapture runaway slaves, but the Indians had adopted the runaways into their families and refused to give them up. Few crackers owned slaves, but many made money returning runaways to their owners. Although a few well-to-do settlers owned them, it was hard to own slaves in Florida where there were Indians and slave settlements ready to help and receive the runaways. Many escaped slaves tried to reach a black township near St. Augustine. Sometimes they were captured by the Indians, who often accepted them as one of the tribe, while other Indians made them their own slaves.

Cracker cowboy, Wilson Hoquid, center, with Seminoles, Billy Bowlegs, left and Tommy Doctor, right. Phot courtesy of the state Bureau of Archives and Records Management.

* * *

Crackers learned to live off the land as many practical people do. They used whatever was available to them as well as what knowledge the Indians provided. The cowboys and crackers were also influenced by the Spanish and had their share of renegades. In fact, when the U.S. marshals began to control crime in the West, members of famous outlaw gangs sought safety in the Everglades and its adjacent islands.

Both the cowboys and the crackers used tomato cans to make their coffee. Western cowpunchers used mesquite wood for their fires, while Florida crackers cooked their coffee with fires made from rich heart pine. Both cowboys and crackers drank from tin cups and ate on tin plates. The menus were primarily the same, beans and biscuits cooked over open fires. Iron pots were covered with ashes to bake the biscuits.

An occasional foray into the southern woods provided swamp cabbage, coontie root, and blueberries for a change in diet. The western menu was enhanced by mesquite beans, berries, and pine nuts (also known as piñons).

Crackers used food as a bargaining tool with the Seminole Indians who were always hungry. On a cattle drive, baked sweet potatoes and fried salt pork were used to buy safe passage to Punta Rassa, the port of departure for cattle on the hoof—the live cattle. On the return trip through Indian Territory crackers fed the Indians again in order to slip their bags of gold safely home without being detected.

In the West, however, this was not done. I think cowpunchers would fight their way though an ambush to get their cattle to market or to move them to a greener pasture.

Cattlemen in both areas had other problems as well. In the South, there were insects and diseases that created problems. In an attempt to solve some of their problems, Southerns imported a more disease-resistant breed of cattle called Brahman to be bred with local stock. Still there were the persistent sand flies, now called "no-see 'ems," and gallinippers (large mosquitoes) so big that you would think that you were in Alaska—where they were the thickest—instead of Florida. Almost all crackers had had a bout with malaria because of them. In the West, a breed of cattle more resistant to the cold eventually was imported from England and Ireland. Both region's efforts to upgrade their stock proved successful.

The Western cowboy had his trouble, too. He dared not step into his boot before checking for a scorpion. And if that weren't enough, there were coyotes, cougars, wolves to fend off after the buffaloes were decimated.

The crackers of Florida defended their herds against red wolves, panthers, and bobcats. In addition, they were troubled further by the terrain. It was marshy, wet, swampy and a large part of it was uninhabitable. Oftentimes the humidity was so high that food, clothing, and even shoes mildewed.

The Western counterparts had the opposite condition. It was often very hot, dry, and extremely cold. There was a shortage of water, treacherous mountains to cross, and often their cattle froze. The cattle of the South, on the other hand, could be swallowed up in quicksand or lodged in a bog until they died.

In spite of it all, Florida and western cattlemen managed very well and were happy. They danced the two-step to music played by guitars, fiddles, harmonicas, and even dulcimers. When singing, accompanied by these same instruments, their songs dealt with everyday problems of loneliness and heartaches. Their plaintive melodies seemed to help them accept and deal with the harshness of reality.

Most cowpunchers dressed in ordinary cowboy dress when there was a shindig, a Sunday church singing, or a night out on the town. Saturday nights were howl nights and all cowboys usually quenched their alcoholic thirst to their satisfaction. On special occasions the gentleman cowboy of the West sported a tailor-made outfit that was spectacular. With his bolo tie and ten-gallon hat, he was "king of the walk."

The Southern fellow wore the traditional garb of the townspeople to funerals and weddings, but most often he wore the typical clothing that identified him as a cracker. His wardrobe included his ten-gallon hat and his hand-tooled leather boots with spurs. Sometimes he wore chaps, but always a bandana. He carried with him a lasso, a rifle, a whip, a bedroll, and a saddle complete with bridle and reins. His horse was usually a cutting horse that more often than not, he had broken and trained himself.

The whip he carried was specially made of braided cowhide. Whenever he cracked his whip, he wanted it to sound loud and function as intended. A skilled cracker could cut the head off a rattlesnake with one crack.

Having observed and studied both types of cowboys, I am particularly impressed by the crackers.

Old Behemoth:
A Hog-Chompin' Gator

In the tradition of front porch stories, my cousin Herbert Wesley Rosser told me this one that took place between 1915 and 1917 about his father, my uncle Charles Halo Rosser.

"Charlie, I ain't kidding you! That gator's so big he can chomp down on one of them hogs and leave half of 'em un-et. And that's no lie!" exclaimed Angus, a neighbor of my uncle Charlie Halo Rosser. "I want you to get your gun and kill him before he either eats all them hogs or before he chases them all away!"

"Aw, Angus, you ain't a fooling me, are you?" asked my uncle. His neighbor was known to tell tall tales.

"I swear I ain't afooling anyone."

"All right, I'll be there tomorrow morning and we'll have him all skinned out by noon."

"You'll know ifin it's the right one when you see him asunning on the lake bank. He's twice the size of most gators!"

With that, Angus, left.

Charlie had planned to go fishing, but when he had a chance to catch himself that big of a gator, he thought fishing could wait a day or two.

The Angus Hog Farm was on the edge of the Everglades where feral hogs were rounded up and sold. Most of these hogs were descendents of the swine brought over from Spain several centuries before. They had reverted to a wild state when they escaped to freedom and rooted up the ground everywhere they went, as they still do. When they were killed for food, their hair was so wiry that even by using a razor one had trouble shaving their bristles off, so early settlers called them razorbacks.

Early the next morning, Uncle Charlie picked up his shotgun, loaded it, and headed toward Angus Hog Farm. He didn't care much about that smelly place, but he wanted to see this monster Angus was complaining about.

Angus was waiting for him at his cattle-guard gate. A hog or cattle gate is made with fallen logs or timber layed down with spaces in-between. The wood is placed over a dugout pit, and should a hog or cow try to cross it, the animal's feet would get caught between the wood sections and the hog or cow would be trapped.

This stopgap procedure worked for small operations, but if a rustler really wanted to steal the cattle, he'd tear down the fence and frighten the cattle to make them run.

The two men took a dirt road that headed into the backwoods where Angus's razorbacks were corralled. Whenever he had an order to fill, he'd drive his hogs just like cattle to market. He had to be as careful as a cattle rancher about thefts because as late as the first World War, hog rustling was a good business.

Soon they arrived at the lake. Old Behemoth, as the gator had been nicknamed, wasn't on the lake bank as was expected, but Angus's hogs were squealing and running wildly about. Before long they saw him: he was swallowing half a hog that he had just chomped in two. When the gator saw the men coming, he headed for the water. As big as he was, he traveled very fast.

Uncle Charlie took aim and shot just as the gator reached the water. The first shot missed and didn't seem to faze him. Down he went into the pond to avoid them.

Uncle Charlie knew the creature would have to come up soon for air, so he waited. Angus, on the other hand, thinking that Charlie had things under control, went searching for some of his animals before they wandered back into the wilderness.

Uncle Charlie watched for the gator's eyes to appear. "Them gators are a smart lot. They keep their cover," he said to himself. Soon those eyes showed and he aimed his shotgun at them. With a loud blast, the gator's nose splattered into bits that flew into the air. The gator's tail swung wildly back and forth in anger. Then there was no sign of him. He had gone down with a violent lashing back and forth.

Uncle Charlie had wanted to hit him between the eyes, but he wasn't in the right position. He had to wait again for the animal to come up for air. Being a patient man, he waited with his gun aimed and soon as the gator surfaced, another shot rang out and the gator went down. Uncle Charlie felt that he had got him that time. The shot between his eyes would kill him immediately.

Uncle Charlie put his gun down, ran over to the edge of the pond, and waded into the shallow water. He tried to pull the body, but couldn't budge him. He called for Angus to come help him, but Angus was nowhere to be seen.

Thinking the creature was dead, my uncle decided that there was nothing to do but go to the house for help. Angus wasn't at the house, but his brother was, so the two men headed back toward the lake, calling Angus as they went. Angus's brother decided to give out a big, long hog call. Angus heard it and responded. He came running, thinking that there was an emergency.

"Nothing's wrong, Angus. It was the only way we could reach you. We need you to help us down at the lake."

"You weren't kidding, Angus. That gator is so big I couldn't even move him in the water. You two will have to help me!"

When they reached the pond's edge, the gator was nowhere to be seen. His body should have been floating.

"Do you reckon you just stunned him, Charlie?"

"Maybe so. I thought I killed him. Let's wait and see if he's still in the water. He's hurtin' and that means he's mad. He ain't got no nose and he's gotta come up for air."

Sure enough, up he came. Charlie ran to get his shotgun, but Old Behemoth, as they called him, disappeared again.

"How many shots you got in him?" asked Angus.

"Four, and he acts like he ain't feeling any of 'em."

"He's still moving mighty fast to be hurt too bad," remarked Angus.

Soon the gator was swimming toward the other side of the lake. Uncle Charlie aimed at him right between the eyes again and fired. This time the gator went under and didn't come up.

The men waited to make sure he was not going to resurface, and all three splashed into the clear water. It wasn't hard for them to see the monstrous creature, but it took all three of them to angle him so that they could pull him ashore.

Suddenly that powerful tail of his swung around. Angus and his brother were pulled under water by the sudden movement and Uncle Charlie barely missed being snapped at by what was left of those powerful jaws and teeth. Luckily, the water was knee deep and they were nearer to shore after having pulled him back.

Again Uncle Charlie climbed out of the water and reached for his shotgun. He waited. When he shot the sixth time, the gator didn't come up. He sank down like dead weight.

Again they waited. The other two climbed up on the beach and sat with Uncle Charlie. Finally, Uncle Charlie said, "Let's get him up on land—now!"

The three men waded again into the pond and began to pull the gator toward the bank. They pulled and pulled, but soon discovered that he still had life in him. His tail began to swing slowly back and forth. Uncle Charlie shot him once more at close range and the old fellow finally gave up the fight. They measured and skinned him before they nailed it up for drying. Old Behemoth was fourteen feet and nine inches long and three feet wide.

"Angus, I gotta tell you again, I didn't believe you when you said it was the biggest gator you ever saw—he's the biggest one I ever saw, too!" said Uncle Charlie.

Uncle Charlie then put a hand up to the sky and counted the number of times his hand stacked up before reaching the sun. According to his reckoning, it was just about midday.

"The job's done, Angus, and by Indian-time telling we did it before noon."

"By George, Charlie, you did it!"

Angus reached out and shook Uncle Charlie's hand.

A Dangerous Friend

Another tale was handed down about my aunt Ruth. It takes place about 1910.

Five-year-old Ruth (one of my mother's sisters) had inherited that Celtic copper-red hair with its accompanying ivory-tinted skin. In addition it was wiry-wavy, and therefore hard to manage. For about two weeks she had been begging for a pet of her very own. The family already had a collie dog and her parents saw no reason for her to have her very own pet. So as a way of coping, her mother had promised her that "When our ship comes in you can get a pet of your very own."

From 1900 to about 1920 there were many types of boats on the Caloosahatchee River: paddle wheels, steamships, tugboats, and even houseboats. There were very few schooners that came up the river although one might see an occasional sloop or a yawl.

Fishing was a fun thing and a good recreational endeavor because it often provided food for the table as well. On one of those bright, sunny days Ruth and her older brother went fishing on the dock that extended fifty feet or more into the river.

From the dock Ruth saw a full-masted schooner coming up the river. She gasped in surprise, dropped her cane pole, and ran down the dock toward home as fast she could. Before she reached the front door she began screaming, "Mamma! Mamma!"

Her mother came out of the house, wiping her hands on her apron.

"What in the world is wrong?" she yelled.

The front door slammed shut behind her mother about the same time as Ruth reached the front steps.

"Mamma our ship is coming! It's down there on the river sailing up this way!"

Ruth's mother pulled her panting child up to her and held her close.

"Honey, that ship belongs to someone else. Our ship has not come in yet. Be patient with us for a little while longer. There will be money enough for many things before too long."

Ruth slowly pulled away and handled her disappointment by saying, "Well, that's all right. I suppose I'll have to 'make do' with my new friend."

For the next week or so, Ruth seemed happy enough. There was no more begging for a pet of her own. She kept talking about her new friend and what fun they had together.

One day when Ruth was swinging on the front porch, her mother came out to string beans. While she sat in the rocker stringing beans by snapping them into small pieces after pulling out the "string," Ruth kept looking around, hoping that her new friend would come.

When her mother finished, she went inside.

Ruth continued to swing and look. Finally her friend came for the expected visit.

Her mother heard Ruth talking to the visitor who never seemed to answer. She decided she wanted to meet Ruth's friend and find out who she was and where she lived.

Ruth's mother walked quietly to the front screen door and looked out on the porch. She could easily see her daughter's back, but she could not see the friend. She remained there waiting and watching. Suddenly, she froze in horror.

Ruth had allowed a copper-colored pit viper snake to wrap itself around her neck and dangle loosely about. The snake's color was the same color as her hair.

Fearing for Ruth's life, her mother stood motionless and very quiet. She dared not even move for fear of the copperhead's striking.

Finally after unwinding, the snake slithered over to the rocking chair. Ruth moved over to the chair and the snake climbed up into her lap. Ruth began to sing it a lullaby while she rocked back and forth and stroked its scaly body. Slowly the snake moved from her lap down onto the porch and soon disappeared under the front steps.

As soon as it was safe, her mother rushed out the door and immediately began to examine her child. Ruth did not understand what was happening or why her mother acted so upset.

When Ruth's mother was satisfied that Ruth was not bitten, she seated herself in the rocking chair with Ruth in her arms. She began telling Ruth about how dangerous it was to play with snakes. She wanted Ruth never to do such a thing again.

The next day Ruth and her mother went to visit a cousin who lived nearby. When they departed for home, Ruth was allowed to take one of their cat's kittens. On the way home, Ruth looked up at her mother and asked, "Mamma, did our ship finally come in?"

She didn't listen for her mother's answer. As far as Ruth was concerned, the ship had arrived. She finally had a pet of her very own.

Jesse James's Remnant

This is my version of a popular story about "Mollie and Dallie," twin daughters of a man named Malcolm Green. It was told more often than any other about the infamous outlaws that came through Southwest Florida. It was of interest to our family because of the Hendry House where Jesse James's former cohort stayed. The Hendry House belonged to my grandfather and had been used by officers stationed at the fort during the Civil War.

* * *

"But, Dallie," Mollie complained.

"There's nothing more to say, Mollie. That man is just not the right one for you!" said Dallie. "You know nothing about him. For all you know he may be one of those Texas outlaws that are supposed to be heading down here to Florida."

"That's just a lot of nonsense. He's just about as much a gentleman as I've ever seen," stated Mollie emphatically.

"I'm going to tell Papa about this, Mollie. It is for your own good."

"Don't you do it! I'll run away with him if you do. The folks will want us married in church. You know how they are."

Mollie tossed her head in defiance and left the room. She walked out on the spreading veranda and plopped herself in the swing. She loved John and she was beginning to think Dallie was jealous. Dallie's friend, Tom, hadn't asked for her hand like John had. *She has no idea how much I love him*, Mollie thought.

"Tom is not the marrying kind," she reminded Dallie again, "but John is one in a million. That's why Tom left. You won't ever see him again. Anyway, he's gone and that's that!"

She remembered Tom's desire to farm on one of the keys off the coast. He had said that he wanted to plant an orange grove—or was it tomatoes?

Just think how happy John and I will be living here in Arcadia near the folks, she thought.

Mollie spent the rest of the afternoon swinging back and forth dreaming. She would see John that night at the church social and would tell him about Dallie's meddling. Dallie couldn't possibly know how it felt to have your heart singing when the man you love is near.

The twin girls were very pretty in their organdy dresses. Each carried a basket of goodies to help out with the refreshments at the social. Everyone was having fun singing, dancing, and drinking homemade lemonade.

John twirled Mollie around real fast. Her head began to spin, and when she fell into his arms on the dance floor, several of the chaperones gave her a disapproving look. *He makes me feel like a princess. I just tingle all over when I'm near him*, Mollie thought. John noticed the chaperones' disapproval and whisked her out of the room as the waltz played faster and faster.

"Mollie, let's run away tonight! I don't want a big wedding, do you? I could saddle up a couple of horses and we could ride over to Fort Myers and be there by morning. Then we could get a license and be married before noon. How about it?"

"John, I want to tell you about Dallie. She's meddling in our affairs. She wants to tell Papa about some gossip she heard about you and Tom. She's going to stop us from marrying if she can."

"No, she won't. We'll just slip away tonight. How about it?"

John's tie was bothering him. He loosened it and then pulled it off. In the moonlight Mollie could see a bad scar when he unbuttoned his shirt collar. She did not mention it, though, as he pulled her close to him and kissed her tenderly on the lips.

She felt that magic tingling come over her as she slowly pushed him away. She replied softly, "Yes, yes, yes!"

"I'll come by your house right after the social. Bring enough clothes with you to last a week."

Without saying another word, he jumped from the church steps and disappeared into the night.

Mollie slipped out the back door of the church, not knowing that Dallie was watching. Dallie followed her down the street keeping far enough behind not to be seen by her sister.

I must hurry, thought Mollie. *When John comes, I want to be ready*. She packed her satchel, changed her clothes, and quickly wrote a note, which she intended to leave on her bed. Since her father was asleep, she knew he wouldn't wake before morning. She was ready, but John did not come.

Where is he? I'm ready, but I feel that something is wrong. I wonder what?

Finally she heard hoofbeats. The house was quiet—too quiet. She tiptoed down the stairs and was just about to open the door when she saw Dallie with her father's gun.

"Turn around and go right back up stairs," Dallie said.

"No! Let me pass."

Mollie felt the barrel of the muzzle-loader against her back.

"Not one step farther. I've found out that John is one of Jesse James's gang. I won't let you go," said Dallie.

But Mollie pushed her aside and ran toward the two horses and rider waiting in the shadows. Dallie did not fire, instead, she began to yell; their father came running.

"Mollie is running away with John! I should have told you before, Papa, but I thought I could make Mollie listen!"

As soon as Malcolm Green could, he saddled his horse and raced after the fleeing couple. His horse was fast enough to overtake them, but just as he came within distance, a shot rang out. Then another followed by another, and both he and his horse fell.

"John, please let's go back! Father may be hurt!" cried Mollie.

"Keep riding and don't stop until I tell you," he shouted.

They rode for several hours. The horses were wet and lathered. "Now, we'll stop," said John.

Mollie was shaking. She was so cold and afraid that she could hardly get off her horse.

"Aren't you going to help me?" she asked.

"Get down yourself. You've already caused me more trouble than you're worth."

With that he spit and grabbed another chew of tobacco. He was no longer the gentleman she had known.

"Now, we can't go back to Arcadia. The law will be after us for sure. Come here, gal."

Mollie climbed off her horse as best she could and wandered over to where he stood. He pulled her close to him.

"Drat the luck, Mollie. When we get to Fort Myers, we'll have to keep moving unless. . . ." His voice trailed off to nothing.

With that he pulled her down onto the grass and kissed her hard. She protested, but he slowly removed one garment after another from her rigid body. In the moonlight, she lay bare and breathless. She wanted to scream, kick, run, or do anything except to yield to his passion.

"You sho' are a pretty little chick! I wanted you the first time I ever saw you. You'll be a lot more fun if I can catch you. Why don't you run?"

Mollie was in such a state of shock she couldn't move.

"Move, I tell you. Move!" he roared.

Mollie lay on the ground whimpering like a hurt pup. She felt something sting her that cracked as it hit.

"Move! You cracker! This here whip is itching to draw blood."

Mollie pulled herself up off the ground, but fell forward when she tried to run.

"My but you sho' is purty with nothin' on."

With that he came over to her and pulled her to the ground. She fainted.

The next morning Mollie awakened to find herself on the ground, naked and bleeding. John was sleeping nearby. She could remember nothing except the racing horses and the shots. She felt sure that her father was hurt, maybe killed.

No time to think. Get dressed and run! she reckoned.

The whiplash had burned, but it wasn't deep. She quickly dressed. Her body ached. The pain was intense when she tried to walk.

I'll saddle the horse and get away before John wakes up!

She moved slowly and quietly. She was never sure just how she did it, but she was up on the horse and ready to go when John awoke.

"Ah-ha! The pretty little bird is trying to fly! Oh, no you don't."

He tried to grab the reins, but she was already racing away through the scrub oaks and palmettoes. She had no idea where she was going. She was going to get away no matter what happened! She hadn't gone far when her horse reared up and bucked. She was thrown over a clump of palmettoes and landed in a bog.

"I can't move without sinking. I'm in quicksand!"

The horror of being sucked down into the mud seemed a good way out of her troubles. She felt a sense of relief, but it was not to be.

Through the bushes and palmettoes, she heard John coming. He was beating the bushes as he approached.

"You gotta be in here somewhere! That horse hightailed it like he was a deer."

Then he spotted her. She was no longer fighting, but to her amazement, she was no longer sinking either.

"Ah, there's the little bird. Why she's caught in the bog!"

He disappeared but soon returned with a log. He shoved it into the brackish water near to where she was.

"Grab hold and don't let loose!" he yelled.

Mollie didn't move. "Do as I say! You are my woman now! Hurry up! I might crack my whip again."

Mollie obeyed. She was exhausted.

John pulled her out of the water and helped her brush the muck off. "I see that you are a fast learner. You just do as I say and you won't have no more trouble with me. You are a sight! Can't tell whether you're white or black. Makes no difference. I like 'em either way."

Mollie's saddlebag was on her fleeing horse, along with her satchel. She had nothing to clean off her face. Her hair was straggly and matted with mud. For just a moment John seemed to be the gentleman she had once thought he was. He took his handkerchief and wiped off her face. He held her chin in his hand and looked her in the eyes.

"Dammit, woman, I love you!"

He led the way back to the campsite. There he helped her up on his horse and the two of them began to hunt for the other horse. John whistled and before long the horse came cantering back.

"We'll be in Fort Myers soon. The Hendry House is where we'll put up for a couple of days."

The couple forged the Caloosahatchee River at Alva. The water was deep, but it was not very wide there. They would reach Fort Myers by following the cattle trail the ranchers used.

As soon as Mollie was across the river, she tied her horse to a small pine sapling near the river's edge and plunged in. She splashed about and began to clean herself and her clothing. Just as she was ready to climb out she saw two large eyes coming toward her. John called to her, "Watch out, there's a 'gator eyeing you!"

Even though she was wet and weighted down by her clothing, she stepped quickly on the bank before the gator could grab her.

She shook her golden hair and began to wring the water from it. Soon she was back on her horse and the two continued on the trail. They had not gone far when three Seminole Indians stepped out from behind the underbrush. They pointed at John's saddlebag and then motioned with their hands that they were hungry. One patted his belly and smacked his lips. John had thrown a few day-old biscuits in his saddlebags, in case of an emergency. He reached in and tossed them each one. As soon as they began to eat, he motioned to Mollie to get moving.

"We'd better make tracks and hurry up about it," he called to her. "Them injuns have been known to cause trouble."

Around noon they pulled into the old fort and headed for the Hendry House. When they had bathed and put on clean clothes, John led the way to the courthouse. There in front of the justice of peace they took their wedding vows.

"Now, you are my woman officially."

Mollie was glad that he had kept his promise, but she felt that she had made a bargain with the devil. She had no reason to believe that she had made a good marriage.

That night when they lay in bed, she asked John about the scar on his neck.

"Well, that is one whale of a story, Mollie. I was caught by a posse and strung up to hang along with a couple of buddies. One of my buddies heard about the hanging. He followed the posse and hid in the mesquite. The posse strung us up, mounted us on our horses and then spooked them. They left us for dead and rode on. My buddy came out of the bushes. He saw me stuck in my saddle with the hanging rope around my neck. He figured that my horse had not raced forward like the other horses but had rushed forward and then stopped. He cut the rope from around my neck. I was alive but badly burned by the rope. My horse had saved my life. It was Tom Watson who rescued me."

"Is Tom the buddy who cut the rope off your neck?"

"Yep. I owe him one for rescuing me. He was a good friend of my friend, Belle Starr. That's how I met him."

"Dallie said you were a member of Jesse James's gang. Is that true?"

"That ain't generally known. How'd she find out?"

"Maybe Tom told her. Could be that sheriff friend of hers told her."

"If he did, then I ain't as safe as I thought, but no one can prove anything. All they can do is talk. I got all the money I need safe in the bank. Tom's money is hidden out yonder on Marco Island somewhere."

Soon John was snoring. Mollie's mind was still in a turmoil, even though John was treating her like a lady again. Soon she, too, fell asleep.

They were awakened early the next morning by the steamboat's whistle. John was up and dressing hurriedly. He wanted her to hurry, too, since he had decided they would leave Fort Myers and head on down into the Keys. He wanted to find Tom.

Mollie had never seen a big steamboat before. The paddle wheel was churning the water and she heard music playing.

"That's a calliope," said John. "The steam from the ship's boilers make it whistle that way."

"It sounds like a pipe organ!"

They hurried aboard, but just as Mollie was about to step upon the ship her heel caught in between two boards.

John rescued her by untying her ankle-length slippers, dislodging the shoe, and carrying her onto the ship himself.

They found their cabin and soon the steamer was headed south to Chokolokskee, on Marco Island, where Tom was farming. It was a beautiful day. The water was calm, the sky a deep blue, and the air was cool off the water. She wanted to be on the deck. Porpoises were swimming alongside the ship in their beautiful rolling way. Sea gulls and pelicans, hoping for a free meal, were following in the wake of the boat.

As they neared Chokoloskee, John became agitated and began to pace up and down the deck. He had a scowl on his face and a wild look in his eyes.

The ship docked and their bags were unloaded. John was eager to talk to Mr. Smallwood, the owner of a general store, so they hurried down the wharf. Mollie waited outside the door, while John climbed the steps that led to the trading post. Soon he came down with the news that Tom was away, so they had to go back to Fort Myers. Luckily the steamship was still tied to the wharf. John made arrangements for them to return, so they boarded the ship again.

When in Fort Myers, John left her at the Hendry House while he went off for provisions. He proceeded to equip himself with a mule, a wagon, and supplies enough to last a month. He told Mollie that they would homestead some land so they could farm.

Soon he and Mollie were in a wagon, headed back toward Alva. There they forged the river once again and headed south following the river until it reached Yellowfever Creek. He then followed the creek along its bank until the water began to run clear and provided a secure, easy crossing. Nearby was a natural clearing with several huge oak trees. There he stopped.

"Here's your new home, Mollie."

Mollie looked about. They were miles away from anyone, alone, and with nothing to shelter them from the elements.

Mollie gasped. Then she sighed, and finally realized that her life would never be the same again. There was no escape. Before her lay her future in its raw and ugly reality.

"What's ailing you, woman?"

Mollie could not answer. She wanted to cry. Her dreams were dashed. There was nothing left for her but to accept life with this strange man who called himself John Littleman.

Days passed before she could feel anything. She did as she was told, she said nothing, and slowly turned herself into an obedient, childlike person. John had bought supplies from Henderson's Country Store in Fort Myers. They cooked in an iron pot, washed dishes in the creek by scrubbing them with sand, and slept on the bed of the wagon.

John chopped enough wood to keep a fire going during the night. When the mosquitoes were bad, he moved the wagon so that the smoke would cover it while they slept. With mosquito nets, quilts, and a pillow, they managed until he finished their lean-to shelter. It had no flooring, but at least it kept the rain off during the regular afternoon rains. They didn't have to rush to cover their sleeping gear when the sky clouded over.

John was good with his rifle. He killed and dressed a deer. He showed her how to smoke the meat like the Indians did, and made sure that they had swamp cabbage or other foods that the wilderness provided.

Slowly Mollie adjusted to living off the land. She was lonely much of the time, but both of them kept so busy that time went by in a hurry. She learned to cope with John's strange moods. Whenever he began to pace, she became like a little scared child.

One day they heard a horse riding through the woods. It was the circuit rider preacher. He had heard that people were living up on the creek. He came by to invite them to come to church over at Bayshore.

Mollie was so glad to see another human being. She felt like a caged animal. It must have been at least a month since she had seen anyone but John. She felt ashamed of the way she looked. Her only two dresses were beginning to show signs of wear. She had to wash in the creek and hang their clothing on tree limbs to dry. However, she graciously asked the preacher to sit on a tree stump. (They had cut down two trees with a crosscut saw to build the lean-to.) There was nothing to offer him to drink, but she did ask him to stay for dinner. He looked around the campsite and seemed to think he had better get on to visit some of the other squatters. Of course, he didn't dare to call them squatters. He called them homesteaders.

After visiting with John a while longer, he mounted his horse and pledged to visit again when he was making his rounds.

* * *

Slowly the woods gave way to their hard work. A one-room rough-sawed wood cabin, built up off the ground, soon emerged, with a fireplace and a thatched roof. The floor was made of rough pine, but it looked and smelled clean after Mollie scrubbed it down with her own homemade lye soap. Her broom was made of broken-off branches, tied together with grape vines. It served its purpose, and was often used to shoo away the flies whenever John was eating. She always fed him first; she had what he did not want.

Their table consisted of a door that had been salvaged from a house that had burned. John had made four legs for it. Two home-made benches were placed on the sides of the table, and a field crate or two held the tin plates and cups. They often used a fly catcher plant's blossoms to catch the flies. Flies loved its sticky-honey-filled flowers, but they were caught if they sampled the sweets. The only door to the cabin had to be left open for ventilation most of the time. A large double bed was covered with mosquito netting. This was such a joy to Mollie after having lived out in the open for so long.

John had built her a wash table out in the middle of the creek where the water flowed rather rapidly. It was less than waist-high. The washtray, or table, was covered by the running water. She could use her own lye-soap and a scrub brush to clean the clothes. Next to that was a tray-like tub that held enough constantly moving water so that she could rinse the clothes up and down. Of course, she had to wring them out by hand. The running water of the creek kept her from having to use tote water from the creek. She could wash dishes or clothes just as easily.

To clean the iron pots, she used creek sand and elbow grease. The sand she used to scour washed away quickly. There was always enough boiling water because it was easier to keep the fire in the fireplace going than to have to build another fire.

When she was washing clothes one day, a gator slowly and silently swam toward her. His attack was quick and the large demon-like creature pulled her down and under the water. Mollie struggled and screamed. John came running with his rifle. The gator was pulling her over to the creek overhang, but a shot from John's gun stopped him. John jumped into the water and forced Mollie's arm and shoulder from the gator's jaws. When she was free, he pulled her up on the creek bank and treated her wounds, which surprisingly were not life-threatening. However, she carried those terrible teeth-mark scars with her until her death.

After caring for her, John pulled the dead twelve-foot gator out of the water, skinned it, and nailed the skin up on the side of their shack to dry.

* * *

Meanwhile, back home, things had not gone well for her twin sister, who was left alone after their father had died that horrible night. Without a provider, money was hard to come by. So Dallie married the handyman and she and her husband headed south, hoping to find Mollie. Someone in Fort Myers told them that Mollie and John lived on the other side of the river.

One summer day, early in the morning, Mollie looked out over the meadow and saw someone coming in an ox-drawn cart. She cupped her hand and placed it over her eyes to see better. She then waved and started running toward the cart. Dallie saw her coming and jumped off the cart and ran to meet her. The two sisters held each other in embrace for a long while. Then slowly they pulled apart, looking at each other closely. Gone were the days of plenty. Each sister was weather-beaten and worn from hardships, but no one could destroy their indomitable desire to survive.

They pulled back from each other and began to laugh. What a joy it was to be together. Neither had to say a word. As usual, they seemed to know what the other thought and felt.

Mollie was the first to speak. "We may have lost everything, but we'll always have each other."

She pressed Dallie's hand between hers. Dallie's other hand covered her hands. "We thought we'd never find you, Mollie."

Mitchell had brought the cart to a halt and he joined Dallie. "Mollie, do you remember Mitchell?"

"Of course. How are you?" Mollie reached out to shake his hand.

"We're married. He's been so good to me!"

John came out from the cabin and growled, "What you folks doing here?"

"We came to see Mollie. You act like we're not welcome."

"You're not. This here's my place. You can't stay here. Get going before I start shooting."

"John, please. Don't act this way. She's all I have left in the world. We are sisters," begged Mollie.

"You heard me. Git going."

The two sisters parted. Dallie turned to Mitchell and held on to his arm.

"Sorry to have troubled you, John," said Mitchell.

With that the two of them climbed into the cart. Mitchell took hold of the reins and they pulled away, headed in the direction they had come.

Mollie ran after the cart, but she hadn't quite reached it when she heard the whip crack. She stopped dead in her tracks. The whip cracked a little closer. Then one last crack came down hard right behind her.

She couldn't see her sister's face, but she knew that Dallie was crying. Mollie didn't cry, though. She couldn't cry anymore. She thought that if she had been a dog, she would have crawled back with her tail between her legs. Mollie didn't see Dallie again for a long time. Then one day, after John relented and let her go to church, Mollie spoke to the preacher about her.

"Have you seen my sister, Dallie, or do you know anything about her?"

"Indeed, I do. She and Mitchell are homesteading about five miles toward the river on the other side of Yellowfever Creek. She's getting along fine."

Mollie's heart sang out in happiness. "Could you give her a message for me?"

"Be happy to oblige."

"Tell her that I'm coming to see her soon."

With that Mollie went into the church and sang her praises to the Lord. While the others listened to the preacher, Mollie prayed and prayed, "Lord, please help me."

When the service was over, John was waiting for her in the wagon. The preacher came out to see John.

"Mr. Littleman, I have a message for you from your friend, Tom Watson."

"Then give it to me!"

"All right. He says to tell you he wants to see you right away."

Mollie climbed up on the seat and then John took a chew of tobacco, and spat.

The preacher turned to greet someone and when he did, John yelled to the mule.

"Giddyap!"

When John pulled up outside their cabin, he told Mollie that he had business to do and left in a hurry. She saw him leave with the whip cracking and the mule was trotting faster than she had ever seen it go. Down on her knees she fell and prayed, "Thank you, Lord. I knew you'd help me."

It was early in the afternoon when Mollie headed out. She took a little bundle with her. She had no idea how to reach her sister, but she headed down the wagon trail to the church. The preacher was gone and the church was locked. She sat on the church steps and began to pray. I'll just keep walking on this wagon trail. I'll come to someplace. Surely the trail will lead me to help. She walked and walked. About sunset, she saw a cabin very near the trail, and there were people sitting on the porch. As she walked toward the house, someone yelled, "Howdy, ma'am! Are you lost?"

"No sir, I'm not, but I could use some help if you'd be so kind."

"Gladly, ma'am. I'm at your service. Come sit on the porch with us. Ain't it a nice evening?"

Mollie's feet were hurting her. Her high-top boots were not made for walking. She gladly accepted the offer and was soon seated in a rocking chair. "What can I do for you, ma'am?"

Mollie had to think for a minute. She was not accustomed to asking for help. She didn't want to make more trouble for herself by telling him her problems with John. Finally she said, "I'm trying to locate my sister, a Mrs. Mitchell. Do you by chance know her?"

"No, ma'am I don't. Do you know where she lives?"

Mollie explained to him as best she could about her sister's homestead and its location.

"We're not far from the river. I have a launch moored down there. You're welcome to stay the night with us. I'll take you where you want to go in the morning. Maybe we can find your sister."

The man held out his hand. "The name is Williams. This here's my wife, and these are our young'uns."

"My name is Mollie Littleman. I live up on Yellowfever Creek."

"Yep. I know your old man. What's he doin' letting you walk over here ? You havin' trouble or sumpum?"

"He's been called away. The preacher told me that my sister wants to see me, so I am trying to go to her."

This answer seemed satisfactory and the matter was dropped. Mollie spent the night and early the next morning she and Mr. Williams set out to find Dallie. The ride down the river didn't take long. Soon they passed Yellowfever Creek, and several houses on the river front. "This here is the Fox home. Let's see if they know your sister."

Mr. Fox did know the Mitchells and was willing to take Mollie over to their homestead. "Thank you, Mr. Williams. When my husband gets back, I'll have him come by to thank you personally," Mollie said, trying to make them believe that everything was fine.

Soon Mollie was in front of her sister's place. It looked more like a prairie mud house. Grass grew over an overhanging ledge. Under it was a room sheltered from the sun and wind. The door was shut, but smoke was coming out the chimney, so she knew Dallie must be there. Mollie thanked Mr. Fox and walked slowly toward the cabin. She knocked gently on the door.

Mitchell opened the door. "Mollie! Come quick, Dallie! Look who's here!"

It was like old times. Mollie and Dallie shared their happinesses and sorrows. Time went by quickly. Finally, Mollie couldn't contain herself anymore. "Dallie, guess what? I'm pregnant."

"Oh, Mollie. Does John know?"

"No. I'm afraid to tell him. You don't know how good it feels to be able to share my secret. I don't know what John will do. I'd like to run away, but now that I'm this way, I'm going to have to rely on him."

"You can stay with us, Mollie."

"No, I don't trust John. He'd find some way to get me back."

"Where is he now? How'd you get away?"

"He's off to Chokoloskee to see Tom Watson. Remember him?"

"How could I ever forget? Oh, Mollie, how did we ever get into so much trouble?"

After she had visited for several days, Mitchell offered to take Mollie home and put in a garden just as he had for Dallie. Mollie gratefully accepted both offers. Soon they were in the ox-drawn cart and fording the creek. It wasn't too far to their cabin if they crossed the creek rather than going up the river.

Mitchell plowed up a plot. Both Mollie and Dallie planted seeds and shared more secrets.

"Mollie, what do you do when John changes and becomes mean? You'd now be dead if you hadn't done something to protect yourself."

"Come, I'll show you. I get away from him. So far he's not found my hiding place. He's been looking, though."

Mollie led her to an area that was about a quarter of mile up the creek. Three or four big oak trees were growing close together. "This is where I hide."

"Where?"

"Come on the other side of the tree and you'll see a small hole. I put my foot in it. Now watch me."

Mollie put her foot in the opening and pulled herself up onto a low hanging limb. Then she secured herself on the limb and climbed up further. Down in between the trees was a most wonderful hidden spot. Water could drain out and it was sheltered from the wind, rain, and most of all from view.

"How did you find it?"

"One day I was desperate. I saw John coming. I had to hide in a hurry. I climbed up here and just accidently discovered it.

"Early one morning, after being here all night, I looked up overhead. There was a panther sleeping on the limb above me. When I moved, he moved, too, and was gone before I knew what happened."

"Is John ever kind or good to you?"

"He seems to go along fine for awhile. Then I think he'd even treat his own mother terrible. I think he's very sick."

"Did you ever try to get away?"

"Many times. I finally adjusted to his spells."

Later that day, Mitchell took Dallie back home after tearful good-byes and promises to let the sisters see each other again soon. Mollie tended her garden and waited for John's return. This garden was all the farming that ever was done. Whether John ever intended to farm was a matter of speculation.

Six weeks later John finally returned and brought Mollie a gift. "Don't you like the pretty dress I brought you?"

Mollie fingered it. It brought back memories of times that now were like dreams.

"It's pretty. Thank you, John."

"Is that all you can say?"

Mollie smiled sadly and said, "It was sweet of you to think of me. I hope that you will be happy when I tell you about something very special to me."

"What's that?"

"I'm pregnant."

"After all these years? Can't be mine. You been playing around on me?"

"Oh, John, how could you?"

She ran out the door and into the night. All the pain that she had not been able to feel seemed to have finally found an outlet. She sobbed bitterly as she ran. Suddenly she tripped over a large oak tree root. She hit her head as she fell, then she began to roll downward toward the creek.

Stunned and beside herself with grief, she did not try to stop what was happening to her. The splashing water shocked her. She just sat there in the cool water. It wasn't long until terrible pains began to seize her. She slowly pulled herself up and tried to climb the creek bank, but before she could, another pain hit. This time she screamed.

When John heard her scream, he came running. He saw her lying in the water like she was drowned. He quickly picked her up and carried her into the cabin. As he realized that she was losing the baby, he sat on the edge of the bed and placed her in his arms, and began to cry. "Mollie, forgive me. Please. I'm so sorry."

* * *

Ever after that, John was a different man—that is until a strange illness came over him and he realized that he was going to die. They had been married for more than twenty years. They lived frugally and for the most part, John seemed to have all his needs met. He never became the farmer he said he wanted to be. Mollie's needs never were met, but she managed to adjust and find happiness in many little ways.

That terrible day he found out he was going to die, he hitched the mule to the wagon and took off. Late in the afternoon he returned. He was surly and gruff. "Come here, woman."

Mollie came over to the table where he was sitting.

"I want you to see something." He opened up a large leather satchel. It was full of greenbacks. Never had Mollie seen so much money. He proceeded to take it out by the handfuls and place it on the table. There was another smaller bag that he emptied, too.

"This is the money we started with, and this is what we have accumulated." He had made two stacks.

He gathered up as much money as he could carry and went directly to the fireplace. He threw it all in to burn. He made several trips back and forth until it was all gone.

Mollie was so stunned she could not move. Not one muscle did she move to save the money. It was as though she couldn't believe what was happening.

He came back to the table and pulled out some legal papers. "Do you see these papers? I'm going to burn them so you can't ever benefit from them."

Mollie had no idea what the papers were or what they may have entitled her to inherit. She did know that whenever he wanted something he got it, but he never wanted to do much for her.

He took those handful of legal papers to the fireplace and threw them in.

"Now, Mollie, I have some news for you. Come sit here by my side."

He had to tell her twice. She seemed unable to understand what he was saying.

"Do you remember when we were married in Fort Myers?"

"Yes."

"That marriage was no good. I was already married to a woman out in Kansas. You have lived with me the same as if we were married, but you were never my wife, you were never married to me."

He looked at her with a wry smile. The next day he was dead.

* * *

Mollie continued to live in the cabin they had built until she died. She never knew whether or not she owned it. No one ever questioned her right to live there.

Her sister, Dallie Mitchell, lived on their homestead across the river until just before she died. Troubles continued to plague Dallie and Mitchell. They were so poor after their oxen died that

Mitchell had Dallie hitch the plow to him. He pulled the plow like a mule while she operated it.

These are the kinds of people that survived, despite all their troubles and heartache, just to get a toehold in the pristine wilderness.

Foraging Pays Off

This story is based upon an actual incident that shows the creativity and self-reliance of my Aunt Juanita Sherrill. If anyone could live off the land in Florida, she and her husband, Lawrence, could. They lived in a small one-room house that they built themselves. They enlarged the house as they could afford to, and by the thirties, had a comfortable little house on land they bought from my father. They began their own family soon thereafter. This story takes place shortly after they were married, about 1930.

* * *

"Lawrence, I need your help," Juanita called to her husband.

"I'm all yours," declared Lawrence as he folded up the newspaper where he had been scanning the want-ads.

"It's my turn to entertain the ladies from the Garden Club next week. I'm trying to think of something different to serve."

"Like what?" he asked.

"Oh, I don't know. Something that won't cost much."

"Now, that's a hard one. The last time I went shopping with you, I promised I'd never complain again about how much it cost us to eat."

"Well, things haven't improved. The pantry is nearly empty, and we have already used up most of our canned goods."

"Chicken is out. We've only three hens left and they are still laying. At least we are blessed with eggs. I'm going to let one of the hens begin setting on her eggs."

"How about rabbit?" asked Juanita.

"Haven't been able to shoot one this season. It'd take too many squirrels to feed all those folks."

"Oh dear! We've just got to come up with something soon."

"I've checked the garden. Sweet potatoes are not ready yet. There are sunflower heads, garlic and onions hanging up to dry. Corn's stored in the bin and peanuts are drying out. The new crop of greens is just coming up," stated Lawrence.

Juanita pulled her apron up and untied the strings. She wiped the sweat off her forehead and grabbed her old straw hat. She slipped off her house slippers and pulled on her old worn walking shoes.

Just like everything else—worn out. I wish Lawrence hadn't been laid off. It's been so hard, especially on him. There's just no work and no prospect of getting a job since the plant closed, she sighed.

"I'll take another look in the pantry before I check on the peanuts and corn," she said as she looked up on the near empty shelves. She saw some black walnuts she had gathered in Alabama last summer. There was cornmeal, two kinds of flour, salt, dried huckleberries in a two-quart jar, a big jug of vinegar, and a bottle of honey. Six cans of Carnation milk were left. She shook her head.

After a quick survey of the barn, she saw the heads of sunflowers hung on a line to dry. She also saw the garlic and onions tied together and hanging on loaded strings. She felt the need to think. She always thought best on her feet, so down the rutted sand road she began to walk.

> ## Persimmon Chews
>
> 1 cup dark brown sugar
> 1 cup of uncooked persimmon pulp
> 1 cup of English walnuts
> 2 egg yolks
> 1 tablespoon butter
> 1/4 cup of confectioner's sugar
> 1/4 cup of black walnuts chopped
>
> *Combine sugar, persimmons, walnuts, eggs and butter in top of a double boiler. Cook over boiling water 25 minutes stirring constantly. Cool for one hour. Form into walnut-sized balls, roll in confectioner's sugar and black walnuts. Refrigerate for an hour before serving.*

She wished her friend, Hazel, hadn't come by this morning. She always wanted to know everything, but she seldom really listened. Juanita had to tell her that what she was serving was a secret and she wasn't going to talk about it. Hazel would have to wait like everyone else to find out. How could Juanita tell her when she didn't know herself? She wasn't going to tell her that they were so down on their luck. Again Juanita sighed. She stiffened her back.

Her feet seemed to sink deep into the sandy ruts as she trudged forward. It wasn't long until she noticed some wild onions growing between the ruts. She pulled one up. At that point the wheels in her brain began to turn, and she began to pick all the onions.

These will be good with those cooked leftover lima beans, she thought. Earlier in the day she had thought about gathering some poke salad, but she realized it was too late in the season. The leaves would be tough and bitter.

As she walked on she noticed cattails growing along the side of the pond. There was watercress, too. *That's an idea, I'll walk down to the creek to pick the cress there. It'll taste good with these onions.*

She looked again at the cattails. She thought about how good those fresh young cattail buds were when her mother had cooked them. They were eaten like, and tasted like, corn on the cob. *Too late in the season for them. Pollen is already forming.*

Her mind was still churning—now she was planning a menu for the Garden Club from the bounty of the land.

"I could have watercress, salad and swamp cabbage," she said out loud. Immediately she began looking for a suitable sabal palm, also called a cabbage palm. It had to be just right, not too tall, and one that needed to be taken out. She would locate it and then come with Lawrence when he chopped it down with his ax. She allowed herself to dream about how it would be done. He would have to chop away all the fronds and cut it down to the heart to get the large white tubular boot. Then he'd have to slash down the side of the boot with a knife and pull off layer after layer of white bitter growth. Finally when it was beginning to become tender, he'd taste the top edge of the last layer to see if it was sweet. If it was sweet, then the job was done. The sweet, tightly packed cylinder was ready to be cooked or eaten raw.

She was forced back to reality by the swooping of a mocking bird. It shrieked loudly, flapped its wings, and dove at her. It was prepared to attack anything that came near its nest. Juanita continued to walk and think of a novel and inexpensive way to entertain.

The road ended when she came to the creek. The shady old live oaks seemed to invite her to enjoy their cool shade. She plucked the watercress from along the creek bank. Then she stepped into the shade. Her feet crushed the acorns. She stooped down to look at the new crop that lay heavy on the ground.

> ### Sunflower Seed Soup
>
> 2 cups of shelled sunflower seeds
> 3 scallions, including tops, chopped
> 6 cups of water
> 2 packages of instant chicken broth
> 1 teaspoon salt
> 1 grated carrot
>
> *Place all ingredients in a large pot and simmer, stirring, for 45 minutes. Serve hot.*

Now, let me see. If I remember correctly, we can make flour from these acorns like Mamma used to do. She then made it into bread. Oh, boy! Is this ever good! It'll wow them! What a luncheon we'll have! Juanita wanted to begin gathering the acorns right then and there, but she had her arms full. She remembered her mother telling her that white oaks had less tannin in them. She would need at least a peck or more for enough flour to make bread. *I'll go get Lawrence. We can pick them up together.*

When she started back, she noticed bracken ferns along side the creek bank. Nope. No such luck! The fiddleheads had already grown into long fronds. There were no newly-coiled shoots to clip for a delicious treat.

All the way home she thought about the old days when her mother talked about how hard times were. Her mother had told her: *I kept the family alive by foraging. It pays to forage.*

Juanita's eyes lit up. *Now, it is my time to forage and help out.*

Her feet trampled on some wild violets. She thought if it were spring, she'd stew up some of those violet leaves and sugar down some of the violet flowers. Next summer I must remember to gather some daylilies and make fritters like Ma use to do.

Her mind raced on with every step she took. By the time she reached home she was feeling so jubilant that she was becoming excited about the luncheon.

She opened the door and called, "Lawrence, where are you?"

She looked inside the house. He wasn't anywhere to be found. The sun was beginning to set. She thought he would never come home, but just before dark she heard his footsteps.

"Honey, I've scouted around. I think I can gig enough frogs so you can serve frog legs for the ladies," he called.

A happy Juanita ran into his arms. She was no longer depressed or worried. "Oh, Lawrence we are going to have a wonderfully unique meal."

The next few days were very busy. Lawrence gathered the acorns and put them in the wash pot. He covered them with water. Then he built a fire under it. It was filled to the brim with acorns and water. He simmered them for twenty minutes. Then the hot water was poured off and he let the acorns cool.

Next, he cracked the hulls from side to side so that they fell off. The shelled acorns were then returned to the pot.

"They've got to be leached out at least five or six times," said Juanita. When the acorns boiled up, the water was drained off. After six times the bitter tannin was leached out. The water ran clear. She knew the tannin was all gone because the acorns tasted sweet.

"Now, we'll spread them on trays and bake them at 300 degrees until they are dry and brittle. You can blow off the chaff and

Acorn Bread

1 cup acorn flour
1/2 cup cornmeal
1/2 cup whole wheat flour
1 teaspoon baking powder
3 tablespoons cooking oil
2 eggs
1/2 cup of honey
1 cup sour cream

Combine acorn flour, cornmeal, whole wheat flour, salt, and baking powder. Combine egg, oil, honey, and milk. Add mixtures together a small bit at a time. Pour into greased pan and bake for 20 to 30 minutes at 350 degrees Fahrenheit.

pound them to pulp in that big wooden bowl you made for me. The last step will be to grind them into flour."

While Lawrence tended the acorns, Juanita began to husk the dried corn. She saved the shucks to wrap the corn in when she steamed it. Then she grated the hard kernels from the cobs. After rinsing with cold water, the kernels were drained. She added fresh water and let them soak overnight. Tomorrow, she would boil them gently until tender and steam them in the corn husks.

"I've finished grinding the acorns," said Lawrence. "Let's take time out to see what we do next." Then he added, "I think it would be a good idea to go over the menu."

Juanita agreed. "We'll eat salad, swamp cabbage, acorn bread, steamed dried corn, sunflower seed soup, and frog legs."

"What's for dessert?" asked Lawrence.

"I saw some dried huckleberries in the pantry. Does huckleberry pie sound good to you?"

"Great! I'll go get the sunflower seeds now from the barn. I was saving them for the chickens, but I'll share with you. How much do you need?"

"I'll need two cups of shelled seeds. Will you shell them for me?"

"Sure thing. By the way, I saw some ripe wild persimmons near the hammock next to the saw grass where the frogs are. Want me to get you some?"

"Please. I'll make up some of your favorite persimmon chews if I can find the recipe."

Juanita found the recipe, but she wanted to have it on a card rather than having to read it from the heavy old family cookbook. So she wrote down the recipe for Persimmon Chews, then the one for Sunflower Seed Soup, based on an Indian recipe.

Juanita was tired, but she wanted to do one thing more before resting. She went into the pantry, took down the dried huckleberries and the black walnuts.

She remembered how hard it had been to dry those berries. It had rained every afternoon after she had put them on the tin roof to dry. As soon as it would cloud up, she would have to climb the ladder, remove the wire screen that covered them, and gather them up off the clean cotton sheet. It took nearly a week for them to dry, but when some of them were cooked, they were delicious.

Juanita called to Lawrence, "Let's take a break." She poured them hot coffee and placed biscuits and guava jelly on the table.

She happened to look out the window and saw the wild elderberry bush in bloom. She thought about the time her grandmother had served elderberry tea to her when she was a little girl. It seemed so elegant to her then.

"That would make an excellent drink!" she exclaimed.

Lawrence placed the sunflower seeds on the table and asked, "Did I hear you say something about making a wonderful drink?"

"Yep, elderberry flower tea. It's easy to make. All you have to do is pick the blossoms, cover them with water to get rid of the bugs, and drain. Pour more water on them and let them sit for twenty-four hours. You then strain the water and use the liquid after sweetening it with honey and lemon juice."

"I had thought sassafras tea would be nice. I could dig up a root for you and all you'd have to do is boil it."

"Let's make Grandmother's tea for the ladies. I think they would like it better than sassafras tea."

When they finished, they went back to work. At sunset they quit for the day and made plans for tomorrow.

Early the next morning they went to get the swamp cabbage after Juanita gathered all the ingredients for the huckleberry pie. Then she helped by stacking the large fan-shaped fronds and keeping the area clear for Lawrence when he swung the ax. In less than an hour they were back home. Lawrence took off for the woods to gather the persimmons and gig the frogs. Juanita cooked and baked all morning long. She steamed the grated corn and cooked the swamp cabbage, saving some of the raw pieces for the salad. She parched the peanuts and made the acorn bread. She decided to write the recipe down on a card before making the bread so she could clip it to a hanger under the cabinet. It made her cooking much easier.

"Whew! Only one day left!" exclaimed Juanita the next morning. On that last day they cleaned and washed clothes. Lawrence was good at picking up and dusting. All the while she worked Juanita thought of her mother's contribution to the luncheon. "Mamma would have had guavas served in some way, but that is not possible today," she said. "The winters have been too cold for them lately so guavas were all killed off. The same holds true for the coconut palms, but I've heard they were being replanted. They'll grow until the next killing frost."

They worked tirelessly until everything was ready—including the pie. Juanita's freshly-ironed apron was starched. The spotless tablecloth was ready and Lawrence sported a tie. His Sunday suit smelled sweet from sunning. African daisies honored the set table along with her mother's linen napkins with the hand-crocheted-edges .

Hazel Jones was the first to arrive. "Juanita, I've been dying to know what you've been up to. You have been so secretive for the last week or two. You wouldn't let anyone in on your surprise."

"I've been too busy," said Juanita.

"Tell. Come on, tell me what you're having."

"All right. Sit down and be quiet. Promise not to interrupt until I quit talking."

"I promise."

"We're having watercress salad, sunflower seed soup, steamed corn, swamp cabbage, acorn bread, frog legs, huckleberry pie, persimmon chews, parched peanuts, and elderberry tea."

Hazel looked dumbfounded and then said, "Well, I never! Just wait till the girls get a whiff of this!"

Juanita smiled and said sweetly, "This is one meal of a kind. There'll never be another one like it."

Lawrence interrupted, "The ladies are coming. Don't let them come in the kitchen, Juanita."

The meal was a success. "No one has ever served such a unique dinner for us," said the president. "Let's take a vote, ladies. How many of you want these wonderful recipes?"

Every single hand went up. Juanita sighed. She thought, now I'm going to spend the rest of my life giving away Mamma's secrets. Of course, knowing what to choose and how to prepare it was the best of Mamma's secrets. A person could get poisoned if she didn't know what she was doing. I must remember to tell each one to be careful when gathering wild things. Many of them are poisonous.

Later that evening, Juanita told Lawrence, "I wish now that you had let the ladies go into the kitchen. If they had seen those frog legs jumpin' in the fry pan, they wouldn't have thought the meal was so wonderful."

She took Lawrence's hand and squeezed it tightly. "Thanks to your help, we put on a spread that was fit for a king, and guess what? It cost us little or nothing. Mamma was right when she said that foraging pays off!"

Fort Myers Is Discovered by the Famous

Members of the Hendry family were influential in persuading the founder of the *Fort Myers News-Press* to locate in what is now Lee County, and they were also neighbors of one of the city's most famous residents, Thomas Alva Edison. I have childhood memories of the great inventor, but first I will share my research about some of the other great early residents and visitors to the Fort Myers area.

What splendid days were those in the years of 1884, 1885, and 1886 for the small village of Fort Myers. The village seemed to shout "I've arrived!" On August 12, 1886, the town of Fort Myers became incorporated then, on May 9, 1887, Lee County was organized. To give you the flavor of the time when my ancestors were living in the Fort Myers area, I quote, with permission, from sources I've discovered while looking for information about the Hendrys. I was surprised to learn that much of the information came from the extensive writings of F. A. Hendry.

The mid-1880s were marked with the appearances of special people and special events. Once John Ringling came to see if he could locate his circus here. There was too much opposition from the old-timers and the wealthy winter residents so he went to Sarasota.

Amazingly, the first person of importance to come to the community was shanghaied!

According to Karl H. Grismer's *The Story of Fort Myers*, Stafford C. Cleveland, publisher of the *Yates County Chronicle* in Penn Yan, New York, suffered from ill health during the summer of 1884. His doctor told him that unless he got away from vicious New York winters he could not expect to live to see another spring.

Editor Cleveland straightway made up his mind to go to Florida and, buying some secondhand newspaper equipment, including an old Miehle flatbed press, made his way to Cedar

Keys, then the one and only railroad terminal on the Florida West Coast. One of his friends in New York who had cruised down the West Coast the year before to fish and hunt, told him that Fort Ogden on the Peace River, above Charlotte Harbor, was a community with a future, so that's where he headed.

At Cedar Keys he loaded his equipment on the *Lily White*, a trim, two-masted schooner which then was making irregular trips up and down the coast, stopping at almost all towns along the way. The Captain of the schooner was Henry L. Roan, a resident of Fort Myers.

Captain Roan knew as well as anyone that Fort Myers needed a newspaper and when he learned that he had a bona fide newspaper editor on board, and a whole newspaper plant to boot, he made up his mind that Editor Cleveland would never get to Fort Ogden—not if he could help it. So instead of going to Charlotte Harbor and stopping first at Fort Ogden, as he ordinarily did, Captain Roan headed straight for Fort Myers.

Sketch of turn-of-the-century cat boat used to off-load goods from schooners to the wharves. Used with permission of artist, Patti Middleton, and the Englewood Historic Society.

Arriving there, the tricky Captain called "the gang" together, to inform them of the notable personage on the *Lily White* and told them to get busy. The gang did—all members of it: Captain F. A. Hendry [my great-grandfather], Howell Parker, Jehu Blount, Peter O. Knight, Marion Hendry [my great uncle], Taylor Frierson [my grandmother's brother], Tom Langford, C. J. Huelsenkamp, Ed L. Evans, Carl Roberts, and one of the gang's newest members, W. P. Gardner, a rabid Fort Myers booster if there ever was one.

They rushed to the dock where Editor Cleveland was patiently waiting for the schooner to pull out again and gave him the works. Eloquently they told of the wonders of Fort Myers and in glowing terms they informed him of its tremendous possibilities for growth. As for Fort Ogden—shucks, that tiny place never would amount to anything! Right here at Fort Myers, they chorused, was the place for Editor Cleveland to settle down, set up his newspaper plant and become rich and influential.

Captain Hendry guaranteed him 300 subscribers for a year. Gardner said he would pay six hundred dollars to help him meet initial expenses. Parker, Huelsenkamp, Frierson and many others promised they would be regular advertisers. Evans and Roberts told him they would handle the job of setting up the plant—without charge. Almost overwhelmed by the offers and by the attention he was getting, Editor Cleveland capitulated. His equipment was unloaded and installed in a small frame building at First and Jackson.

On Saturday, November 22, 1884, the first issue of Cleveland's paper, the *Fort Myers News-Press,* appeared. It was said to be one of the finest papers published in Florida at that time, and it was instrumental in the development of Fort Myers. It was also his influence through the paper that many, many notables came through Fort Myers or settled there, including Thomas Alva Edison. Grismer continued:

> Following the shanghaiing, that same winter another event occurred which seems to prove that destiny was at work.
>
> Thomas Alva Edison was visiting St. Augustine. It was a wet, miserable winter there. He had come for a vacation to rest and relax in the sun. When he had made up his mind to return home because of the bad weather, someone suggested that he go to Fort Myers, where it was warm and sunny. He took the advice and went there with two of his friends: A. Smith, and E. T. Gilliland. He traveled by rail to Cedar Keys, and engaged Captain Dan Paul's Yacht, *Jeanette,* for a cruise down the west coast. On the yacht was Nick Armeda, a sixteen-year-old, who was familiar with all the developments going on in that area. He told him about the cable office that had recently opened. Edison, being an inventor and interested in all kinds of communication devices, wanted to see the office. When a young man, Edison had been a telegraph operator, so he wanted to check things out.

George Shultz was the station operator. He was delighted to have Edison visit him and told him all about Fort Myers. Edison was particularly interested in the history of the Indian wars and the surrender of Billy Bowlegs (the Seminole chief who helped to end the Seminole War). He became so interested that he wanted to visit the small village. Arrangements were made and it wasn't long until he was in Fort Myers. Edison was delighted with what he saw. Grismer elaborates on Edison's reactions:

> That evening he strolled through the small town and was deeply impressed by its tropical beauty, its solitude, and the friendliness of the people. It appeared to be an ideal spot for a winter home.

So interested was Edison that he made inquiries about riverfront property for sale. An enterprising fellow found a thirteen-acre tract belonging to Samuel Summerlin, which had sold for five hundred dollars a few years earlier. Edison said if the price were right

Top: Thomas Edison in front of his winter home in Fort Myers, Florida, 1917. Courtesy of State Bureau of Archives and Records Management.

Center: Thomas Alva Edison (right) and Henry Ford on post card.

Bottom: Thomas Alva Edison post card, on the occasion of his 84th birthday. February 11, 1931, Fort Myers, Florida.

he wanted to buy it. A year later he purchased the property for $2,750. In those days, that was a tremendous amount of money, but Edison thought he had made a good purchase and bragged about it for years. The transaction was to become one of the most important real estate sales in the history of South Florida.

After Edison owned the land, he ordered enough lumber from Maine for two prefabricated houses, and had it shipped to Fort Myers. While the houses were being completed, Edison and his bride stayed at the Keystone Hotel.

In *Yesterday's Fort Myers*, Marian Godown states:

> Because cooking odors disturbed Edison, he ordered twin houses, one containing the bedrooms, living room, and work areas. The other, the dining room, kitchen, and guest quarters.

> When the houses were completed, they returned north where he ordered equipment for the Fort Myers Laboratory. He ordered a 40-horsepower steam engine and a dynamo and had them shipped to his "Seminole Lodge," the name of his estate. He returned in 1887 and started working on his electric-light invention.

In March 1886, Edison promised the city that he would provide the lamps to light up the city the next winter. And on March 27, 1887, some lights were turned on briefly, but there were two problems. According to Cleveland's *Fort Myers Press*, on April 21, 1887, the first one was:

> The dynamo to be used in lighting the town of Fort Myers by electricity arrived one day last week. As Mr. Edison is very busy and his stay short, we have our doubts as to whether he will light Fort Myers by electricity this year or not. They are very busy at the laboratory and can hardly spare the time to put up the lamps, etc. which are also here and ready to use. However, the plant will be put in operation in good season next winter and we'll rejoice.

And, there was a second problem: The townsfolk feared that the lights would keep the cattle awake. It wasn't until Edison returned to Fort Myers, almost thirteen years later, that he made the offer again. The lights for the city finally did go on January 1, 1898.

Fort Myers News-Press, on January 1, 1898, relates:

> A soft bright light suddenly appeared in all houses and stores connected with the electric light plant and for the first time electricity was used as a lighting power by the general public in Lee County. After an hour or so the lights dimmed and went out. Adjustments had to be made to the "complicated machinery." But soon the current came back on again and everything went fine until midnight when the current was again shut off, this time for the remainder of the night. Connections with the hotel were made four days later.

All night service was provided only for the hotel. For all other customers, the current was shut off promptly at 11 p.m. Old-timers recall that the lights in their homes always blinked several times exactly at 10:45. That was the signal the lights would go out 15 minutes later.

My great uncle, Capt. Fred Menge, and his brother, Conrad Menge, were owners of the Menge Brothers Steamboat Line. For awhile they monopolized the river traffic. The boats in the line included the *Suwanee, Thomas A. Edison, Uneeda, Anah C, Gray Eagle, Ralph Barker, Riverside, Seminole, Titanic, Yansa, Corona, Ada Mae,* and *Dawn.*

According to Spessard Stone:

Author's sketch of Suwanee *stern-wheel steamer that Henry Ford had Conrad Menge rebuild and install at Greenfield Village, Dearborn, Michigan, in memory of his friend, Thomas Alva Edison*

Capt. J. Fred Menge was a close friend of Thomas A. Edison and Henry Ford. One of the traditions of Ford's arrival at his winter home in Fort Myers was in former years a footrace with Capt. Menge, which the auto magnate usually won. Edison engaged the *Suwanee,* a two-deck stern wheel about 75 feet long, between 1905 and 1913, to take his family and friends on a cruise for two or three days or a week. At his insistence Capt. Menge and Conrad personally ran the steamer.

Florence Fritz in her *Unknown Florida* writes:

The *Suwanee,* of the Menge Brothers of Fort Myers, made the historic first run after which their *Queen of the Glades* made regular four-day runs to the Everglades and "canal regions."

What trips they were! *The Suwanee,* piloted by Capt. R. W. Dupress and Fred and Conrad Menge, was a stern-wheeler. It had 13 staterooms and excellent cuisine.

Up the winding romantic river the *Suwanee* would churn her stately way—around countless bends, through orange groves, pineapple, and banana plantations, through prairie and glade.

She steamed slowly so passengers might observe the exciting tropical vegetation which sometimes met across the narrow jungle stream. Palms, moss-hung oaks, isolated homesteads, steamer-landings of settlers came into view and were passed. There were wild birds, and alligators sunned on the banks. Deer occasionally came down to drink. Far beyond was the mysterious land of the Everglades.

At night, the *Suwanee* was tied up along the river bank, for it was dangerous to navigate the twisting river in darkness. Once moored, a delicious supper was served in the spacious dining room. After that, the room was cleared of furniture and fiddles were tuned up. There was dancing—quadrilles, waltzes, two-steps and Virginia reels.

These were never-to-be-forgotten journeys, beloved by Henry Ford, Thomas Edison, and all who ever sailed the ancient river.

Alfred Jackson Hanna and Kathryn Abbey Hanna wrote in their book *Okeechobee*:

The *Suwanee's* most famous passenger was Thomas A. Edison, who being very fond of fishing, chartered the boat regularly each season during many of the winters he was working in his laboratory at Fort Myers. Her revered decks carried many a happy passenger when round-trip weekly schedules were maintained between Fort Myers and Fort Lauderdale. Her Okeechobee days were ended when the hurricane of 1926 blew her ashore near Moore Haven. Yet, even here the *Suwanee* served purposes not always as useful as unique. Children delighted to play in her hull; hoboes found a free night's lodging in what was left of the lower deck, and town drunks sought refuge there to sleep off the effect of their orgies. Finally she was towed up the canal and dismantled, her timbers sold, and her engines sunk.

Even so, the *Suwanee* proved to be as indestructible as a cat with nine lives. Because of Edison's devotion to and wide use of the boat, Henry Ford engaged Conrad Menge to raise her engines from their watery grave and build a replica. Menge constructed the new hull on the old Riverways of Menge Brothers and shipped it on flat cars to Michigan the new

The steamship Thomas A. Edison, *which traveled the Caloosahatchee River, between Fort Myers and La Belle, 1909. Courtesy of State Bureau of Archives and Records Management.*

Suwanee, with resurrected and reconditioned boiler and engines. Mr. Menge followed and put her in perfect running order on a small river in Henry Ford's Greenfield Village. *The Greenfield Village Guide Book* explains that this little river is the *Suwanee* and that nearby is Stephen Foster's house. But no aid to the imagination is needed to recognize Okeechobee's much-loved steamboat, the *Suwanee*.

* * *

Stories abound about Edison and the other inventors who were creating and enjoying the new technology of the times. Edison even became involved with agriculture and experimented with plants to see if he could make rubber for tires from goldenrod. According to *Florida, a Guide to the Southernmost State:*

> Shortly after Edison had established his Fort Myers home, Henry Ford bought an estate adjoining that of his friend. The Ford Estate, 2200 McGregor Boulevard, is enclosed, like his neighbor, with a high picket fence; the unpretentious house is hidden from view. Ford soon joined Firestone and Edison in forwarding the experiments of the Edison Botanical Research Corporation and spent a great deal of his time at the old Hendry home near LaBelle where he liked to take long walks accompanied by his secretary.

And Grismer relates this story:

> The Motor King came to Fort Myers in February, 1914, accompanied by John Burroughs, the noted writer and naturalist, to visit Edison. Before he left Detroit he sent an order to the Fort Myers Ford dealer to have three Tin Lizzies ready for him on his arrival. Ford and Burroughs came in on Monday, February 23, and were greeted by a crowd of more than two thousand persons. They were escorted to the Edison Home by every automobile owner in town—all 31 of them. The parade was headed by the three Fords Henry Ford had ordered. He gave one of them to Edison, the second to Burroughs, and kept the third for his own use. For many, many years whenever he came to town thereafter he drove the car around Fort Myers. He was asked often why he didn't replace it with a newer model and always replied, "Shucks, why should I? A Ford never wears out."

> Edison spent his later years searching for a substitute for rubber. He experimented with various plants, including goldenrod, which turned out to be a good substitute.

> When he had ideas for solving a problem or creating a product, he jotted them down in a sketchbook. Then, he would call Fred Ott, who cranked up his Model T and hurried off to the shop to have a sample or model made by the next morning.

There were always stories about Ford and how he did not want to waste a penny, but he was always doing great things for people.

In the book titled *Florida, A Guide to the Southernmost State*, (compiled and written by the Federal Writers' Project) is this information:

> As Edison extended his activities, The Edison Botanical Research Corporation was established here.
>
> The Federal Government, in conjunction with Henry Ford and Harvey Firestone, sponsored the research work. Edison spent long hours making tests of flora that might be used to provide an emergency rubber supply if tropical markets should suddenly be closed to the United States. More than 500,000 tests were made on various plants and trees, and the common goldenrod was found to have great possibilities. In the course of his experiments Edison cross pollinated a small goldenrod and a giant variety, 14 feet tall, native to the Everglades. Using this hybrid, he eventually evolved a rubber-making process that could be adopted commercially.

I Remember Edison

During this time, when I was seven or eight years old, Edison came over to our farm, along with Henry Ford and Harvey Firestone to see the goldenrod grown on our acreage. They arrived in an open door sedan. I thought Edison had the biggest eyes I had ever seen. Our visitors- picked some goldenrod samples and left.

In the late 1920s, we had a chance to see Edison's laboratory on a Sunday afternoon. Edison had ordered some plants and there were too many for him to use. Since we had a large unplanted area, we were asked if we wanted to have some. This is where the Australian pines, planted in front of our house and in the back field, came from. I loved to climb to the top of them and swing in the breeze. I finally quit when I realized how much it worried my mother.

The thing that impressed me most about Edison was his inquiring mind. It was open, all kinds of ideas, welcoming the usual and the unusual. He tested each and every idea for its validity.

Great Uncle Fred Menge lived next door to Edison and they shared many common interests. Edison was fascinated with the gentle man who was a mystic and was able to heal. Uncle Fred's healing powers resulted from his prayers and faith. Once, Uncle Fred wanted to remove a wart from my finger. He massaged it as he prayed. I must confess I was only pacifying him when I allowed him to pray about my wart. The wart didn't bother me. I thought the whole idea was silly, but he was my great uncle and a dear man, so I let him do it. Imagine my delight, surprise, and even adulation when the wart began to slowly disappear. Within a week, it was gone! He thought the Lord worked through him.

Edison was, unlike many residents in Fort Myers, fascinated with the art of healing and obsessed with anything bordering on the mystic. He had developed his own theories about life in connection with his other theories, such as the Etheric Force—the foundation for the discovery of electromagnetic waves.

He openly acknowledged that he believed in a higher intelligence, but he wanted to test out his theories. It is said that he built a fabulous machine that could record all kinds of sounds at different frequencies. He even claimed to a group of scientists that he had built such a machine, but it was never found.

Supposedly Edison once told a friend that while he was known as a great inventor, he had tried but had been unable to create even a simple life form. He remained fascinated with trying to determine if there was life after death, and told reporters that he was working on a device that was so sensitive that he would be able to pick up such evidence. No one has found a model of such a machine in his laboratories. Such tales like this circulated in our little town. On warm summer evenings, folks would gather together on front porches to talk. They discussed politics, religious movements, and current gossip.

The story of Edison's machine was the topic of discussion one evening. It was rumored that Edison, Ford, and other influential people took the machine out to a graveyard. They wanted to learn if the dead could enlighten them as to the validity of his theories. Edison felt certain that if the spirits of the dead were in their graves, he had a machine that could communicate with them. So he theorized that if they made any attempt to reply to his questions, his machine would record it.

So began the strange sojourn of Edison, Henry Ford, and other interested people into the graveyard with his recorder machine. He did not believe in it, but he was going to prove once and for all whether there was life after death. After all, his machine could record anything and he could speed it up or slow it down.

If this event happened, as it was rumored, it would have been comical to see these learned men out in the graveyard, trying to entice the spirits to talk to them. They pleaded, they bribed, and did everything possible to get a response, but nothing unusual was recorded. When the session was over, I think Edison had proved to himself once and for all that the dead do not come back—let alone talk! Yet, he could never quite understand, nor did he ever quit trying to understand, the mysteries of life.

Recently it was reported that all of Edison's work and papers were stored and locked up after his death. Nothing was disturbed.

In time, these rooms may be opened. Who knows what may be there waiting to be rediscovered. Wouldn't it be something if that mysterious machine was found intact? Stranger still, what if it works?

Here is an opinion offered by Michele Wehrwein Albion, curator of the Edison Ford Winter Estates on May 12, 1995, as to whether this event ever occurred.

> All of our sources suggest that the story originates from a practical joke Edison played on a reporter, who had come to get a BIG story. When he would not leave Edison alone, the inventor gave him the story of a lifetime. However, it has persisted and many believe it true.

> Edison performed another practical joke on visitors to Seminole Lodge, the Edisons' Fort Myers Winter Home. He cut segments of belts from his machine shop and had the staff fry them up, covered with gravy. The steak was served to a guest and masqueraded as Florida beef. Then Edison would patiently observe while the poor victim tried to cut up his/her steak.

* * *

I did not see Edison again until his eighty-fourth birthday at the opening of the Edison Bridge, built in his honor. He had escaped the crowd and was walking across the bridge. I remembered him and hoped that he would remember me. When I caught up with him and tapped him on the arm, he looked down at me and smiled, but hurried on. I was just another stranger to him. I did not talk to him because I knew he was hard of hearing. I'll never forget his bushy white hair that the wind on the bridge had messed up. I thought that it looked like Mother's kitchen mop!

Florida's Second Johnny Appleseed

When people think of the beautiful palms along McGregor Boulevard in Fort Myers, they usually think of Thomas Edison. Edison is credited with planting them, a visual legacy we enjoy today.

Edison had been carrying on many experiments and had made friends with the citizens of Fort Myers. On April 16, 1907, the city council accepted Edison's offer to plant and care for royal palms on McGregor Boulevard. The first palms, imported from Cuba, died. Seven hundred more were bought from E. E. Goodno, who dug them out of the Big Cypress. Many of these died as well.

Edison once again bought 250 royal palms in 1913. This time they survived, and in 1914 he bought 178 more. The town established a park commission in 1915 to care for the upkeep and fertilizing of the palms. The real "man behind the palms" was my Uncle Jimmy—James E. Hendry, Jr. (1878–1955).

James E. Hendry wasn't really my uncle, but the relationship is complicated and almost sounds like a brainteaser. He was my father's double first cousin; his father and my father's father were brothers. The two Hendry brothers married Major Aaron Frierson's two daughters. The children of each brother became double cousins. Their children, I think, would be called either first or second cousins. No matter, I chose to call him Uncle Jimmy. And I called his sister, Isabel, Cousin Izzy. In the South, it was proper to address one's elders with respectful titles such as uncle or aunt.

Uncle Jimmy was trained in business practices, but it took him awhile to find himself and use his talents. While he was cashier at the Bank of Fort Myers, he became interested in semitropical plants. It wasn't long until he went into business with Cousin Izzy's husband, Arthur. W. Kelly. Kelly had a forty-acre tract on McGregor Boulevard. They called their business the Everglades Nursery and specialized in palms.

The *Fort Myers News-Press* dubbed Uncle Jimmy as the man behind the palms in an article written February 22, 1983.

While Thomas Edison seems to get most of the credit for the royal palms lining McGregor Boulevard, other Fort Myers residents played a major role in seeing that the trees were actually planted.

The inventor had the idea of lining McGregor Boulevard with the stately palms that made it famous, and he offered to pay for the first mile-long planting. But after that, it was up to others to extend the "Boulevard of Palms."

Nurseryman James E. Hendry [Uncle Jimmy] was the pioneer of beauty who contributed the main effort that made McGregor into a horticultural landmark.

It wasn't until Hendry shamed the city into taking care of the Edison palms that they began to flourish. Hendry acted as a human watchdog for the palms, driving up and down McGregor, noting which trees needed fertilizing, spraying, and watering, and calling them to the city's attention.

In part as a result of Hendry's badgering, the city appointed its first park board in 1915. With Hendry as chairman, one of the first tasks was to care for the Edison palms. He noticed that many palms died from bud rot. This fact made him interested in finding a cure for this disease.

James E. Hendry, Jr., courtesy of Sara Nell Gran

In an article by the *Fort Myers News-Press,* dated February 19, 1981, I found this information:

When a disease called "Bud Rot" threatened the palms and the town faced a loss of the whole palm population, Hendry found a cure by treating the trees with manganese. He saved thousands of them, replacing those killed at his own expense.

Although his name became synonymous with palm culture as the years passed, Hendry tinkered with other tropical plants always trying to bring out more of their beauty.

His nursery career was noted by the Southwest Florida Historical Society's story printed in the *Fort Myers News-Press* March 10, 1955:

But the great epoch that he represents began with the cutting that a ship's captain brought back from Brazil and presented to his grandmother which grew into Florida's first purple bougainvillea. Prospering and spreading, the plant soon covered much of the home, which stood on the site of today's Fort Myers post office, and visitors came from afar to admire it, but Young Jim was not content. He demanded other colors and shapes for the beautiful plant.

Years later, by a method of hand pollination that he invented, he solved the problem. It was only one of many such triumphs. In tribute, he was named winner last spring of the national Johnny Appleseed award, the precious accolade bestowed only on the great and gifted among those who take nature's miracles and compound them with their own dreams.

Date palm and orange trees on grounds of James E. Hendry's home in Fort Myers. Circa 1880s. Courtesy of State Bureau of Archives and Records Management.

As time passed, his imagination and industry tilted with other eternal varieties that seemed unconvincing. Nematodes, those ruinous pests that are mankind's most relentless enemy, were attacked and routed from root stock of fragile gardenias with the result that the "scarce 100 plants" of his early days multiplied themselves and became the pride of thousands of families.

Again the *Fort Myers News-Press* gives us another great story, "Granddaddy Gardenia" by Lee Melsek, which appeared on Sunday, May 18, 1975:

In 1925 a botanist gave the tree to Jim Hendry's [III,1909–1984] father, the late Fort Myers horticulturist James E. Hendry, Jr., as a gift. At that time it was a little clump of green foliage whose species name, Veitchi Thunbergia, was probably longer than the tree.

Royal Palm avenue in grounds of Thomas A. Edison winter home. Courtesy of State Bureau of Archives and Records Management.

The tree was a native of South Africa, and its new home on Fowler Street made it the first gardenia tree in South Florida, Hendry said.

According to Hendry, his father began grafting the tree with other species of gardenia trees grown in northern Florida in an effort to make its sensitive body immune to the life-sucking nematodes that prey in South Florida soil.

Hendry's father owned a nursery, and Hendry remembers that as a boy we used to pick the gardenias off the tree for corsages.

By the 1940s, Hendry said the little tree spawned thousands of other trees and the perfume of the little white gardenia flower was becoming a popular fragrance in the yards of area residents.

The senior Hendry kept grafting his little tree by cutting chunks from the understock and fitting it with other species, using beeswax to mold the two together.

The Veitchi Thunbergia species became the only species of gardenia tree to be immune to the dreaded nematodes here, Hendry said.

It became a very tough tree, Hendry said, and the branches of the new South Florida trees became drenched with small white petals.

Through all the experimenting, the original tree kept its stately posture at the Hendry's Fowler Street home, even after the senior Hendry died in 1955 and the grafting ended.

From Marian B. Godown's article "The Man Who Planted the City of Palms" in *News Press* in 1981:

A bit of Hendry horticultural heritage lives on today in Fort Myers in the 'Granddaddy' tree Hendry [Jr.] used in his successful grafting. The tough, little tree was moved to the City Hall parking lot eight years ago after the [original] Jim Hendry house was torn down.

Through his hybridizing of old varieties of hibiscus, Hendry created 400 new shades. He was honored by the American Hibiscus Society; the Fort Myers chapter is named for him.

He was the first nurseryman to propagate indoor-type palms in such numbers that they could be sold at dime-store prices. This practice was considered revolutionary when Hendry started.

Susan Ford, in her "The Quest To Protect Palm Trees," in the February 19, 1981, issue of the *Fort Myers News-Press* eulogizes [my Uncle Jimmy]:

When he died, he was acclaimed across Florida in gardening circles for his five decades of pioneering work in helping to beautify the Sunshine State.

In 1968, the periwinkle Garden Club of Fort Myers donated a prayer garden in Hendry's memory to Lee Memorial Hospital, an institution which Hendry previously had helped landscape.

For over a dozen years, cafeteria diners at Lee Memorial

enjoyed looking at the quiet piece of greenery amid bustle. Two years ago, the Hendry Garden made way for the Support Services Building.

The large shrubs and Palms were sent to other parts of the hospital grounds while the two carved stone benches surrounding the statue of St. Francis of Assisi—once the centerpiece of the secluded garden—now face the busy entrance of the hospital's Doctors Clinic (formerly the emergency room).

* * *

I remember one day when I was living in Phoenix, Arizona, and looking through a flower catalog. Suddenly my eyes saw the most beautiful daylily that Uncle Jimmy had produced. He had named it after his wife, Aunt Dot. Whenever I see some of his flowers, I am enthralled by the beauty he created.

This is the reason he is honored and I must say that one cannot heap enough honors upon one who has blessed the world with such beauty. Surely the Lord smiled upon him and crowned him with such ability!

All That Glitters

On a blustery January day in 1926, "little brother Bill" was born. He was given that nickname the day he was born and until the day he died, he was always called little brother by me.

Old Doctor Winkler drove up to our home carrying his little black satchel. He drove a workingman's Model-T Ford complete with its isinglass and other accoutrements. One of my aunts whisked my other little brother, Harry, and me away shortly after he arrived. Our trusted servant, Kathareenus, stood guard outside my mother's room. She was all atwitter, pacing up and down and about as agitated as I had ever seen her. For all intents and purposes one would have thought she was the one having the baby. She quickly shut the door behind us, seeming to be somewhat relieved at our departure.

Later that afternoon we returned home. Old Kathareenus met us at the door. In her arms was our new, little brother all wrapped up in white and lovingly cradled in her arms.

She let us look at his little red face and then pulled the baby blanket up over it as though she were protecting him from danger. She was in complete possession of him and we felt excluded, although it was not intentional. We felt left out in the cold because we had so looked forward to his arrival.

Little Billy was Kathareenus's baby—not ours. Our resentment grew as she remained in control. We were not even allowed to touch him, look at him, or go near him without her undivided attention.

I'll never forget how Old Kathareenus would grab him up in her arms at his slightest cry. She would pick him up so carefully and tenderly, and then hurry out to the front porch swing with him. Then she would begin to sing. She sang in a loud but comforting voice that was uniquely her own. I don't know how many Negro spirituals songs she knew, but each one carried the lament and intonation of all her black heritage. I can still hear her now as she sang, "Swing Low Sweet Chariot." The swing managed to come down on the "low" and would crest again as she reached "Sweet Chariot."

Bill was "her baby" for two years. By that time he was spoiled "rotten" as Southerners say, but he became the favorite of everyone who knew him. Not only was he a handsome little boy, but he had the largest eyes and the longest eyelashes I'd ever seen. Those eyes had a controlling command about them that enabled him to be and keep him in charge of his adoring audience.

If a child could be called "flamboyant," he was. Everything about him was colorful; I sometimes wonder if Kathareenus's constant attention influenced him so that he wanted everyone to notice whatever he did. He loved to adorn himself with bright colors and things that would attract the attention of others.

One afternoon when I was drawing on our screened-in front porch, he wanted me to sketch him. He wasn't satisfied with the likeness until I put a wristwatch on his arm and a ring on his finger.

I thought it rather comical to note that on one of his last photographs before his death, he sported a large college ring and a gold wristwatch, just like the ones he had wanted me to place on him as a four-year-old child.

Our Bill was a clown and a cutup most of his life. Our grandmother taught him during the first grade. He was quite a challenge—almost more than she could manage at times. Every question she asked the class, Bill's hand went up. If she didn't call on him, he'd yell out the answer, anyway.

Half of Bill's school year was spent outside the classroom. If he weren't standing out in the hall, he was playing or swinging out on the playground. If anyone asked him what happened at school, he'd reply, "Nothing." If pressed for what he did all day, held say, "I played." I sometimes wonder how he ever graduated from high school!

In addition to being a clown, he was a second Tom Sawyer. If he had chores to perform outside, Bill seldom did them. The yard was full of children doing what Bill was expected to do. There were more girls around than boys, but he seemed to be able to get the work done and have fun at the same time.

There was one neighbor girl named Jeannie Powell who was his favorite helpmate. She became quite a joke in the family circle because she was so attentive to his wishes. We called her Jeannie with the light brown hair. She was exactly what Stephen Foster was trying to portray in his song by the same name.

The only real work I ever remember seeing Bill do was to take directions from our brother, Harry, who was interested in flying model airplanes. He either designed them or made them from kits he bought. Bill looked up to his older brother's ability and admired his skill. He constantly bugged him for help when trying to copy one of Harry's model planes. Sometimes he would borrow parts of Harry's things to accomplish what he wanted to do. This created a problem for Harry and oftentimes brought on a fist fight. It seemed to me that Bill could have made things as well as Harry if he had wanted to put in the same amount of hard work and effort that Harry had to exert.

Usually, though, whenever the two boys wanted to do something they did pull together. It was usually Bill's skill with people that enabled them to do the yard work or whatever else had to be done. They could finish up early with all the help that Bill was able to recruit.

Bill possessed a remarkable mind although he always thought he had less intelligence than either Harry or me. He was smarter than either of us in many ways, but things were so easy for him to learn and do, that he did not have to apply any effort at all until later in life. In addition to being smart, Bill was talented in music. The first time he put a trumpet up to his mouth, he automatically shaped his lips correctly. Most people have to be taught. He could play it without any trouble, but Bill didn't like to practice. It was the same with piano lessons, but when he was older, he enjoyed playing his trumpet at church or playing the piano for the sheer fun and delight of it.

Our parents loved music, too. They must have loved it to endure the practicing sessions we put them through. Their favorite time was when we were asked to perform for them while they sat on the front porch after dark. With fireflies darting about and the moonlight creating shadows, they sat on the front porch and rocked away while they listened to our discordant trilogy. I played the piano, Bill played the trumpet, and Harry played the violin. We had our own little orchestra and played all the old-time favorites that people never seem to play anymore. There were Irish lilts, patriotic songs, hymns, and several Scottish tunes that they dearly loved. My Dad's favorite was "Drink to me only with thine eyes."

The noises that came from our house during the day must have driven our neighbors crazy, but they never complained. I think people back then were much more tolerant than they are today. It was especially noisy when Harry tried to play the tuba. I really don't know which was the worse—when he practiced a new tune on his violin or when he bellowed on the tuba. He could make such outlandish squeaky sounds on the violin that we accused him of trying to get even with us by all the noise he generated with his instruments. Even our dogs got in on the act. They would let the neighbors know that they, too, could be melodious! It was especially noticeable every time the fire whistle blew to let the townspeople know there was a fire. The dogs joyfully joined in to do their part!

While on the subject of dogs, Bill once brought home a mange-infected dog, whose owner did not want to go to the trouble or expense of treating it, so offered it to Bill. Bill was a kindly soul and felt sorry for the dog.

It became an issue as to how to treat it because we didn't have the money to take it to be treated. In those days I don't think there were veterinarians like there are today.

We had what was known as "horse doctors" who treated mainly livestock, but even then, we could not have afforded to pay him. My folks tried tar soap and other suggested cures like sulfur and lard. But nothing seemed to work. One day someone suggested that we dip the white spitz dog in laundry bluing. They swore by it as the best remedy they had ever heard of. With the help of Harry and Dad, Bill filled a washtub with well water. Then they added the "bluing," and the dog was properly dipped and dried. It killed the mange, but we were left with the most beautiful blue-haired dog you ever saw. The blue finally washed out, but the teasing persisted quite a while longer.

That wasn't the only time Bill was involved in an episode that was colorful. Being such a social fellow, Bill had friends among the blacks as well the whites.

Our Great Cousin Ruth Parker was a wicked guitar player. She spent hours on end learning to play Negro spiritual songs and accompanying some of the black people who sang for money. One day she talked Bill into joining her. He played his trumpet and I think they must have had what we now call a jazz fest. When they finished that afternoon, she complained to him about a problem. Bill thought our folks knew everything and could help, so he brought her home with him.

Earlier in the day, she had dyed her gray hair as usual with henna dye. Rather than turning her hair an auburn color it colored her hair a fire-engine red. She tried to wash it out to no avail, so she tied her hair up in a handkerchief. Her hair problem went unnoticed by the black women because they often wore a *tignon*, a red handkerchief with the corners tied on the top of their head.

When they arrived home, our folks were kind and understanding, but they knew of nothing other than to dye her hair black or to let it grow out. In time, the color would dim. Of course, she would have done this already had she wanted either of these choices.

She left our house frustrated and unhappy. All the way home she wondered what she could do with her hair. As she neared her home, the idea struck her to use bleach on it. She knew what she would do—she'd use hydrogen peroxide. Once before she had used it to bleach her hair when she wanted to become a blonde. That would make it turn to a bright orange first, then it would become lighter and lighter until she became a blonde. She looked inside her cabinet, but there was no hydrogen peroxide. Now what? She decided to try Clorox bleach. She diluted it down because she was afraid that it would dissolve her hair completely if she used it straight from the bottle.

She could hardly wait to look in the mirror to see what had happened. To her horror, her hair had turned to a beautiful apple green. She felt like crying. She wondered what would happen if she used a little bit more, so she poured out another portion. Again she wetted her hair with the Clorox water. By the time she looked again, it was a softer green than before, but it was still a gray-green. After the third treatment, some of her hair began to fall out. The color was still green—a dirty brownish green. She had by this time resolved to wear a tignon until the green wore off. Several months later, the green had disappeared, Cousin Ruth was happy to have her gray hair back. She never used any dye on her hair again.

The next episode of interest in Bill's life that I remember was when he and some of his friends joined the volunteer fire department. They were to join forces with the regular crew when a forest or field fire would erupt, taking their shovels and burlap bags with them as they reported for work. All went well for awhile, until "one of the volunteers" had the brilliant idea of making some extra money. They were not paid much, anyway; and the more work the more money.

Soon the fire whistle began to blow quite often. The dogs performed admirably and the regular crew had more than enough help to extinguish all the fires. Soon, it was reported that the police were becoming suspicious about the number of fires. Anyone caught setting a fire would be soundly dealt with or punished. The fires stopped just as suddenly as they started. No one ever knew who was to blame and if they did, I don't think anyone would have told.

About this time, World War II was declared. Everyone was patriotic in those days. Both my brothers went into service. Harry's poor eyesight kept him out of the Air Force, so he went into the artillery and Bill went into the Navy.

This was the first time in his life that Bill could not be in control. He could neither play nor goof off. He was stationed on an oil tanker and he did see the world, but at what expense! One of his friends was swept overboard in the Arctic and froze to death before he could be rescued. Other times he prayed for safety when there was fear of being torpedoed or dashed to pieces in a fierce winter storm that tossed his ship forty or more feet up in the air and then nosed it down into the depths.

He seldom ever talked about his experiences on the tanker, but he did tell me about this episode. On the ship during war time, there was no tailor on board to adjust or alter their uniforms.

Bill had spent all of his money on his last shore leave and needed some for supplies. All his buddies were broke as well, so they weren't able to help him out. Bill needed money desperately. He thought and thought of a way to earn some. He happened to look across the galley where he was working and saw one of his shipmates wearing a uniform much too large for him. This guy seldom went ashore. Bill thought he might have money stashed away; so he walked over to him and eyed his suit rather critically.

"Would you like your suit altered?" he asked.

"You betcha," the sailor replied.

"I think I know a way I can get it done for you."

With that Bill left him and went to visit his petty officer. He told him that he knew how to operate a sewing machine and wanted to know if there was one on board.

"You can sew?" he asked. "Well, for goodness sake why didn't you say so?"

"I just did," Bill replied.

"Come with me."

They went down a few steps and into a large storage room. In one corner, there was an old treadle Singer sewing machine. As soon as Bill saw it, he knew how he was going to obtain the supplies he needed.

"You know how to operate this?"

"Yep."

Bill sat down and threaded it up. There was a spool of white thread in one of the drawers. There was also a piece of practice material for evaluating stitches. He sat down and tested the stitches out for the officer. Guess who was his first customer?

Bill had learned how to use the old family machine when he was making a Halloween costume one time out of sheets. Mother had showed him how to use it. His ghost costume did not win him any honors, but now his skill was going to do so! After tightening up the petty officer's skivvies, he was in business. From that time on until they reached port, Bill's spare time was spent altering uniforms and bell-bottom trousers.

Finally the war was over and Bill used his GI bill to attend college. His heart was not in his studies, however; it was more on the young ladies. He spent his time entertaining them and enjoying life as usual. That is, until he met that special lady he wanted to marry.

Jeannie "with the light brown hair" had married someone else by the time he returned to the states, but he found Stella. She became the one star in his existence. From the time he married her until his death, she received all his care, attention, and love. Nothing else seemed to matter to him.

Bill had two sons, William II, and Robert Louis. Son, Billy, graduated from The Citadel. Bobby graduated from the United States Naval Academy at Annapolis. Both became Marine officers.

After Bill's marriage, I saw little of him or his family for the next fifteen years. We were not living near enough each other to get together very often. Can you imagine my surprise when my little brother, the little boy who played all the time, became dean of students at Boise State University?

I wasn't the only one who was surprised! All Bill's hometown friends were surprised, but the one most surprised was Bill, himself. Had anyone ever predicted when he was a child, that he would gain recognition as a scholar or educator, we all would have laughed. Even Bill would have laughed.

When Little Brother decided to settle down, he did so with a passion, as his accomplishments show. He never realized how much he had to offer. Or, maybe it was true he knew how much he had to offer but refused to make it a reality by proving himself in a competitive world. It can be said with great authority that when he decided to go to work, he made most of us look like we were the ones who were playing.

Though he sought "gold and all that glitters," I think what Bill was really seeking (what he really wanted) and finally found was to be known as just a regular guy. Perhaps it may best be expressed by hearing the love of his life sing, "He's just my Bill."

Section Two

Stories from other front porches

Excerpts from the writings of F. A. Hendry

My great-grandfather, Capt. F. A. Hendry wrote a number of articles and letters to the editor about his life, the draining of the Everglades and other important subjects of the day. The following are excerpts of some of these historic pieces.

The Jacksonville-Times Union originally printed F. A. Hendry's letter to the editor "Fifty-seven years in Grand Old Florida." It was reprinted on December 12, 1907 by the *Fort Myers News-Press.*

I have just read from the able pen of Mr. Sidney Herbert a very interesting letter, "Progress of the Florida Railroads," which put me in a reminiscent mood.

I enjoy very much the writings of these old-timers. It is hard for the present generation to realize the vicissitudes, trials and inconveniences through which the old-timers have passed. It is those old-timers who can fully realize the marvelous changes during the long period of a half century. It was in the winter of 1850, my father, James E. Hendry, moved from Thomas county, Georgia, to Hillsborough county, Florida. I, at that time, was a vigorous youth of 17 years, and acted in the responsible position of engineer and conductor of an ox team, and had a clear right of way the entire run of about 500 miles. The schedule was so well arranged that there were no collisions, no break downs or smash ups. The goods were all delivered in good order at the terminal. There were no bills of complaint or rebates. This was 57 years ago.

In reviewing the conditions then and now, our minds naturally ran to railroads and what they have done for our fair State. During the latter '50s I heard my first railroad speech. It was made in Tampa by Geo. Call, a cousin, I believe, of our beloved Wilkerson Call. He was a brilliant man and stirred up Tampa on the railroad question. I remember well that meeting. Our dear old landmark, Jas. McKay, Sr., presided at that meeting. That famous old railroad charter, from Amelia Island to Charlotte Harbor, with a branch to Cedar Key and Tampa, was the only road then being discussed. We all know its history. Since that time I have heard many railroad speeches, some of the landing railroads to the skies, other abusing the railroads beyond all common sense and reason. But, notwithstanding the conflicting sentiment pro and con, the railroads have come and have come to stay. Not, however, without great trials and tribulations, and there is no man who has greater reason to rejoice in their coming than the writer and I would greet them with all my hart and soul. I have cast my vote in granting more lands, possibly, to build railroads than any living man in Florida and there is no doubt but those grants of land have been the means by which our State to-day is all checkered up with railroads. The 10,5000 acres of lands given to the railroads has been a mainspring in the building and operating of these roads. It is a source of much gratification to me. . . .[Fifty-seven years ago there were] no railroad crossings, no sign boards with the warning "Look out for the engine when the whistle blows."

Leaving the little town of Thomasville, Georgia, the first point of notoriety was Madison County Court House, now the beautiful, flourishing city of Madison. The next point of interest was old Columbus, on the old Suwannee river, very near the present site of Ellaville. Then came the little town of alligator, nestling among the lakes, now the city of Lake City. Then came the little town of Newnansville, the county seat of Alachua county. In this quiet little town Uncle Sam kept his land office. The next point of interest was the famous Payne's Prairie, having driven over the present site of Gainesville. There was no Gainesville there, not a shop or hack to be seen as I now remember. Payne's Prairie indeed was a point of interest to me. As far as the eye could see was a level expanse of open prairie, clothed with grass, the most luxuriant, all dotted with herds of fat cattle and horses, and clouds of ducks and wild geese. To a youth as I was, it was captivating beyond my power of description. Next point in order was Micanopy, a pretty little town among the shady oaks, and of Indian war notoriety, a town with a history. It was in this vicinity, the admiration of the beautiful and the grandeur of nature's handiwork was felt in my youthful breast. The rich undulating hammock lands, the beautiful silver lakes with their green borders of spatterdocks or bonnets, was inspiring.

Big Orange Lake was the next point of interest and it was a stunner. It was there I saw my first orange grove, not tame and cultivate as now, but wild, just as nature planted them.

[Of the state's roads] It is a source of much gratification to me, and I venture to say all the people of the State, to know that they have done their part nobly in aiding these great public utilities, and to see our State to-day blooming and blossoming as the rose. While I am a great friend of the railroads, and give them credit for the wonderful development of our State, I am sorry to believe that in many instances they have not dealt fairly by the people, and that the people have just cause to complain. This fact has been pretty well established, but the great and vital principle of railroad service should not be condemned for the shortcomings of a few systems. The people who have given their 10,5000 acres of actually deeded lands to railroads feel that they have invested rights as well as moral rights, and the railroads cannot afford to lose sight of this fact. If, indeed, those rights are ignored or overlooked, the railroads can't be surprised at the representatives of the people passing laws to enforce a square deal. From my standpoint, I feel that the most friendly and fraternal feelings should exist between the railroads and the people. The great advantages the railroads are to the people of the State need not be mentioned in this letter, their name is legion.

It was in the latter '50s I had occasion to make a trip to Thomasville, Georgia. I was then living at Fort Meade, Florida, and rode horseback 90 miles to Melonville, very near the present site of Sanford. There I took passage on Captain Brook's steamer to Jacksonville. Then an there I saw my first railroad, a brand new road, now the Seaboard system. I traveled on that road to Lake city. The railroad had just been completed to that point. There I took the state and traveled to Madison thence on stage to the Savannah road to Thomasville. Returning I traveled by state to Monticello. There I took the railroad to Tallahassee, and there on to the oldest road in the State to Saint Marks, where I took passage on a weekly steamboat line to Cedar Key and on to Tampa and from there 45 miles overland on horseback to my home on the beautiful Peace River. This was the best that could be done then. Think of it now, in this day of quick and steady transit. I can make the same round trip in 48 hours.

[He describes returning to Polk County after "the great war."] The rich undulating hammock lands, the beautiful silver lakes with their green borders of spatterdocks or bonnets, was inspiring.

Big Orange Lake was the next point of interest, and it was a stunner. It was there I saw my first orange grove, not tame and cultivated as now, but wild, just as nature planted them. Passing through the dense hammock lands bordering that grand old lake, these wild orange trees were most beautifully interspersed. Look where you would, and there the deep yellow oranges hung like apples of gold. They were the bitter-sweet variety, good enough for anybody. My pen is not able to describe the scenery as I saw it in that day.

Ocala was the next point of interest. It, too, was a very little town, a city in embryo, now the Brick city of our State, situated there among the tall oaks, hickory, beech and magnolias.

The next point of interest was Dade's Massacre. The signs of mortal strife were not old. There I slowed down and trod lightly upon that memorable and sacred spot. If I did not, I should have bared my head, bowed in humble respect to the noble patriots who sacrificed their lives upon the altar of their country. No other points of much interest did we pass except the crossing of the famous Withlacoochee and Hillsborough rivers, until we reach our point of destination, 22 miles east of Tampa on the Alafia river. There we settled in a wild wilderness country and began life anew in a new country. . . .

Immediately after the great war I was a delegate from Polk county to our new State constitutional Convention, and Uncle Sam furnished the transportation, and I took an old slow war transport from Tampa to Saint Marks. Many similar trips of these kinds I made before the days of quick and ready transit. No use to mention that to-day South Florida, with her incomparable climate, can furnish the markets of the North with her millions of fruits and vegetables, fresh and crisp from grove and garden.

Let us stop cursing railroads and foster them, and by so doing we encourage them to give us a fair and square deal. Let the laws be wisely enacted to meet sporadic case of railroad ingratitude,

Very respectfully,

F. A. Hendry
LaBelle, Lee Co., Fla., Nov. 23.
Reprinted by permission of the Fort Myers News-Press.

BLOCKADE RUNNING IN DAYS GONE BY

By Captain F. A. Hendry (Fort Myers News-Press, Feb. 4, 1909)

There was a day when this great and glorious country of ours, now so happy and prosperous, was rent in twain by the most perplexing political problem that ever a free and independent people was confronted with. Great statesmen racked their brains and made strenuous efforts to solve it, and reconcile the contending forces. Civil and pacific influences were as futile in resisting the tempest of political disturbances as pitching chaff against a cyclone. Physical forces were resorted to as the sol arbiter and almost like magic, our beloved country was engulfed into a civil war, the like of which has no parallel in the annals of civil warfare. Pending this strife the events and incidents of the following story were in substance narrated to the writer:

It was during the darkest and most perilous days of our country's history, away back in the early sixties, that every port and harbor of the southern states were blockaded by the federal government. The object of this blockade was to prevent any vessel from taking any person or thing from the Confederacy, or taking anything out into foreign countries. Thus it was that the southern states were penned up, guarded and watched and cut off from any communication with the outside world.

Southern chivalry, daring and determination, was a force when brought into activity very difficult and hard to control. Frail vessels, old and unseaworthy, of every class were hastily fitted up and manned by brave, daring and experienced sailors for the purpose of running this blockade and to bring into the Confederacy many of the actual necessities, including medicine, surgical instruments and implements of warfare.

The cotton raised in the southern states was a commodity in great demand in all foreign countries, and the south had plenty of it ginned, baled and stored, but there was no market for it except to those daring men who risked their lives, their fortunes and liberty in running the blockade. Every pound of cotton captured by the Union forces was condemned as contraband of war, confiscated and sold for the benefit of the Federal government. Millions of dollars found their way into the Federal treasury through this source. Thus it was that the penned up and blockaded confederacy was paying the bills to defray the expenses of a terrible war being waged against it.

After this terrible war was ended satisfactorily to the Union, the South having worn itself out fighting for free men's rights, the congress of the United states piled it on to the South in a double dose by fixing a war tax upon all cotton raised within the limits of the United States, which meant the Southern States, thereby forcing a vanquished enemy, stricken with spoil and poverty, to practically pay the entire war debt.

It was during this war and blockade period the Federal government found that it was up against a difficult proposition to prevent the southern people from running the blockade, dangerous and perilous as it was. Few people in Lee county today know that its territory was a field of some of the most daring adventures in the history of blockade running. Just outside and near the Sanibel light house, a Federal gunboat was stationed, under orders to intercept and capture any vessel or person who dared to pass in our out. There they lay in the full enjoyment of the sweet influences of the most delightful climate on the face of the globe. Little did they know that while they were there watching and waiting to capture any poor devil of a Confederate that might attempt to pass, that there was a long wagon train of mules and oxen en route to Charlotte Harbor, laden with one hundred and seventy-five bales of cotton, designed for the Cuban market.

A few wealthy cotton planters living in Marin and Sumter counties with their gin-houses full of the precious lint, took it into their heads to run the blockade. They employed a sea captain, a regular dare-devil of a fellow, who feared neither God or man, and was the owner of an old superannuated schooner then secreted near Cedar Keys. They furnished him money to fix her up in fine shape, and this he did, and employed a crew composed of men in whom he could trust, and two of the best pilots to be found, who knew every nook and corner along the Gulf coast. When fully prepared for the high seas, the captain received orders to sail down the Gulf coast and slip into Estero Bay, passing the Federal blockade boat in the darkness of the night, which he did, passing right under the muzzles of its guns and into Estero Bay and up inside, through a tortuous channel and anchored it in the vicinity of Mound Key. To make their hiding more secure the topmast was at once taken down, and the main mast and rigging clothed with palm leaves and other tropical foliage so that the vessel presented more the appearance of a cluster of forest trees in the distance than a ship's mast. At that day, Estero was hardly known except by coasters and there was no more secret place in all Florida. It was then that one of the pilots, who knew the route thoroughly, was dispatched to Charlotte Harbor to report that the schooner had reached its hiding place and ready to take its cargo. Lighters and craft of every kind were hurriedly brought into use, and in about two weeks every bale of that cotton was snugly stored on board the schooner, and she was ready to make her dangerous and hazardous voyage across the Gulf of Mexico. Then followed a period of suspense, watching and waiting for suitable wind and

tide, liable to be discovered and captured at any time. Watches and spies from this schooner spent much time out towards the blockage boat. This was done to avoid surprise should the Federals discover their whereabouts and make a search. It was a perilous service and a great strain of suspense.

One day, while thus waiting, the wind and tide bid fair, and it was determined that in the darkness of the coming night, they would make the break and risk making their way once more by the Yankee gun-boat.

The captain desired to personally make an examination of the channel leading out to the high seas, note the shoal places and to see that the coast was clear, ordered the ship's yawl manned with two oarsmen, and taking one of the cotton planters with him (there being three of these pioneer cotton planters going along to sell their cotton) to see that the job was well done, and rowed down the Estero river, making notes of points, and objects along the shore line. They were not armed, except a common axe, taken along to use in chopping some small twigs with bushy tops to stick down at some shoal points, when to their astonishment and surprise, a beautiful little sail boat, flying the Union flag, turned a point just ahead and in full view of them. It was then the captain demonstrated unusual tact and quick decision. To attempt to evade the Yankee sail boat would cause suspicion and lead to their capture. The captain knew that the sail boat belonged to the blockade gun boat and would report having seen them, and that a search would be made at once, and he determined in an instant

to capture the sailboat. He ordered his oarsmen to pull with all possible speed toward the sailboat, and signaled the sail boat to come about, which it did, and at the top of their voices asked what he wanted and who they were. The captain answered that they were refuges from rebel tyranny en route to the blockade boat, and wanted to be towed, as they were all fagged out. Of course, said the unsuspecting Yankee, come alongside, and we will tow your old yawl for you. You are very kind indeed, said the rebel captain, and as the yawl came along side, he seized the axe, sprang on board and demanded an immediate surrender. The sail boat with only three men on board at once became the prize of a common blockade runner. An undesirable prize indeed. It was not the policy of blockade runners to make captures. They never had letters of marque and reprisal and to make seizures or captures placed them in the attitude of pirates on the high seas, a crime punishable with death by all nations of the earth.

This capture, while it was a bloodless one, and a very simple, quiet one, was one which nothing but blood could atone. It took but a few minutes for that splendid, well rigged sail boat to take the whole party to the schooner. The captain called the owners of the cargo, the three old cotton planters into private council. He stated the case correctly, telling them that he had per force of circumstances placed themselves in a very dangerous attitude. That he was ready at that moment to sail, that the tide and wind was favorable as could be desired, that it was dangerous to remain where they were another day, that they had captured a fine boat and three prisoners, but it would never do to attempt to go out upon the high seas with those prisoners aboard, but something must be done and done quick. The boat can be disposed of easily enough, but the prisoners, what shall be done with them? We are in a terrible dilemma, the case an extreme one and it requires extreme remedies. You know, said he, that dead men tell no lies. They are the only living witnesses against us. Their living testimony would hang everyone of us, and I do not propose to take any risk. I will never raise my anchor or sail this boat with these prisoners on board. The three old cotton planters were brave men, noble-hearted men with pure southern blood coursing through their veins, incapable of doing a mean trick, and they were dumbfounded to find that their captain was such a desperate, low-down wretch, possessing such little regard for honor and human life. The one cotton planter who was along when the capture was made was wrought up to a high tension and said: "Captain, do you mean to kill those persons who so confidently surrendered to us this afternoon?" The captain said: "You know what I said and I mean it."

"Well, sir," said the old planter, "those prisoners shall not be hurt, not even a hair on their heads, unless it be done over my dead body. I am responsible to those captured men for their safety and I am ready to die in their behalf. Turn them over to me personally and I will take them now to your schooner and sail this night to Charlotte Harbor and from there across the country to Tampa and deliver them to the confederate authorities. Give me one of your pilots and I am off." And in a few minutes two men in charge of three prisoners were fairly splitting the water en route to Charlotte Harbor, and by daylight were far away from the danger of the Federal gun boat.

Part II

By Captain F. A. Hendry
(Fort Myers Press,
Feb. 11, 1909)

The prisoners, together with important war despatches and U.S. mail galore, were all safely landed in Tampa a few days afterwards. It was then and that same night the topmast was replaced, and the forestry was thrown from the main mast and rigging. The anchor was raised form its long resting place and the vessel clothed with all the canvas necessary to drive her with great speed across the gulf of Mexico. With no lights and just enough sail hoisted to glide safely with the wind and tide, the schooner quietly glided out to ea, passing under the very guns of the blockade gun boat. On that boat, as they glided by was a big festival occasion, the band and other music was in full force. They were having a regular carousal, an old Beltashazzar time we read of in the bible, but there was no handwriting appearing on the walls of that ship's saloons, no Daniel to interpret it and tell them that there was one hundred and seventy-five bales of rebel cotton passing by, worth in Cuba one dollar per pound.

The pilot soon informed the captain of the schooner that they were safely passed the gun boat and on the high seas. Then it was that the full sail was hoisted and the schooner fairly splitting the sea with all the breeze should could carry. By the time old sol showed his face in the eastern horizon, the schooner cast anchor between Key West and Dry Tortugas, where war vessels seldom every passed. The day was spent in rest and recuperation from the mental strain through which they had passed during the past twenty-four hours.

The old planters and the captain of the schooner were genial and pleasant companions per force of circumstances, but the events of the evening before, relative to the prisoners, greatly lessened the high esteem they had entertained toward the fearless and desperate captain, but had no fears as to his loyalty to the hazardous scheme they were engaged in or to the southern cause. All was serene and quiet during the day. Occasionally a lonely sail boat was seen in the distance voyaging to and fro. Late in that afternoon the breeze freshened and was favorable. Orders were given to raise anchor and hoist sail and steer across the Gulf of Mexico, on a due course for the safe and neutral harbor of Havana. Very soon the schooner was under great strain from the load of canvas she so proudly carried and she was fairly splitting the deep, blue water of the Gulf of Mexico.

Everybody on board was feeling good over the happy anticipation that they would have a safe uninterrupted sail across the Gulf that night, and by daylight cast anchor in Havana harbor. It was then those bright prospects were marred. The watchman cried out, "steamer to the south-west!" All eyes were instantly turned in that direction and saw a cloud of smoke evidently from the smoke stack of a large steam boat. Ominous, dangerously ominous and distasteful was that cloud of smoke. The time has come for this captain of the schooner to show of what stuff he was made. Danger and peril was no new thing to him. All eyes were fastened upon him, reading his every action and emotion. He seized his glasses and took his stand, turning the lens upon that steamer. Steadily he watched the course and outlines of that ominous looking craft. A stern, determined look was the captain's common mood, now intensified to a remarkable degree. He called to the man at the wheel to keep her off, but soon countermanded the order and said keep the ship upon her course, "that steamer is a Yankee gun boat, she is in search of just such game as we are, she is a propeller, and with this wind and sea room we can out run any vessel which carries her power in her stern." This statement was seasoned with language common to a Mexican border desperado, and unfit to print.

The captain then ordered every stitch of sail stowed away for emergency, hoisted to its proper place, and it was then the schooner was put under all the strain she could possibly bear, every seam and joint was put to its test and that old once-superannuated schooner was called upon by the force of the sail and wind to do the service of her youthful days. The course of the two vessels at the converging point brought the man of war almost or quite in range of her heavy guns, and at that point the gun boat let drive a shot which almost reached the fleeing schooner. The captain looked like a demon and cried out: "Shoot and be d—d," and ordered the flag of the confederacy hoisted to his mast head. Soon the gun boat was directly in the rear of the schooner and the race for life and liberty was on. The destiny of that schooner and cargo, was well as the men on board, depended or rested with the wind. It was then the captain and all the men on board began to realize that they were not only simple innocent blockade runners, but had committed the terrible crime of piracy in capturing the United States dispatch and making prisoners of three of Uncle Sam's loyal subjects [the prisoners, a cargo of one hundred seventy-five bales of cotton were mentioned in the prior week's story.]

They supposed that the gun boat then chasing them was the one stationed at Sanibel, it was possible that the sail boat captured by them had been recaptured en route to Charlotte Harbor the night before and that the Yankee gun boat under whose guns they had sailed, were in possession of all the facts and hot on trail. There was many forebodings, surmises, uneasinesses on board that schooner. The loss of the boat and cargo, when compared with being confronted in a United Sates court martial with three men captured, whom the captain wanted to kill and forever set aside and silence their testimony in human courts, was a small affair. The wind tempered, as it were, to the shorn lamb—did not albeit —it was a race royal. The firing continued brisk and lively all night long. The whizzing shots fell harmless into the gulf of Mexico, there to rest upon its fathomless bottom as relics of the fiercest and hottest race ever run upon its boisterous bosom. The schooner behaved well, the wind freshened and she ran liked a scared wolf, with a hungry pack of hounds at her heels, as the light of day shown forth with all its glories from the eastern horizon sailed into Havana harbor. As the heart panteth for water brooks, so panteth the fleeing schooner for the safe and neutral waters of that Spanish port. 'The firing was heard long before the schooner reached that port, and a 'Spanish man of war steamed out of port, saw the situation and dropped in between the fleeing and pursuing vessels, practically saying to the Federal gun bot, "it is enough, stay thy hand."

* * *

[Both boats reach Havana harbor] After the usual regulations and red tape the Federal gun boat was allowed to enter, and was assigned a place very near the blockade runner. There they lay side by side and in speaking distance, one with Old Glory unfurled to the tropical breezes, one with the Stars and Bars, the emblem of the confederate States, each with equal rights. Those two flags represented the best blood and best element that ever crossed swords. Sad the thought that it was brothers of one country, brothers in blue, brothers in gray, brothers in blood, terribly arrayed against each other. From each deck the captains gracefully saluted. In the streets of Havana the gray and the blue met and mingled together. In the saloons they ate and drank together. Pleasantries passed gracefully between them. Socially they were friends, each avoiding to mention the terrible chase across the Gulf or the troubles at home. Within the Confederate captain's breast, however, there was a smoldering volcano. That fearful chase and those deadly shots were not forgotten, and like the dynamite or nitroglycerine, the least little friction would touch him off. On one occasion the Yankee captain of the gun boat, with too much Spanish rum inside, and possibly not knowing the hair-triggered rebel captain very well, made a terrible mistake when he drank to the health and success of the Federal government, hoping that Richmond had fallen and that old Jeff Davis was in Irons. Quick as a pistol flash, the rebel captain, instead of drinking his glass of grog, dashed it into the Yankee's face and proceeded to kick him out of the saloon. This little unpleasant incident brought about an estrangement between those two gentlemen during the remainder of their sojourn in Havana..

The cargo of cotton was sold and discharged under the eyes of the Federals. A return cargo was purchased and placed on board the schooner, under the same conditions. Nobody knew, except the captain and owners of the cargo, when the schooner would sail, and nobody knew her pint of destination when she sailed, except those men. No clearance papers were demanded by the Cuban authorities as confederate blockade runners were permitted to enter and depart at will and pleasure. It was one night, however, when conditions were favorable, she did sail out from under the guns of the Federal gun boat and before the gun boat could take out clearance papers and give chase, she was half way across the Gulf en route for some Florida harbor and succeeded in evading the vigilant watch of other war vessels and sailed safely into the waters of charlotte Harbor, and safely anchored about the mouth of the Peace River. Runners were despatched for teams of any and every description and the cargo conveyed far into the interior, passing the counties of Manatee and Hillsborough. This was one of the very few successful adventures of blockade running. There were valuable packages in that cargo, the most valuable was hospital store; medicine, drugs and surgical instruments. There were packages of coffee, an article for which southern people possess great fondness; tea and fine liquors, and so many other articles which contribute to the comfort of man, especially the sick and the wounded and the dying, were in that cargo. Those things were greatly needed, not only in and on the battlefield, but by non combatants, women and children and the aged and infirm at home. The Federal prisoners, of which there were a great many thousands being held by the Confederacy, were dying for the want of those comforts, which could not be administered unless procured through this perilous and dangerous method of blockage running.

The most pathetic appeal was made by the Confederate authorities, to the Federal government to send those things so much needed through the lines, with ample guarantee that they would be used solely for the welfare and comfort of the Union prisoners which was peremptorily refused. This fact is hard to believe when we remember the noble hearted men at the head of the Federal government in the person of the lamented Abraham Lincoln.

The United States government in its thirst for blood hanged poor Captain Wurze because so many Union prisoners died at Andersonville, Ga., while the Federal government was responsible for that terrible mortality. Refused to send these comforts and to cap the climax refused to exchange prisoners with that promptness that humanity demanded. Capt. Wurze, the martyr, recommended to the Confederate government when exchange was so wantonly delayed to parole the prisoners and send them home, which recommendation was sanctioned and endorsed by some of our leading generals, but from some cause was not done. War always carries with it many dark pages in history, but this, the hanging of Capt. Wurze and refusing to send medicine and comforts to their own prisoners, and the delay in exchange of prisoners, is one of the darkest found in the history of the great war between the States.

Blockade running during the dark days of our history must not be looked upon as a low order of profession or livelihood, or a sort of smuggling. It was commendable and most worthy and those who engaged in as it should rank in the highest order in the list of noble men.

Very respectfully submitted,

F. A. Hendry

Pensacola Journal, Sept. 2, 1906.

Reprinted with permission of Fort Myers-News Press

DRAINAGE OF THE FLORIDA EVERGLADES

F. A. Hendry, for Fifty-six Years a Resident Along the Frontier, Who is Thoroughly Acquainted With the Situation, Makes Able Argument in Support of Governor Broward's Plan

Excerpts of a letter by Capt. F. A. Hendry of La Belle, Fla, who for thirty years was a member of the Senate or House of the Florida Legislature, and who is a man of great patriotism and devotion to Florida, will be read with a great deal of interest, as he is one of the best known men in the state. He was a director on the board of the Hamilton-Disston Drainage Company, which company was at work eleven years digging canals in the Kissimmee Valley and Florida Everglades, and he is probably the best posted man in the state on the subject of drainage. [He is apparently responding to a letter by a Mr. Hendrick].

Mr. Hendricks' Letter

La Belle, Caloosahatchee River, Fla. August 30.

Editor Pensacola Journal:

The Times-Union of August the 10th talking about Gov. Broward and his drainage methods truthfully says: Is it not strange that the men who are to be most benefited by the collection of this (drainage) tax are fighting its collection through the courts and fighting it successfully?" Your writer believes that it is strange.

"They are not asking the State to drain their lands. They are only asking to be let alone." The writer understands that these men to be benefitted are organized forces formed into some half-dozen syndicates owning about three and a half million acres of these lands to be drained. The other half belongs to the State, private individuals and to our public schools. "They are only asking to let alone." Nobody wants to meddle with the fee simple to these lands but there are other interests involved about which we want to talk.

Want Lands Drained.

About two hundred thousand acres belong to a class of citizens of our State who want their lands drained. The school board want their lands drained. Now if these latter three classes of land could be drained and leave these corporations out, since they have cut such a dash, we would manage to do so and let those big fellows do their own drainage—which they would not do because they can raise all the money they need on the face and faith of this vast acreage whether it is covered in water or not.

"They are only asking to be let alone." That is just the idea. That is just what the Seminoles of Florida say. "Let us alone. We want no schools, no books, no lands. Me hunt, me fish, me kill 'gators skin 'em, me kill otters plenty; me get money. Me want no white man talk, Washington man bad. Me want to be let alone."

We poor men who live out on the frontier and those of us too, living within the pales of civilization who are burdened with our families to support, when the tax collector comes around would like to be let alone, but we are not.

An illustration.

Jones and Smith owned a whole section of land, Jones one-half and Smith one-half. It was swamp land, very rich and fertile, but worthless without drainage. A small lake was near it. This lake kept this section of land too wet for agricultural purposes. By opening a canal or ditch a mile long this lake cold be lowered and kept lowered and the whole section of land thoroughly reclaimed. Jones was a farmer, Smith, a speculator. The taxes on this land were very low in consequence of its worth-condition. Smith kept his mortgaged to raise money to speculate upon, lived high and in another state and was a gentlemen of ease and leisure. Jones asked Smith to join him in cutting a ditch to get clear of the water which continually overflowed their lands. Jones wanted to clear his land and cultivate it, as it was very rich. Smith, with much complacency and unconcern said: "No, just let me alone, I don't want to go to that expense; let this land be; if we drain it and make it so valuable as you say the blasted

199

county commissioners will raise the assessment and the taxes will be more than I want to pay." Jones said: "I want my land drained and I want to cultivate it, but to drain my land drains yours, too, and you should bear an equal burden of the expense." Smith replied: "Just let me alone." Jones asked the legislature to pass a law, a drainage law, which it did, and the land was drained under that law, and Smith has to bear his share of the expense.

Would Benefit All

The lowering of Lake Okeechobee six or eight feet means the drainage of all those lands belonging to the corporations , the private lands, the State lands and the school lands. And it is strange, as the Times-Union says, that the six corporate land holders with their three or four million acres of land kick at their drainage and rush into the United States court and pray, as they never prayed before, "to be let alone." Are the people of Florida to be thwarted in this great drainage scheme because six big land companies say "we want to be let alone?"

One of the cardinal points of democracy is to do the thing which is the greatest good to the greatest number. Certainly the people of Florida are democratic to the core. What did the Legislature of Florida, composed of one hundred of its very best men, do? They passed a law, a drainage law, carefully studied, carefully worded and wisely voted upon. Was this all? No, three-fifths or more of them passed a resolution on proposing to amend our organic law, making clear the way for extensive drainage operations. Three hundred men, representing forty-five countries of our fair State and thirty-two senatorial districts ask the people of Florida, at our next general election, to ratify this resolution. Shall we do it or rebuke them by turning a deaf ear to their request, give credence to all this literature coming to us through the mails gotten up by a bureau organized by the six big corporate powers and vote it down? No indeed, if the writer knows the people of Florida and he thinks he does, they will adopt that Constitutional amendment.

Purely Selfishness

"Want to be let alone." They care nothing for those of us who are periodically overflowed, our fruit trees killed, our truck killed, our grazing swamped by that great fountain head (Okeechobee Lake) which is to be controlled and lowered by our drainage commission. They seem to care not who sinks so they swim.

It must be understood that the writer does not hate the big land owners. . . .

Originally printed by the Pensacola Journal in 1906, permission to reprint give by the Pensacola Journal.

TRIP TO CUBA

Impressions Of The Country and Customs Of The People Who Still Cling To The Ways Of Their Ancestors

[by a *News-Press* editor, a guest of the Hendrys]

This account of a trip to Cuba appeared in the weekly Fort Myers Press over a period of four weeks beginning in the issue dated February 7, 1901 and concluding with the issue dated February 28, 1901. It was transcribed by Larry Wiggins for publication.

Home Again

The Hendry party, who left Fort Myers on the 5th of January for a trip to Cuba, returned here with one member less last Friday, after a varied experience in the Queen Isle of the Gulf. The returning party were Mr. Jas. E. Hendry, Sr., and wife and three children, Fred, Isabel and Clarence; Mr. Bard L. Hendry, wife and baby; Mr. J. E. Foxworthy and wife, and the editor of the PRESS, who was an invited guest of Mr. Hendry. James E. Hendry, Jr., remains at Cardenas, Cuba, where he will look after the cattle interests of his father and brother. Bard also brought back with him a destitute Cuban boy, whom he will look after and give an education. A large volume could be written of the varied experiences of the party while in Cuba, and we propose to give our readers some of the impressions of Cuba as we find it today. We saw much that was new and surprising to American eyes, but we found on returning to Fort Myers that our experiences were of a much wider range than we had

realized. There is an old adage that you must go away from home to hear the news. We must dissent with this view, for we are thoroughly convinced that the place to hear news (?) is right at home. As a rule we pay but slight attention to the idle gossip of the street, but in this case it seems that what was evidently started by some wag as a good joke, was taken seriously by quite a number and spread broadcast over the land. Therefore we wish to state right here that none of our party were incarcerated in Cuban dungeons, their pictures as yet do not adorn the rogues' gallery of Cardenas or Havana, and the streets did not appear to come up and meet any of us as we walked about, in fact, we are all in love with the pretty isle lying south of our own dear peninsular, and such matters as have been brought to our attention since our arrival home could never have happened and to be in earnest we will state once for all that there is not a single word of truth in all the rubbish. So much for things that did not happen, and now we will endeavor to give some facts of our trip.

Off For Cardenas

The good schooner Wave, owned by Messrs. Hendry and Langford, was in waiting at Punta Rassa for our party of twelve on Saturday morning,

January 5th. The Wave is practically a new vessel throughout now and one of the staunchest vessels that plies the Gulf, having recently been thoroughly overhauled at an expense of $12,000. Besides being fitted with cattle pens to carry 200 head of stock, she has a large and comfortable passenger cabin that will accommodate twelve persons, and our party were made quite comfortable during the entire trip.

Capt. Ben Cary with a trusted crew of experienced sailors manned the vessel, and the large American flag was flying from the peak of the topmast in honor of the owner being aboard. A light northern was blowing at the time, which promised a good trip southward, and when the lines were cast off at 1 p.m., the sails rapidly filled and we glided swiftly out of the harbor of Punta Rassa and by the Sanibel light.

Our trip to Key West was far from lacking in interest. The Wave moved through the water at an eight mile an hour clip, and the varied changes of the waters of the Gulf as the changes of light or dark green were developed by shallow bottom and suns rays were being commented on when an object of darker hue suddenly appeared on the surface. The watchful eye of the Cuba sailor-boy Papey had first discovered the dark object, and his exclamation, "Devil fish," brought all hands to that side of the deck, but the monster of the Gulf had passed us far astern. But just then its mate made its appearance within twenty feet of our ship, and all had a fine view of the monster octopus of the deep, which must easily have measured twenty feet across. This little diversion occurred off Naples.

The sailors had strung out a couple of heavy trolling lines for King fish, and after awhile there was a snap on one of the lines, and Captain Ben hauled in the stout line with no little exertion and swung a 25 pound King fish aboard which was turned over to the cook, who dished it up in slices, nicely fried at supper.

The Wave was making steamer time across to Key West, reaching the northwest bar long before daylight Sunday the 6th. To make it more pleasant for our party of land lubbers, a number of whom had already experienced those queer sensations that the motion of a ship produced, he took a turn off to the eastward to avoid "laying to" in "stays" at the bar, where a heavy sea was rolling from the effects of the northern. With the appearance of daylight the bar was crossed, and the island city that has the honor of being the extreme southern town of the United States was reached by breakfast time.

It is plain sailing for a Captain to take a vessel from one American port to another. When he starts for a foreign port it is different, however, for he runs up against the red tape regulations that hem about all things maritime. Our knowledge of navigation laws has been greatly enriched by our recent experience, and we can now fully appreciate the responsibilities of a sea captain. Every false step made lays the vessel liable to a heavy fine, and it is easier for a ship to be fined $1,000 than for an editor to have a suit for libel

on his hands, and the latter is as easy as falling off a log.

Capt. Cary had his clearance papers, passenger and crew list, invoice and a dozen of other papers all duly prepared by 10 o'clock Monday morning, January 7th, and with favorable breezes still blowing from the north we set all sails for Cardenas, Cuba, one hundred miles to the southeast, the distance being slightly farther than Havana, but is made in just as good time going over on account of the advantage of sailing with the Gulf Stream.

Going out of the harbor of Key West the transparent waters disclosed the marine life at the bottom of the Gulf. The finny tribe could be seen darting about at a depth of 15 to 20 feet, and huge sponges, coral, etc., made a grand kaleidoscopic picture as the vessel glided out to sea through the main ship channel.

Before us lay that mysterious current that all land lubbers dread on account of its noted record as a disturber of man's digestive organs. Even before the Gulf stream was reached the Wave was rolling in the heavy sea, and the passengers were turning pale and succumbed to the elements, and even this scribe, who counts himself a pretty good sailor, parted with his supper without the least provocation.

Every one felt better when, on Tuesday morning the 8th, the harbor of Cardenas was entered. It is one of the finest natural harbors in Cuba, which is saying much, as the island possesses many fine harbors. A long peninsula makes out into the sea, curving in such a way as to give safe anchorage inside

the harbor extending up from the outside light for a distance of thirteen miles to the wharves of the city. By nine in the morning we had docked, but had to remain aboard until the quarantine officer, customs officer, etc., had examined our papers and cargo, and given us a clean bill of health. These details were eventually disposed of and our first landing on Cuban soil was made on the grounds of an immense sugar refinery, which has been standing idle since the little set-to that Uncle Sam had with Spain or perhaps since the insurgents started on the rampage in 1894 or '95. This great refinery which consists of a number of high buildings and immense tanks, is making preparations to remove the rust from the machinery and open for business again.

Cardenas

Cardenas is a city of 26,000 inhabitants, situated on the north coast of Cuba, some ninety miles east of Havana. From where we lay at the dock the impression was conveyed that there were but few low buildings, as the city is situated in a valley that appears below the sea level, and one wondered where the inhabitants could be hiding out. A walk of a few hundred yards soon enlightened us, for before we knew it quite a share of the juvenile population were following at our heels after the manner of the small boy when the circus strikes town. It was the first intimation we had that we were living curiosities or monstrosities. Mr. Hendry and his stalwart sons looked like the Broadway squad in contrast with the Cubans around them, and the writer "sized up" to the best of them. The ladies of our party were great objects of interest at once.

We read the paper at home and we feel conceited enough to believe that by one bold stroke Uncle Sam has Americanized the entire island of Cuba. But our pride receives a shock when we come in contact with the people we have liberated from the Spanish yoke. Here is a city 100 miles from the shores of our country, and scarcely a dozen Americans among the entire 26,000, and this includes the American officer acting as collector of the port, Rev. Mr..... and Miss...., Presbyterian missionaries. Very few of the Cubans speak any English, but we were fortunate in meeting Mr. Juan Castro, who has been often in Ft. Myers purchasing cattle, and whose home is in Cardenas. Our experience with the store keepers for the first three days would prove as entertaining as Innocents Abroad, had we the gift of Mark Twain, and besides, our time and space will not permit of going into details.

On every hand were what appeared to be fully equipped bars. Strictly speaking they are cafes, where coffee, lunches and even a complete meal may be had. They seem to be connected with all kinds of stores, unless it is a dry goods store. Grocery and provision stores, bakeries, hotels, and all restaurants have these bars located on the premises. Coffee and wines are the principal indulgences of the Cubans, and evidently the wines take the place of water as a table beverage. The ladies of our party did not fancy the Cuban beverages, but spent no little time in trying to secure some ice cream. This was before some of us learned how to talk Spanish, and the result was that everything from brandy down to milk was offered us for the desired article. James and the writer raked the town over hunting for a public bath. The nearest we came to it was in the leading hotel, where they had a large stone bath tub, but no water in sight, and we could only get a cold bath by waiting until manana (tomorrow). We finally enjoyed the privilege of a bath in the Gulf with a norther blowing in, for the trifling expense of $1.50. After this we suppressed our desire for a "banos" until we reached Havana, where the fine baths made up for our seriocomic experiences in Cardenas.

Cardenas before the recent war was an important exporting town, and shows evidences of a good business point, as it goes in Cuba. The principal crop exported is sugar, very few ports surpassing it in this commodity. The plantations are again turning out their crops of cane and the sugar mills are starting up, and it is estimated that one million bags of sugar will be exported this season.

The city is regularly laid out in straight streets and avenues. Everything is of rock, for this is a rocky country, and a few miles back from town a mountain perhaps 1,000 feet high looms up. The streets are made of crushed rock and are very good; the stores and residences are all of crushed stone formed into a concrete, while the roofs are made of clay tiling, overlapping each other, making a serviceable but rather clumsy looking roof. Stores and buildings are all one story in height, the public buildings, clubhouse, churches, etc., being the only exceptions. You may tell a store from a residence at once from the fact that all residences have iron bars protecting the windows, which are always fastened. To unaccustomed eyes this seems very strange, but it is universal, and the same custom exists in Havana. The entrance to these residences have immense solid doors, large enough to drive a locomotive through, but these large doors are seldom opened, there being another door of ordinary size cut into the larger one, which is used for ingress and egress. Thus it is that a residence has much the appearance of a prison on the outside. The explanation of this plan of arranging dwellings is that Cuba being a climate of practically summer temperature throughout the year, the dwellings are made to admit all the air possible, the windows being thrown wide open at night, and the iron bars are intended to keep out intruders. The rooms have all very high ceilings, wide passageways running through into large court yards, so that all portions of a dwelling are reached by the breeze that invariably blows over this sunny land. The interior of the houses are all of stone, even the floors being stone, except with the richer class the houses have marble floors.

Besides having a good harbor, Cardenas is connected by railroad with Havana; also with Cienfuegos and intervening towns. The depot and train shed does credit for a town the size of Cardenas, but the prettiest thing about the depot is a well kept flower garden. The locomotives have the appearance of engines used in this country twenty years

Ella Kathryn Hendry

ago, but the cars would scarcely be used to move live stock in. They are divided into three classes. The first class coach would even be frowned at on the Lakeland and Punta Gorda branch of the Plant System, which has had to submit to all the outgrown rolling stock of the other lines of the system. The first class cars contain seats of rattan, the second class "coaches" have plain wooden seats with backs, and the third class coaches wooden seats without backs. The fare is 5, 3, and 2 cents per mile respectively.

Cardenas, like nearly all the balance of Cuba is 100 years behind the times. Still there are a few modern things, such as a good electric light system and an up to date market. In fact Havana has nothing in the way of a market building to compare with that in the city of Cardenas, and for that matter few American markets are as well arranged. It covers perhaps a couple of acres of ground, is built in a square; two stories high, surmounted by a beautiful dome, with a large courtyard in the center, and all the stalls are kept neat, clean and airy. On the ground floor are the fruit and vegetable stalls and cafes, while on the upper floor are the meat stalls, each stall being enclosed by wire screens, which are only opened through a small sliding screen not more than a foot square through which the meats are passed to the customer. It is a model in its way, and is one of the redeeming features of the impracticable Cubans.

[Next week we shall give our readers the continuation of the description of our visit in Cardenas and to the sugar plantations and fine pasture lands. This will be followed with an account of our trip out of the harbor, (which was the scene of one of the first encounters in the Spanish-American war) and up the Cuba coast to Havana, in which city we remained nearly two weeks, and which we will describe as rapidly as we can find space for same.-Ed.]

Part Two

Near the center of Cardenas is Mercada plaza, in the center of which is a good statue of Columbus, four magnificent royal palm trees standing as sentinels forming a square about the metal production of the great navigator and discoverer. The square is beautifully laid out as a park, with seats for the public. On one side of the square is an old Catholic Church, with the date 1846 on it, and on the other side is a large hall and club building.

One of the customs of these people that early attracted our attention was the manner of dining. In the business houses where a number of clerks are engaged, meals are served in the stores. Every day at 10 a.m. and 4 p.m., the hours in which breakfast and dinner respectively are eaten, long tables are set in the stores and hearty meals are eaten. The workmen who start to work early in the morning lay off for breakfast between 10 and 11 a.m. The uninitiated would readily conclude that all the stores had restaurants connected, until the truth is learned. The hours above named are those in which all the people dine, those whose business compel them to rise early partaking of coffee and fruit early in the morning, but the man of more leisure confines himself to two meals a day, but our observations lead us to conclude that more is consumed in these two meals than we who indulge in three meals devour altogether, for the breakfast served is more a combination of breakfast and dinner or lunch.

We noticed but few ladies shopping during the day in Cardenas, but at night numbers may be seen in the stores and promenading the streets. The old Spanish customs are still adhered to, and a young lady is never seen on the street unaccompanied by her mother, and the young man courting a young lady is kept beyond the iron bars until an engagement is agreed upon, and then he may only see his fiancee in the presence of the family. One of our party on seeing the many pretty girls looking through these iron bars as if they were prisoners felt as if he ought to draw his pistol and battle his way to their rescue.

We witnessed a couple of funerals in Cardenas but as we will touch on this feature more fully in our Havana chapter, we will not dwell on the subject here, suffice it to say that these two funerals appear to be the extremes of poor and rich, for in one case the dead body was carried openly by a few men and a few followers, while the other had all the grand display for which the Cuban people are noted, the hearse being an elaborate affair with golden plumes, the six horses being harnessed in gold and red, and the driver being attired in a livery that makes him the most conspicuous individual in sight. Then followed the mourners in carriages, all men, not a lady being seen, the particular funeral that we witnessed having many carriages in line without any occupants, and they are evidently

204

there to add to the pompousness of the affair.

Like Havana, Cardenas is well supplied with hacks, being the only means of public conveyance about the city. These hackmen charge 20 cents Spanish money for a ride from one point to another in the city, and if you stop only a minute for a cigar another 20 cents is charged. This is very reasonable when it is considered that the 20 cents Spanish silver is worth only 13 cents American money. Carts are used for hauling all classes of goods, and instead of placing the bit in the horse's or mule's mouth the iron substitute set against the nose of the animal often cutting deep into the bone and flesh. The loads that are placed on these animals is something wonderful. The roads about Cardenas are in many instances too rough for carts, and the farmers bring their produce to market in packs that almost bury the faithful little animal as if it were an inanimate thing and squats down in a heap on top. These ponies are as docile as a camel, and remind one of the patience of the creature of the desert.

Visit to Sugar Planations

We remained in Cardenas four days, one of which was spent by the men in a visit to some sugar plantations and pasture lands some fifteen miles to the southwest of the city. Mr. Castro was our guide on this occasion. There were six in the party, all mounted on Cuban ponies. All of them are expert horsemen with the exception of the Press editor, who was at a great disadvantage, for about the only mount he is familiar with is the tripod. But he was out to take in the sights, and wasn't to be scared by a small matter of a 35 mile ride, although his previous experience as an equestrian was gained from a total of about ten miles riding. Luckily, however, for this pencil pusher the Cuban ponies have a way of pacing that makes riding a simple matter (for a while) and besides Mr. Hendry took compassion on us and when he discovered signs of fatigue held back and gave us an opportunity to hang on with the balance of the party. As for the pony, he also took pity on us and was as good and gentle as he could be.

We have still a very vivid recollection of that ride, only some how or other the rocky road to Dublin is strongly associated with these recollections. We have never had the pleasure of going over the famous Irish thoroughfare, and wish to state right here, if it in any wise approaches that of the rocky road out of Cardenas that we propose to pass.

Our route led us by the cemetery a mile out, and for a mile or so more the road was good. On either side of the road a wall of stone runs, and growing high above the pile of rocks were great cactus and a plant that resembles the pineapple plant in every way and could easily be palmed off as such, but is only a wild shrub, the fruit of which is very small and worthless.

Suddenly the well-defined road disappeared altogether, and in its place were several trails worn down by the ponies and mules which travel it, for we were now among the rocks, and the trails wind around the small boulders, which literally cover the earth, in serpentine fashion, the horses picking their own way and choosing the trails with the least obstruction. It was impossible to travel here faster than a walk, and so we went on in single file, with the newspaper fellow bringing up the rear guard, but hanging on like grim death, for if the experience was somewhat trying to him, the novelty and scenery more than compensated for the lack of a more easy mode of travel. One had little time to think of bodily ills in the rapture created by the grand royal palm groves which now dotted the landscape. If a more stately or grander tree grows on this green earth we do not know of it, for here the royal palm is seen in all its native beauty. Up in the air they grow as straight as an arrow, the trunks as perfect, symmetrical and smooth as to cause the sculptor to bow at the shrine of Nature, and admit that all his art could never produce its equal. We saw these trees planted in straight avenues, growing to a height of 50 and 60 feet, and then we passed through the rocky country into the rich clay soils that have made of Cuba the great sugar producing country, and then these royal palms became giants, rearing their heads to a height of 75 and 80 feet, a sight in itself to repay one for the trip. We saw nothing like these trees in any of our subsequent travels about Havana, although that city boasts of its wonderful growth and variety of palms.

A couple of hours ride (during which we passed many farmers on the road to Cardenas, sitting on their little ponies or mules, with great packs of produce almost burying the animals out of sight) brought us to the pasture of Mr. Castro, where the Cuban cowboy rounded up some of the cattle for our inspection. There were familiar brands and marks on these animals, which instinctively our Florida cattle men examined, and it was evident at once that many of the steers were from Lee County, but such large cattle never came from Florida, for these were fat and sleek and weighed up in the neighborhood of 800 lbs. Mr. Castro declared that when placed in the pasture a few months previous they were unfit for beef, and that the rich grass of this pasture has caused the change from a poor 300 pound steer to the fine animal we saw before us. Mr. Hendry, who by the way, is one of the best judges of a steer in the State, was much interested in the stock, as were also the boys. That there are great opportunities in Cuba for stock men there can be no question.

Our guide now led the way for a visit to the sugar plantation belonging to Mr. Castro's brother. A short ride soon brought us to the edge of the cane fields. We were disappointed! We had pictured the Cuban sugar cane fields to be great stalks of the succulent stocks, and here were stalks immature and not more than half a dozen feet high. But this disappointment was of short duration. We found that this first field was only young cane and would not mature until later in the season.

Nothing but sugar cane and royal palms were to be seen now as far as the eye could see in any direction. We rode on to the heart of this great plantation, consisting of 7,000 acres, we halted at the great sugar mill, where there is a small village composed of the employees of this plantation. A rest on the cool verandas of the big residence soon cooled us, and we could enjoy the Cuban mill scene to its fullest extent. Here were the typical Cubans in their native dress, white and black, in the lightest summer raiment, straw and Panama hats and white cotton or linen suits.

After a short rest Mr. Castro escorted us through the immense sugar mill with its great engines, several sets of crushers through which the cane passes, until it comes out so dry that the bagasse is fit for fuel at once, and is so used, being carried on endless belts from the crushers to the furnaces. These engines reached up to a height of 30 feet. Then there was the centrifugal machinery, all of immense size, and to explain all the machinery to be seen in this great mill would require much space, but the green cane is taken in at one end of the building from the cars which bring it from the field, and passes through the various processes of grinding, boiling, etc., until it finally comes out through a sluice-way in the floor overhead and sifts into sacks or barrels as the sugar of commerce.

This particular mill was just preparing to start grinding, and we were deprived of the opportunity of seeing it in operation. The adjoining plantation of 5,000 acres was at work grinding but we did not have time to go over to see it.

This particular plantation of which we write, was not destroyed by the insurgents during the war. The owner was on friendly terms with both belligerents, and the property was thus spared from the torch.

The large residence was however used by Spanish officers for their headquarters, and during an attack by a skirmish party of insurgents, one of their number, who was firing upon the band from the tower of the building was neatly picked off by one of the Cuban sharp shooters, his body rolling down the flight of stairs to the landing below, where the blood stains are still to be seen. Shots are also seen imbedded in the stone front where they lodged when being fired at a group of officers sitting on the veranda.

There is a store connected with this plantation, and like all stores in the Cuban towns, a chef is included in the roll of employees. We had partaken of a cup of coffee and bread before leaving Cardenas, so when Mr. Castro invited us to "breakfast" at about 11 o'clock, we were all ready for the hearty meal which was served.

We saw a few small orange trees growing on the premises here, but nothing in the citrus or other fruit line to compare with our own fruit trees, not excepting the mango or Avocado pear. Of the latter we saw some with immense trunks, but they appeared to have seen their best days, and were in anything but a healthful condition.

This plantation is traversed by private railroad tracks, which extend through the plantation to the mill, and on to the bay, which lies close by where the sugar is loaded on vessels direct from the cars.

At high noon our little ponies were again saddled by farm hands, and once more we were off, our guide now being a Cuban negro cowboy, astride a mule, who lead the way through the field into the wild country. The cowboy was not aware of the fact that one rider was almost rattling the teeth out of his head in his endeavor to keep his seat in the saddle, or he might not have gone off at such a smart pace. The riders were strung out along the road through the cane fields for several hundred yards, for now we were in the midst of the matured cane, which was so high as to hide from view the riders ahead. The stalks were very thick and grow to a height of ten or twelve feet. We were told that this cane had rattooned from the same roots for ten years. There appeared to be miles of this kind of cane, and it grew to this size without the aid of fertilizers of any kind. The climate and rich clay soil was the combination that produced this crop and which has made Cuba famous for sugar production. Our party were forced to utter many exclamations of surprise as they rode through the tons of rich cane that would soon go into the mill to be turned into sugar, maybe to find its way to our own State of Florida.

We noticed a man plowing in passing along, and the primitive way in which the soil was turned shows how backward these people are. The plow was a wooden affair with a very small plowshare and a very long beam. The man was holding the plow handles, a small boy was leading the oxen hitched to the plow, and a woman was doing the driving, and the entire outfit was moving along at a funeral pace. We saw a great many fine, large oxen, but the manner in which they are yoked together seemed cruel. The yoke is fastened over the horns, instead of about the neck as in this country, and the oxen

are compelled to haul heavy loads, doing the pulling with their heads instead of the better way of allowing the strain to fall on the powerful shoulders of these patient animals.

We now emerged from the cane fields into a field of grass. The country became quite rolling, and gradually we ascended to higher altitudes, until we rode over hills five hundred feet in height. The range of mountains plainly visible from Cardenas were still some distance off, and the peaks were still high above the ground we were passing over. The country here was most beautiful and picturesque, stone farm houses being passed here and there. Over the hills and down into a rich valley we cantered, and now the luxuriant Guinea grass grew to a great height, and a horse and rider were soon hidden in the tall grass. This pasture was at one time planted in sugar cane, but the insurgents had burned the cane fields, and only straggling blades of cane were visible in the heavy grass to bear proof of the once fertile fields.

It was principally to see this pasture that Mr. Hendry was taking this trip possibly with a view to purchasing ultimately, but an option was secured on the land with the right to stock it with cattle for a time, and it was the plan of Mr. Hendry to keep his son James on this range and for himself and son Bard to ship their cattle over from Florida, and fatten them on this pasture before placing them on the market.

The entire pasture was ridden over. A stream of pure water meanders its way through the field, royal palms grow in all their grandeur and beauty, and

the grass is rich and rank, making it in every way an ideal spot for a pasture.

We stopped at a farm house on our return for a drink of water, and found a Key West family settled there. They were operating a large apiary, and had some orange trees growing, but the fruit was either sour or bittersweet, and again we were disappointed with the fruit trees. The ride back to Cardenas consumed about two hours (they seemed a lifetime to this writer) and the distance home appeared to have grown five times as long as it was in the morning for we were thoroughly tired out, and hailed the livery stable with delight when we finally reached it and the ride was over, but despite the trying ride we enjoyed the novel trip and would even go through more for the sake of the experience of that day.

Much more might be written of Cardenas and the surrounding country, but we must hurry on to matters that may be more interesting to our readers.

After four days pleasantly spent at Cardenas the Wave set sail for Havana, Saturday morning, January 12th. The wind was fair but the trip to the westward had to be made against the strong current of the Gulf Stream, which sets in close to shore here. The sail down the harbor was full of interest. We passed close to the point where the first American officer lost his life in the Spanish-American War. Ensign Worth Bagley, who was killed with several of his men on board the torpedo boat Winslow, which was lured into the harbor, and then fired upon from a masked battery on shore. The Winslow it will be remembered was towed from under the heavy fire by the brave officers and men on the small tow boat Hudson, belonging to the "Mosquito" fleet. The gun boat Wilmington lay at the entrance of the harbor, finally closed in and silenced the masked battery with her four inch rifles. Afterwards the armored cruiser New York and battleship Indiana appeared in the harbor and taught the Spaniards a lesson by leveling the buildings on the docks and causing the Spaniards to keep quiet for the balance of the war at this point.

The long peninsular making out from Cardenas was rounded after a two hours sail and our course now lay down the coast, the Captain laying in as close to land as he felt it was safe to do, which was about two miles off shore. There was plenty of water to sail close in, but sailors prefer to give the rugged Cuban coast a wide berth, and feel safer when they are well off the coast.

As we sailed along every head was intently gazing over the side of the vessel. It was not "mal de mer" this time, but the bottom of the Gulf that was the attraction. The sponges and corals of the Florida reefs were not discerned, but the beautiful colors of the rock bottom were vividly brought to the gaze at a depth of 60 and 70 feet. An anchor was discovered by one of the crew, at the bottom. The vessel was sailing swiftly along at the time, and a floating buoy was thrown out to mark the place. Then the lifeboat was lowered, and we scrambled in with some of the crew, armed with long cables and grappling hooks. The anchor could be plainly seen at the bottom, which appeared about 20 feet down, but before the grappling hooks reached bottom 64 feet had been played out. The anchor was grappled several times, but could not be budged, and had to be abandoned.

As we sailed along we continually scanned the coast with a pair of powerful marine glasses, through which we could see houses, and even cows, horses and men, but the country here seemed almost barren of any crops and appeared very rocky.

Thus we moved along with the mountain range of Cardenas always in sight, even when we were off the city of Matanzas, which harbor we passed at 3 o'clock in the afternoon. We now regretted that the vessel had not cleared for Matanzas instead of Havana, but under the marine laws the vessel could not enter this port now, unless in distress, without the payment of a $500 fine. So we regretfully sailed by the city made famous in the late war as the place where the Spaniards would own up only to the killing of an old mule in the severe bombardment of Admiral Sampson's fleet of powerful war ships, led by the New York and Indiana.

Saturday night was spent in sailing up the Cuban coast, the Captain putting farther out to sea after dark for greater safety, but not so distant but that the glare on the heavens of the electric lights of Havana, Matanzas, and Cardenas could be plainly seen at one time, the three cities being ninety miles apart. After this we retired to our berths to dream of Morro Castle and the city of Havana.

Sunday morning, the 13th, all were up bright and early, with the exception of Mr. Foxworthy, who was down with a touch of malarial fever. The rugged coast now jutted out in strongly defined capes as we near the harbor of Havana. The wind now began to rise and it was evident that a norther was close at hand. Gradually it shifted to the west, compelling us to beat to windward, the Captain making a short leg out to sea and a long leg along the coast to give us a close view of the shore.

Our good ship took on new life as the storm increased, and we eagerly watched the approach to Morro Castle, which now was plainly visible. The sea was getting rougher every minute, and it was a grand sight to see the waves dash up against the rocks, sending the spray high up in the air. By the time Morro Castle and the mouth of the harbor were reached, the norther had broken out with great force, and thus we escaped a severe gale that washed the coast of Cuba, sending the big Ward line steamship Vigalancia and several sailing vessels on the rocks. The gale sent us scudding into the harbor at full speed, giving the tug which had come out for a job the go by. A long pilot boat, propelled by eight strong oarsmen swung skillfully alongside while we moved at full speed and a Cuban pilot boarded our vessel, directing her to her anchorage within a few hundred yards of the wreck of the U. S. battleship Maine.

Part Three

Havana

Our chapter last week ended with the dropping of the anchor of the Wave in Havana harbor. Our party were all interested and excited in the scene before them.

Vessels darted about in every direction. Before us lay the city of Havana; between our boat and the city lay the wreck of the Maine. Nearer to us was the little city of Regia, and down at the mouth of the harbor, Morro Castle and Cabana Fortress were in plain view. Even Mr. Foxworthy could not resist the temptation to rise from his sick bed and survey the animated scene and historical sights that met our gaze on every side.

No sooner had the anchor chains ceased to rattle and the sails taken in when one of the quarantine launches steamed alongside and a physician boarded us. A hasty examination of crew and passengers, and we were given a clean bill of health. From this on throughout the day the Wave seemed to receive a great deal of attention from the Government officials, the health officers and custom house officials being Americans. First the custom house launch would come alongside, then more doctors, next the harbor police, etc. The thing continued until it became quite annoying. Finally one of the Cuban harbor police was placed on our boat and left there, a position he occupied for three days. He was a Cuban from Sagua la Grande and informed us that it was the law, to place an officer on every vessel in the harbor. After several days of this kind of business we were at last left to ourselves.

One of the first welcome sights to greet American eyes as the harbor is taken in, is to see the stars and stripes flying from all the forts in the harbor and the Government buildings on shore. Old Glory never looked prettier than it does flying from Morro Castle and Cabanas, and we felt so proud of our country's flag that our twelve-foot flag was daily flung to the breeze from the mast head, which also helped us to get aboard when we required the services of one of the small harbor boats, known as bum boats, and all we had to tell the boatman was 'Gallata Wave', and they understood that the Americano schooner was meant.

But while the American flag is now the most prominent in Havana harbor, the orange and red flag of Castile is scarcely to be seen at all. The flag that once bid defiance to the world in this harbor is now only to be seen flying from a modest flag pole on the big floating dry dock in the harbor, which under the terms of peace Spain was permitted to retain as her property, and which she has been endeavoring to sell to our Government, but without success. Aside from this dry dock the flag of Spain is seen only on Spanish vessels coming into the harbor, a line of steamships still running to Havana from Barcelona and other Spanish ports.

But our excursion to the Antilles was not to be entirely of pleasure. Our troubles began on Monday morning after our arrival. Mr. Foxworthy had a high fever, and it was deemed best to call a physician on shore. That was a fatal mistake and caused our party no end of worry. By the advice of Tampa friends in Havana a Cuban doctor was summoned. He examined the patient and declared it was not necessarily a fatal case but most serious, and to add to his alarming verdict, he gave orders that Mr. Foxworthy must be sent to the marine hospital, Los Animas, within a half hour, and sure enough by that time the ambulance from the hospital was in waiting on shore and Mr. Foxworthy was bundled up, taken from his family, and driven to the hospital, where he was placed in the yellow fever suspect ward to await developments.

The gloom on board the Wave was so thick you could cut it with a knife. Miss Tillie went into mourning at once, Mr. Hendry looked the picture of despair; kindhearted Mrs. Hendry cried and became indignant in turns, and the rest of us were filled with sympathy over the trouble that had come upon us. The fact is that it was really the best thing that could have happened for Mr. Foxworthy, for he received the very best treatment at the hospital, and besides, had two pretty American young women to nurse him, and when this fact was discovered James and this scribe tried to fall sick and get sent to the hospital, but they had no such luck.

Yellow fever or no, Mr. Foxworthy was at the hospital, and there he had to remain for eleven days, so his personal experiences of Havana is confined principally to the Hospitale Los Animas. Here the peculiar rule under which the island of Cuba is temporarily governed was seen. It was neither American nor Cuban rule, but a conflict of the two. While Uncle Sam is suppose to have full control of all the high places, the Cubans fill every subordinate position, and it is evident that the latter have a peculiar way of showing their gratefulness to the Americans, for it seemed that every thing was done by them to make as much trouble for Americans as possible, in fact, if the truth is admitted, there is far from a cordial spirit existing today between Americans and Cubans, but of this we may speak later on.

At first only Capt. John Cary (we should have mentioned that Capt. Ben Cary had been summoned home to Key West on account of the illness of his wife, and that his brother John had come on and taken his command) was allowed to visit Mr. Foxworthy, as he was an immune, but after a day or two Bard and Miss Tillie were permitted to visit the patient, which seems strange if this was a case of yellow fever. Mr. Foxworthy had no symptoms of yellow jack at all, and daily improved, but a board of five Cuban physicians sat on his case daily for four days, and solemnly declared that he had yellow fever, and gave him a certificate to that effect. So 'officially' Mr. Foxworthy has had yellow fever, but you can never make any one of our party believe it.

Our readers will pardon us for dwelling on these matters which may be of no interest to them, but as we are writing more of the personal experiences of our party than any attempt to give a stereotyped description of Cuba, we must write of misfortunes as well as of the more pleasant reminiscences.

A few cases of yellow fever had lingered in Havana late into December, but the cool weather of January rid the city entirely of the disease. We made our first visit to the city on the Sunday afternoon of the day of our arrival, and we must admit that we at first imagined that Mr. Mike Robe was lurking around every corner in waiting for us, but in a very short time he was out of our minds and we gave him scarcely a thought. We were advised not to go out in the city after sundown, but we soon discovered that to see Havana in its most interesting phases the time to do so is under the glare of the electric lights, for it is at night when the social side of these people is shown.

And while we are mentioning yellow fever, let us remark here that after roaming all over the city of Havana, which only a couple of short years ago was noted as one of the filthiest places in the world, we unhesitatingly assert that today it is one of the cleanliest cities that we have ever been in. Especially is this true outside of the streets bordering the bay, where the heavy traffic makes it very difficult to keep the streets swept clean, but even here dirt is not permitted to accumulate. Go where you will and everything looks sweet and clean to an astonishing extent, and it does not appear possible for disease of any kind to gain a foothold there. This excellent sanitary condition of the city is due to the rigid laws prescribed by Governor-General Wood and the American officers under him, and give cause to hope that before a great while epidemics will be stamped out of the island.

Havana has been so frequently described to the readers of American newspapers and magazines that it is not our purpose to enter into a detailed description of the place, but more with a view to writing of those features that particularly impressed us, touching more on such changes as have taken place since the American occupation. Of course the peculiar houses and narrow streets of the old city are always objects of great interest to the sightseer. In the business district the streets are just wide enough to admit two wagons passing each other and some of the sidewalks are so narrow that one person has scarcely room for a foothold. In passing along these streets the rule is to travel single file, and then one is constantly compelled to jump down into the street and back to the walk to allow pedestrians going in the opposite direction to pass. Even in some of the principal retail shopping streets, such as Obispo O'Reilly and Obrapis Streets, running from the bay to the Prada, or leading boulevard, the streets are very narrow, and the many ladies who frequent this district must find much inconvenience in getting about.

Obispo Street may be said to contain the finest shops in the city. From the Governor-General's palace to the Prada is a row of stores on either side of the street that contain as fine a class of goods as may be found anywhere in the world. The dry-goods, millinery, art stores, bric-a-brac, novelty goods, jewelry, photographers and many other establishments of the kind center here. A general view of the street and the outer appearance of these shops does not strike one favorably, but on entering the rich display of imported goods attracts immediate attention. Broadway and Sixth Avenue shoppers would be in delight here, for the class of goods in the finest establishments are such as are to be found in Paris, London and Berlin. Cuba being the land of summer the display of fans is the finest in the world, several stores priding themselves on having the largest stocks of these goods carried by any establishment.

That Havana must be a city of great wealth, despite the stormy period it has passed through is evident from the expensive class of goods carried by these stores, for after all the principal patrons of these establishments are the ladies of Havana - the rich Spanish families and better class of Cubans, whose residences are richly and handsomely furnished, and the ladies wear rich and stylish clothes.

To the visitor from the large American cities this feature may not seem extraordinary, but to a Floridian at least it is a subject for comment. No such sight can be seen in Florida as the display of finery that is made by the ladies of Havana. Such a display can best be seen at a grand opera night at the Tacon Theatre, the leading theatre in Havana, and one of the largest in the world. It is then that the beauty of the Cuban capital is out on dress parade. The annual horse show at Madison Square Garden may show more stunning and stylish costumes, but we doubt whether so many pretty women can be seen there at one time as come forth to attend the opera in Havana. Now, girls, don't think we do not admire the American girl, for she's all right, and if she used one-half the artificial devices that her Spanish and Cuban sister does, she would undoubtedly be simply bewitching, for that to no small degree adds much to the beauty of the women of Havana, for they have the art of using powder and other articles used by them down to a science, and for that matter even the men are addicted to the powder habit.

At the present time the best means of transportation for getting about Havana is by means of one horse cabs. They seat three persons and have a top in the shape of a hood, and being low afford protection from the sun. These cabs charge 20 cents Spanish money to carry two persons from one point in the city to another. The wise man will always have his American money changed into Spanish silver for pocket change in Havana, the five dollars American exchanging for $6.75 in Spanish silver, so that in paying 20 cents Spanish for a hack ride the American value is only about 13 cents. There are no less than 5,000 of these hacks in Havana, so it can readily be understood that they are a popular mode of conveyance. A change is soon to come, however. At present there are only three horsecar lines in the city, and not an electric road is in operation in this city of 300,000 inhabitants. But electricity is about to make its entrance into Havana, for many miles of track have already been laid throughout the leading thoroughfares, and the trolley poles and wires are being put in place, so that in a very short time electric cars will be running all over the city. This will force the several omnibus lines out of business and interfere to a great extent with the business of the hacks.

After a few days in the city we found that we could get around with but little trouble, and soon picked up enough Spanish to direct hackmen, etc. The city was crowded with American visitors at the time we were there, and we found some American establishments that aided us to get about. Then to, we ran across some Florida friends, who made things pleasant for us.

Our party put up at the Florida Hotel a portion of the time we were in Havana. It is a very well conducted hotel as Cuban hotels go. Like all Cuban buildings it has a large courtyard extending up through the building. The rooms open on the galleries around this court, and the dining room extends around two sides of it on the second floor. The floors throughout are of marble. Our first meal was not relished. It was dinner served at 5:30 p.m. The food was not served in courses, but one article at a time, and as one dish was disposed of one waiter removed the plates and another was ready for your next order. After a few meals we got the hang of things or rather became accustomed to it, and rather enjoyed this mode of serving meals, especially as we succeeded in catching on to the menu with the assistance of a waiter who understood a little English. During our stay at the hotel Havana was visited by the cooler weather of the winter, the thermometer registering 68 degrees. That would be a pleasant temperature even in a Florida home, but Cuban houses were not built to keep out cold and are always cool and airy, even in summer. So our first night in this hotel was anything but a pleasant experience. Our room contained a good set of walnut furniture, but only a small rug on the cold marble floor, and the bed - whew!- but it was like sleeping on a clothes line! It was an iron bedstead with a spring, and for a mattress there was something like a quilt about one inch thick, while the covering consisted of a sheet and counterpane. It was as neat and clean as it could be, what there was of it, but that wasn't enough to go around, and as there was no electric bell we just lay there, and went to sleep dreaming of being shipwrecked in the Arctic regions. Don't expect to find any feather beds in Cuba.

On Sunday morning we went to church before breakfast, partaking of that meal at 12 o'clock. A walk of a few blocks from our hotel brought us to the Cathedral on Empedrado Street, the most beautiful church in Havana, and where the remains of Christopher Columbus were buried until they were shipped to Spain just before the late war. There are many fine Catholic churches in Havana, but few of other denominations, and a visit to any of them is always interesting, images of the Virgin Mary and the Saints, in glass cases and rich furnishings being found in nearly all of them.

Sunday evening is the time selected when nearly every one is out promenading or enjoying themselves in other ways. The great sight is on the Prada with the center of attraction being the Central Park. Here on Sunday nights great throngs of people congregate, many occupying the iron settees in the park, while a regular procession of men and women marches past, the walks being crowded with the moving throng. It is one of the sights of Havana to see this turnout, and should not be missed. In the center of the park is a bandstand and every Sunday night a concert is given by a band of fifty pieces, every member of which belongs to the police force, and it is a novelty to see the men in their natty blue uniforms, white gloves and wearing their clubs, playing splendid music for the pleasure of the public.

The Prada is a boulevard that leads from the Colon Park to the Punta, or point on the open Gulf just opposite Morro Castle, which is only a few hundred yards across the bay. It is a double driveway with a promenade shaded by beautiful trees in the center while the homes of the rich line the drive on either side. Every afternoon Havana swelldom is out for a ride along the driveway. We were informed that we would see many handsome turnouts, but we were disappointed on this score, for the carriages do not rival those found in large American cities. We saw one fine automobile, and that appeared to be a great novelty, and the only one to be seen.

The large hotels and theatres cluster about the Prada and Central Park, the finest of these being the Hotels Inglaterra, the Pasaje, Hotel Telegraffo, and the Tacon, Payret and Albisu theatres, besides the Spanish and other clubs, making it the center of the social life of the city.

There are many fine parks in the city, but the finest is the Colon (Columbus) Park situated at the beginning of the Prada. It covers a square about sixty acres in extent, and the pretty walks are lined with cocoanut, royal palms and a luxuriant growth of flowers and shrubs, making it a veritable tropical garden that is a great attraction to visitors from the states.

We enjoyed rides to all the principal points of interest, our party being indebted to Mr. Fred Lykes, formerly of Tampa, who is in business in Havana with his brother James, for a drive to the Colon Cemetery and other interesting points. The drive to the cemetery was made through Tacon Park, past the Principe Castle, one of the many forts situated on a high hill, and thence through a beautiful country for several miles to the massive entrance arch of the cemetery. There are a number of fine monuments in this cemetery, but as a rule they are not to be compared with the monuments in our large American cemeteries, with one exception, and that is the noted fireman's monument, which is undoubtedly the finest work of art to be found in any cemetery. It was erected in honor of 27 firemen who lost their lives in a great fire some years ago in Havana, the likeness of each of the fire heroes being shown around the base of the monument, while the top, which must be close to forty or fifty feet in height is surmounted by an angel holding in her arms a dying fireman in his fire uniform. Many figures bearing on the event commemorated are placed in the corners of the monument, and altogether it is a magnificent work of art, and a splendid tribute to the men in whose honor it was erected. There. is a handsome chapel in the cemetery, and the grave of the only Cuban General, Galixio Garcia, is very plain with a small monument. Close to the fireman's monument is the spot where dead sailors of the Maine were buried, only one body still remaining there, the rest having been removed to Key West.

The ride home was through the suburbs of Carmelo and St. Lazarus, with the gulf in full view. This is a beautiful drive, and many public buildings are passed. Scattered at intervals along the water front are many fortifications erected by the

Spaniards during the war with the United States. The names of some of these forts are Chorrera and Punta Brava, both mounted with modern guns, a little further on is the Santa Clara battery and the Reina battery. Judging from the number of cannon to be seen on all sides, one would believe that the armies of the world could not have taken Havana by bombardment, for you stumble across forts in every direction that you turn.

Our ride led us for a great part of the way close to the water's edge, and a grand sight was thus afforded us in witnessing the sea wash up against the rocks and break into fountains of water 20 and 30 feet in height, the high wind carrying the spray in a fine mist over us as we drove along. Our drive took us by the state penitentiary near the Punta, where there is another battery of guns, and on through the business section to the ferry, where our party crossed the bay to Regia, and rowed out to the Wave.

Part Four

None the least of the interesting sights in and about Havana, is to watch the ever changing scene in the harbor. From where our good ship lay we had a splendid view of all that transpired in the bay. We had an awning rigged on the quarter deck where we could sit in comfort and watch the maneuvering of the great steamships and sailing vessels. We could tell long before a vessel arrived in the harbor that a ship was coming in by watching the signal flags on the signal tower on Morro Castle. These signals told the class of

vessel and its nationality, and were hoisted as soon as the vessels could be made out at sea. These signals were for the information of the pilots, tug captains and port officers. Every vessel that comes into the harbor must anchor in the place designated by the pilots. The Plant and East Coast steamships usually anchor near the same buoy, within a few hundred yards of the Maine. They never go up to the docks. Passengers and freight are transferred by small steamers and "bum" boats, and engaged in this work was our old Fort Myers friend, the little steamer Clara, which is now used as a transfer boat in Havana harbor. The Ward Line has a steamship arriving in this harbor nearly every day, either from New York, New Orleans or some of the West Indies. The Morgan Line steamships are also coming and going almost daily. Then there are lines direct to Spain, Mexico, etc., to say nothing of the scores of great tramp steamships coming in with coal, cattle, hay, grain, and other heavy freights. The Herrera and Munson lines are companies running to ports along the Cuban coast, and these lines have docking facilities. Every dock in the bay has a vessel loading or unloading there, and only the stern of the vessel lies against the dock, to occupy as little room as possible.

The little sail boats known as bum boats cover the water in every direction. The owners are licensed to carry passengers about the harbor. The law sets the charge at 20 cents, but like all Cubans they will make you pay five times as much unless you make an agreement with them beforehand. They clustered

about our vessel in numbers waiting for a passenger, but we were permitted to use our own boat to go to the Regia shore, where we took the ferry boat across to Havana, but our boat was not permitted to be rowed across the harbor to Havana.

One of the grandest sights that we witnessed while on board the Wave in Havana harbor, was during the norther, which blew with great force for several days. A tremendous sea was rolling outside, and as the mountainous waves would strike the rocks at Morro Castle they would dash up in the air as high as the top of the lighthouse.

Visit to Maine*

On January 22nd we went ashore to the office of the Captain of the Port, Lieutenant Commander Lucien Young, U.S.N., and secured a permit to visit the wreck of the battleship Maine, "with the understanding that no souvenirs shall be removed therefrom." So that afternoon our party rowed over from the Wave to what remains of the ill-fated war ship. It was a sight to stir the fighting blood in the veins of any true American. There lay the noble vessel partly out of water, the great steel plates torn apart as if by some mighty superhuman power. The vessel looks much like the photographs shown of the wreck taken after the explosion, except that since then she has sunk at least ten feet deeper in the mud. One of her great swinging davits rears itself out of the water, her military mast still stands, but she is so torn up that it is almost impossible to tell which is her bow or stern. We crawled all over the steel girders and through holes made in the plates. Everywhere that a paint surface

213

presented itself some visitor had scribbled his name and it was a regular register of American names. The clause in our permit that no souvenirs should be removed was evidently intended as a joke, for everything that could be removed from any portion of the vessel above water had been carried away. The Captain of the Port himself visited the wreck with a party of ladies, while we were there, and brought a machinist along with hammer and chisel to cut off some of the bolts from the riveted plates, a difficult piece of work which required some time. The ladies of our party were presented with some of these souvenirs, and we were given permission to secure what we could. So after the Captain departed we made a sharp search, and the penetrating eyes of our Spanish sailor boy, Paby, discovered several pieces of brass pipe lying on a section of the ship, apparently two or three feet under water. This sailor boy as a rule does not know what fear is, and would jump into the bay with sharks all about him, climb to the topmast in a gale, or do any daring feat—but he feared to go down into this wreck, for he possessed the superstitions that all sailors cling to, and no doubt imagined he would be drawn under by the outstretched hands of the poor sailors buried in the wreck. But he was finally prevailed on to go into the water with the offer of a coin, and what appeared two or three feet of water, proved fully five feet deep. He secured the brass pipe and also a lot of electric light wires, which our party have brought home with them, each member having a souvenir obtained on the wreck.

The wreck lies in the very center of the busiest portion of the harbor, and is a serious obstruction. The Government will either have it blown up and removed or it will be raised up by a coffer dam being built about it and the water pumped out, and then the true story of the explosion that caused the death of two hundred American sailors will be made known.

For the next few days of our stay in Havana we made short excursions to the various suburbs of the city. Regia across the bay from Havana is quite a little city in itself, and the ferryboats are kept busy carrying passengers and teams back and forth, running on a schedule of five minutes, the boats being crowded during the morning and evening hours.

From Regia runs the only electric trolley line in operation about Havana. This line runs out five miles to a beautiful little town called Guanabacoa (with the accent on the "co"), which is east of Havana. It is a town of 20,000 inhabitants. There is a dancing pavilion here, and large crowds go from Havana at night to participate in the dancing.

One of the prettiest suburban drives is that to Cerro, which is an extension of the city of Havana itself. The residences and tropical gardens to be seen going to this place are very beautiful, and a visit to the city would be far from complete without taking this drive.

Morro Castle and Cabana Fortress

On our last day in Havana, Thursday the 25th, we visited the famous Morro Castle and Cabana Fortress, having first obtained a permit to do so from Governor-General Wood. Under Spanish rule visitors were never admitted to these forts, but since they have been under American control a little effort will secure this privilege for the visitor.

We started from the Caballeria wharf in one of the small sail boats, which carried us down to a landing, where the road led direct to Morro Castle. A few minutes walk brought us to the entrance of the famous fort that has played such a prominent part in history almost since the discovery of America, for Morro Castle was first erected by the Spanish Government in the year 1589, although many changes have taken place since then. At the entrance we encountered a guard, one of Uncle Sam's boys in blue, who took up our permit, handing it to us again as we passed out. It was a pleasure to meet our boys, and they gave us all the information that we desired, telling us to go wherever we pleased about the buildings. The soldiers occupying El Morro were a battery of one of the artillery regiments of the regular army, having come from Fortress Monroe to take the place of the Spanish soldiers. The commandant here is Major Grimes, who it will be remembered commanded Grimes battery, which did such effective work at El Caney and San Juan.

We wandered all over the famous fort, visiting the officers quarters, the watch towers, ammunition store rooms, and climbing long flights of stone steps to the bastions, where the Krupp guns lay with their muzzles pointing seaward. Everything is stone and concrete, the walls being very thick. The fort rests on a high ledge of rock, and has a sweep up and down the coast and over the city of Havana, and surrounding country. The artillery boys told us that the guns here were not of the latest Krupp pattern, and that our war ships would have had little trouble in reducing the walls of the fort, for although they were impregnable with the old smooth bore guns, the modern rifled cannon would have soon reduced them to a pile of stone.

We crawled out on the parapet facing the ocean, and looked down into the depths below, for straight below was the water. The light house stands here and upon its front in large letters is the name O'Donnell, and under the name the date 1844. Close to the light house is the signal tower, from which a grand view is obtained of Havana, it being high above the highest church steeple in the city. In this signal station we noted a locker for the flag of every nation, and also one to designate every kind of vessel that moves on the water.

After a couple of hours spent in wandering through the forts we passed out into the road, and proceeded to Cabana fortress, passing the camps of our troops on the way. A walk of half a mile brought us to a bridge, over which we had to pass to gain entrance to the prison in which thousands of Cuban patriots have been imprisoned, many never to see the light again. All this is changed now. The American flag proudly flies from the staff, and American troops occupy the grimy old fortress.

As we passed in the guard halted us, received our permit, and called the corporal of the guard, who told us to pass in and go where we pleased. The soldier boys directed us the best way to see the great prison, for it is one of the largest in the world, having accommodations for four thousand men, although it seemed to us there was room for forty thousand men.

We walked along the high battery facing the narrow channel leading from the ocean into the bay. The fortress has a frontage of 800 yards on this channel, and along its entire exposure are placed heavy cannon at short intervals. The rock here is higher than at Morro Castle, and the city, which is only a quarter of a mile across the channel is seen before you in a grand bird's eye view, every section being plainly in view even to the remotest outlying districts. From here we descended the road to the long tunnel-like prisons, for they resemble nothing so much as long railroad tunnels. The long, main passageway appears so long that the entrance at the farther end seems to almost meet the earth. From the main passageway, small tunnels branch off every 100 feet or so, and these extend back into other and darker prisons. In some there are a few rough wooden benches and tables, but most of the cells were bare of any furniture. It is one of the most wonderful prisons in the world, and by the cutting away of a single bridge, could be isolated from the main land, and escape or rescue would have been a most hazardous undertaking. There were two dark dungeons, but one of these has been filled up by our Government. The other was so dark that we did not feel inclined to explore it to any great distance. This was the place where the Cuban prisoners were executed by the Spanish Government. The labyrinth of cells is astonishing, and one can walk for hours and not see them all.

A small portion of the prison was being remodeled by American mechanics, and we learned that it was intended as a military prison for deserters from the American army, and others sentenced to punishment. Certainly it would appear the irony of fate to imprison in this place, above all others, the men who came to the rescue of the patriots who found a living grave in these chambers of horrors!

A long walk around the outside of the walls of this prison brought us to steep stone steps cut into the rocks, which brought us to the town of Casa Blanca at the foot of the hill opposite the city. Here we found our boatman, and a few minutes sail landed us in the city again. As we passed by the post office, we noted the tree and shrine of Diego Velazque, the founder of the city of Havana, and under this tree the first Mass was celebrated in the year 1519.

But we must close this description of our visit to Havana, not however, without a short account of our last day's stay in the harbor, which proved to be the most miserable of our entire voyage. Luckily for Mr. Jas. E. Hendry, he had proceeded ahead by Plant steamship Olivette with his wife and children, to Key West, and they therefore escaped the ordeal the others had to pass through.

After having pronounced Mr. Foxworthy's little sickness yellow fever, the Cuban doctors had to keep up the farce (which was however, anything but farcical to our party) and therefore orders had been given that the Wave must go through fumigation. Right there and then there was almost a declaration of war between Americans and Cubans, but talking and pleading would do no good, and the more gracefully we submitted the better it would be for us. So all hands were ordered aboard ship Friday morning, and not permitted to leave. Anchor was hoisted and the Wave was towed to the fumigating vessel and tied alongside. The marine hospital men here are all Americans, but they had orders to fumigate the vessel, and did their work thoroughly. The sailors on board the Wave had been there before, and knew what it meant, so they hid their shore clothes in out-of-the-way places where they would not likely be found. But the hospital men were up to some of the dodges of the sailor men, too, and swore and quoted United States quarantine laws as they unearthed clothing hidden in top sails, under the wheel house and other places - but they didn't find everything, oh no; and sarcastically remarked that they never saw a crowd with such few clothes!

Several dozen wire baskets were sent aboard our boat, and into these every bit of clothing and bedding had to be packed, with the exception of the clothing on our backs at the time. This was at noon. When all the clothing and blankets were in the baskets, they were taken on board the fumigating barge and placed in dry steam chests, where they were subjected to a high degree of heat. In the meantime the hatches and cabin were tightly closed and sealed, paper being pasted over any

cracks that would let out air. Then a large steam pipe was placed in the hold and a small pipe into the cabin, and strong chemicals forced into them, and they were subjected to this treatment for 24 hours, compelling all hands to sleep on deck, although the officers on the barge were very kind and allowed Bard Hendry and wife and baby, and Mr. Foxworthy and wife to sleep on board the barge, the latter taking advantage of the kind offer.

Our clothing and blankets were returned to us before night, the linen articles all having a yellow tinge, and the clothing full of creases, just as they had been placed in the baskets. It was a sight to witness every person diving into these baskets, fishing out their own things, and a more disgusted lot it would be hard to find. The sailors made the most of it, and derived lots of fun out of the situation.

Just before noon Saturday, Jan. 26th, the hatches and cabin were opened, and the fumigation was over, but the cabin or holds could not be entered for hours after, so strong was the gas therein. We were then permitted to go. Sails were hoisted and under a strong breeze Capt. Cary maneuvered the vessel out of the harbor, sailing by the Morro and out into the ocean.

We bid good-bye to the Cuban capital, where although we had met with many vicissitudes we had greatly enjoyed the many foreign features to be found there, and would not have missed our trip to Cuba for double the expense and trouble.

What the future has in store for these people we confess is not an easy question to answer.

It may be true that our Government is under a pledge to turn the government of the island over completely to the Cubans, but our observations lead us to the conclusion that it would be a great error to do so at the present time. The Cubans seem to have no love for Americans or foreigners of any class. They appear to realize their inability to cope with outsiders in business matters, and fear the competition of Americans, and so it is very difficult for an American citizen to gain a foothold among them. We believe that they should have a complete system of home rule, with their own officials from president down but the United States should retain a foothold on the island, and should be consulted in all the relationships between Cuba and foreign countries. To do otherwise would seem that we would soon be involved with foreign countries on Cuba's account, and the old troubles that our Government had to contend with during the Spanish administration of the island would again confront the Americans. Some argue, however, that it may be best to turn everything over to the Cubans, and that they will make such a mess of it, that they will be glad to have Uncle Sam step in and take them under the protecting wings of the great American eagle. When that day comes to pass then you may look for a wonderful development in the fertile island of Cuba.

Homeward Bound

Hardly had the Wave passed out into the open sea, when she struck a large wave, head on, her bow going down into the depths and her stern high up on the crest of a wave. We all tried to appear brave, but the color must have left the cheeks of the land lubbers. This gave promise of a rough voyage across to Key West, but was not fulfilled, for the farther we sailed from the Cuban coast the less we felt the high seas, and at midnight the wind had died away, and we drifted in the Gulf stream. After breakfast Sunday the wind came from the west, and the first land sighted was Rebecca Key to the east of Tortugas, about forty miles to the west of Key West. The sea remained rough until suddenly we ran into smooth water and we learned that we had passed out of the Gulf Stream. We caught several king fish running up to Key West, making that harbor just about dark, glad once more to get on land, after a day and a half on the sea.

Head winds kept us in Key West for several days, and while there we visited the graves of the sailors of the Maine, over which a handsome monument has been erected by the citizens of Key West, a separate monument to the dead of the torpedo boat Winslow also standing near by. Thus on this trip we saw the spot where the Winslow was fired on, went on the wreck of the Maine, saw where the dead sailors were first buried in Havana, and their final resting place in Key West.

The cry was all aboard for Punta Rassa on Wednesday morning, Jan. 30th, and soon we were under way and out past the northwest bar. During the afternoon we passed close to the North Atlantic squadron, the vessels having gun practice, and we could hear the roar of the big guns, and sharp snap of the rapid firers, as the smoke ascended in puffs on the western horizon.

Our last night at sea was a calm one, and we made but little headway, so that it was late on Friday morning when we sighted land near Marco. By 11 a.m. we were off Naples, and a few hours with the wind holding where it was would have put us into Punta Rassa. But suddenly the wind shifted to northwest and blew a regular gale, by far the roughest weather we had experienced on the trip. It was now a dead beat to windward, and every ten or fifteen minutes, the Captain who was at the wheel sang out, 'Hard-a-lee' as the vessel went on the port or starboard tack. She tore through the water at a great rate throwing the waves high over her deck and cabin, but her real headway against the gale was slow. The vessel lay over on her beams end as the wind caught her sails, and all were driven below by the cold wind except Mrs. Hendry, who could not be induced to go below during the gale. Only two answered the call to dinner that day, and it was a tussle with the wind, which blew the soup out of the spoons before it could be carried to the mouth. Sanibel Island at last came in sight, and at 7 o'clock at night the anchor was dropped inside the sea buoy marking the channel into Punta Rassa, and though the wind still blew there was no sea and the passengers slept in peace for the night, reaching Punta Rassa early the next morning, where the steamer Plant was boarded and Fort Myers reached on Friday evening just four weeks after the party had taken its departure.

*My cousin on my mother's side, Army Lieut. William Cymro Johns, of Company A, Battalion, USA Engineers, was killed on the USS Maine when she blew up.

An 1880s Christmas in Southwest Florida

By Julia Pate, a cousin of Ella Kathryn Hendry

Christmas in Southwest Florida in the 1880s was unusual—there would be no snow and ice. Sometimes the weather would be cold and some years it would be warm at Christmastime. An earlier settler to the Caoosahatchee region was William H. "Bill" Brown, a native of London, England. He operated a trading post at the edge of the Everglades, which became known as "Brown's Landing." The landing was about thirty-five or forty-miles from Gopher Ridge, which was later named Immokalee by Bill Brown's daughter, Rose Kinnon. Immokalee is a Seminole word meaning "my home." Rose often drove a team of oxen to Fort Myers alone with a load of alligator hides and returned with supplies for her father's post.

The Seminole Indians considered Bill Brown to be one of their most trusted friends. He spoke their language and gave them a fair measure when trading.

It became an annual affair for Bill Brown to have a great feast at Christmastime for his Indian friends. A day or two before Christmas, he would go into the woods near the landing and fire off a huge foot-long firecracker. This was the signal for the Seminoles to gather at Brown's Landing. The Indians came by canoes—standing in the hollowed-out cypress logs. They used long poles to send the boats through the swamp of sawgrass and water. The braves wore black derby hats and long shirts made of hundreds of small pieces of cotton cloth sewn into intricate patterns of brilliant colors. They had traded skins and pelts at Brown's Landing for their derbies.

Since the surrounding land was flooded nine months of the year, the trading post was built on the edge of a swamp on a rise of land. A porch had been built extending out over the water. Similar to a dock, it enabled the Indians to pole their canoes right up the building. When they came to trade, they could throw the alligator hides and other skins up onto the porch for Bill Brown to examine. Besides the hats, another popular trading item was hand accordions. The Seminoles greatly enjoyed sitting on the porch of the trading post as they played hymns on the instruments.

Mrs. Brown and her two oldest daughters would have spent several days preparing for this feast. There were many kinds of cakes baked, and pans of biscuits and cornbread. She was famous for her lemon pies, so she had a supply of them, and pumpkin pies, on hand. Squash, pumpkin, beans, rice, grits and gravy would be prepared. Ears of corn and sweet potatoes were roasted over the coals of a fire, where a wild pig was being cooked to a golden brown. Deer and wild turkey would round out the menu.

The Indians camped around the trading post for a few days and then returned to the Everglades in their canoes—just as they had arrived.

Christmas in the village was celebrated in a different way. In Fort Myers, on the day after Christmas, there was a great Christmas Tournament, patterned after medieval games, with knights and their ladies. Each knight was given a title.

Cattlemen from all over the Caloosahatchee region would arrive—mounted on their best and fastest horses—to try their skill at the tournament or riding at the rings. Tournament Street is said to have been named from these Christmas events held a century ago.

After all the participants had gathered in a vacant field down near the river, the games began. The object was for a rider to use his lance while riding at full speed, to capture three rings, which were fastened on three cross bars about six or seven feet about the ground and about thirty feet apart. The riders were each given three trials. Speed and accuracy were essential.

The night after the games was the Christmas Ball, and the winner led the first dance after crowning his sweetheart "Queen of Love and Beauty."

Firecrackers, sky rockets and Roman candles filled the night air on Christmas Eve while the children of the town presented a play and sang carols in the Methodist church. There was a large oak tree that was decorated and filled with presents.

On Christmas morning, the sharpshooters of the town were given their chance to excel in a contest. They shot at a target at one hundred yards for the prize of beef to be divided between the best five shots. Another contest was held for marksmen who shot for a fine pair of boots.

Eureka! Adventures with Postwar Fishing Company

Written by Hugh Hendry, and edited by his cousin, Ella
Kathryn Hendry

World War II in Europe had just ended. Not too long after the war, Doug, my brother, and I came home to visit our parents who were living in an old two-story house on Fowler Street in Fort Myers, Florida. They had recently moved there from North Fort Myers, which was just across the Caloosahatchee River. My sister, Rosiland, had married a young lieutenant and was living with him at an air base in another city. Louis, my other brother, was working for a hotel on Miami Beach.

My father was called "Gus" and my mother was known as "Maude." Mom and Dad had met in Fort Myers years ago. When they were married, they decided to settle there.

Before getting into my story, I want to tell you about my brother, Doug, and our European Army Adventures.

Doug had landed on Omaha Beach with his outfit, the Fifth Division, which was known for its Red Diamond Insignia. He had fought across Europe and on into Czechoslovakia.

I had landed in Europe after the Battle of the Bulge. I served with the 71st. Division, and had fought across Europe as well, but I was first with the 7th Army. Then I was transferred to Patton's Third Army. Doug was also serving with Patton.

My outfit had met up with the Russians on the Enns River in Austria when the war was over. Doug and I were fortunate in seeing each other once during the war. My outfit was stationed in tents on the Enns River at Styer, Austria. One day, Doug pulled up in his jeep with some of his friends from the Red Diamond Division. Being a staff sergeant, he had somehow managed to commandeer a jeep and travel most of the night for a surprise visit with me, placing himself temporarily on "absent without leave" status.

When we arrived back in Fort Myers after all our traveling and our many adventures in Europe, we were ready for a well-deserved rest. We were anxious to try to put our lives back together, as well. I took a job for a short while with an oil-drilling company testing for wells in Florida. They were hoping to "strike it rich." Doug began working with the police force in Fort Myers.

My father, Gus, better known as J. A. Hendry, had worked as a special investigator for the government at Buckingham Air Force Base all during the war. Later on, he also investigated for the Venice [Florida] Air Base. While working in Venice, he met Jim Hall, a civilian, working as a bookkeeper for the Venice Air Base. Jim was a Southerner, like us. He was single, personable, and very friendly. He made a good appearance with his suntan, brown eyes, and black hair speckled with about three percent white. He was to become one of the characters in my story.

The first character, of course, was my father. He was a great promoter and a "good storyteller." He was a people-person and well liked. His stories of his hunting excursions for geese and wild turkeys were legendary. He delighted in entertaining numerous adults and children over the years.

Our third character was First Lt. Del Grover, a pilot. My father had met him in his investigative capacity. He was twenty-six years old, blonde, with a mustache, slender, and single.

The fourth and fifth characters were Doug, my brother, and I. Both of us were creative in different ways. I was artistic and a problem solver. Doug was very innovative and resourceful. He was also mechanically minded and easy to get along with.

One day while chatting with Doug and me, Dad told us that he had read an article about shark fishing. The article stated that shark livers were a good source of vitamin A. He had also heard that the Borden Milk Company used shark livers as a source for their vitamin A, which was used to fortify their milk. The article's information about sharks interested us all, especially the things we did not know about sharks. We learned that hammerhead sharks had the most potent livers. Potency could be determined by the dark color of the liver. We had no idea that one third of the shark's weight is determined by the size of its liver and that two thirds of their liver is oil.

After investigating the chances of success in the shark hunting business he thought it might be a good thing for us to do.

Both Doug and I were ready by now to jump into another adventure. My father said that he had two friends in Venice, Florida, who were interested in investing money into such an enterprise.

I had saved about $1,200 during the war years and was willing to invest. It was decided that we could start the company for approximately $10,000. Then after it got going, we could make enough money to keep it going and expand it.

At that point we called our first board of directors' meeting. We met in the living room of my parents' home on Fowler Street. All five participants were present.

We decided to name our new venture of shark fishing "The Eureka Products Company." Our products were to be Vitamin A from shark livers, shark fins for Chinese soup, and shark meat for cat and dog food.

Our next step was to incorporate. A lawyer drew up the agreement for the stockholders. He also took care of the other legal details involved. We decided to issue ten shares of stock. Each would be worth $1,000.

Since Dad was founder and president, he was to receive two shares. Doug and I would each hold one share. Because Tim Hall was secretary and treasurer, he would receive two shares. Del Grover, our vice-president, was to receive four shares. He became our largest stockholder because he had more money to invest.

After completing our incorporation, at our next meeting we decided to purchase a used shrimp boat located in Biloxi, Mississippi. When it was purchased, our ship captain could take it down the coast to Bokeelia, which was on the tip of Big Pine Island. This site was to be the headquarters for our company.

We also decided that it was better to postpone buying a boat or selecting a captain until other more pressing concerns were addressed. The most important of these was to investigate how we were going to actually do the fishing, what equipment was needed, where it could be purchased, and the amount of money involved.

I was dispatched to the Borden Milk Company operation in West Palm Beach, Florida. I was to do the groundwork and find out what was needed for our planned operation. I was amazed at all that I had to learn, the planning I had to do, and the various skills and operations that had to be considered.

I observed carefully all the equipment that would be needed. Some could be purchased while others would have to be made. I also made extensive sketches with detailed notes, and made an accurate measurement of machinery that we might want to build ourselves. Finally, I was ready to report to the stockholders and present them with the details for discussion and/or approval.

The things needed for the operation were as follows: Several miles of 3/1611 galvanized chain, possibly more for drop lines;

snaps, swivels, large hooks, fifty-five gallon barrels or drums, and harpoon equipment. In addition to the boat, a pier or dock, we needed a processing plant and its required equipment with things like a boiler, a pressure cooker, and holding tanks.

I was appointed to go to a machine shop and give them an order to build us a cooker that would hold about one hundred fifty gallons of chopped liver and liquid. After a price was agreed upon, the machine shop began turning steel sheeting into making our cooker. This cooker had to have special equipment to do what was needed. It also needed a series of paddles that ran down to the center of the cooker that agitated or thoroughly mixed the caustic soda with the liver as it heated. It needed heat controls so that it could heat slowly as it was being mixed and sturdy enough to run for an hour or more at a time. The mixture would be pumped into settling tanks, where it could be cooled so that the oil would separate and rise to the surface from which it could be drained. The oil could then be skimmed off the top and placed into clean fifty-five gallon drums for shipment.

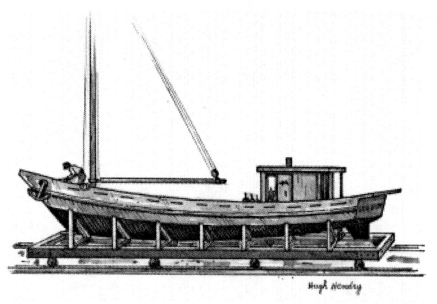

Ocean Queen *at Hansons'*
Boat Ways for a retrofit.
Hubert "Hugh" Hendry, artist.

They were able to construct this cooker within a week's time using my sketches and written instructions.

We placed the cooker, a used boiler, and a meat grinder we purchased into storage.

By again using my sketches and the noted dimensions, Doug and I built a set of settling tanks for separating the liver slurry from the oil. These were also stored along with the boiler, cooker, and meat grinder.

It was now time to think about selecting a captain for our venture and sending him to Biloxi to purchase a used shrimp boat.

Captain Nick Armeda was an old, crusty, gray-haired man who had been a captain on numerous vessels for well over fifty years. He was very good at navigating as well as everything else he did. (As a lad he worked as a deck hand on the ship that Edison sailed on when he came to Fort Myers. He also interested Edison in seeing the cable office that had opened there in 1867.) After being selected, he and Del Grover, our vice president, went to Biloxi to purchase the boat for $4,000.

After looking at boats for a couple of days, they decided on an old seaworthy two-masted schooner, registered under the name of *Ocean Queen*. The craft was seventy feet long, eighteen feet wide, and had a pilothouse near the rear. It had an auxiliary eighty-one horsepower Minneapolis Moline semi-diesel engine under the deck at the rear of the pilothouse. The engine was in good condition. It started with gasoline, but after it was started it could be switched over to diesel fuel.

The *Ocean Queen* had a fantail on the rear, a large winch in front of the pilothouse, and a large hole in the central forward part of the deck. It had a shallow draft of about three and a half feet.

The rear mast pole had been removed for the pilothouse and the forward mast had a large boom swinging from it. This was important for loading and unloading cargo to and from the boat. On the bow, the forward spar had been sawed off since she was no longer under sails. Under the bow, on the port side, hung a rusty two-hundred-pound forward anchor, tied to a large pile of chain that was coiled on the deck.

Captain Armeda and Del Grover piloted the boat from Biloxi, down the Mississippi River southward into the Gulf of Mexico. They turned east toward Florida at the

Ocean Queen *in search of shark bait. Artist, Hubert "Hugh" Hendry.*

mouth of the Caloosahatchee River at Little Sand Island. They proceeded up the Caloosahatchee River, passed Fort Myers, and headed to Hanson's Boat Ways. There the boat was pulled out of the water and thoroughly checked to make sure of its soundness. It passed inspection with flying colors, but it needed to be caulked after the barnacles were scraped off her hull. She was given a complete scrub down, given a fresh coat of copper paint on her bottom up to the water line. Then her hull was painted black and I painted her name on her stern. The pilothouse was painted white, the decks painted green, and on each side of the pilothouse I painted black silhouettes of sharks. When we were done, we let her stay at Hanson's until we could complete our dock and new shark oil rendering plant at Bokeelia, located on the east side of the northern tip of Pine Island.

At that time Bokeelia was a small fishing village. It had a few thousand people, most of whom were fishermen. There was a small store which sold soda pop and general merchandise. The town was considered laid-back.

We needed a place to build a dock and locate our shark plant. The plot of land would have to be on waterfront property where we could build a two-hundred-foot or longer dock that would extend out to deep water. Our plant would be at the end of the pier.

It occurred to us that we might offer a property owner a deal to let us build on his land with the understanding that he could keep all improvements made when we left or if we went out of business. A property owner agreed and signed the necessary papers. He also agreed to let us berth our boat at the foot of the dock in the deep water, about six or seven feet deep. This would be plenty deep for our *Ocean Queen*.

My brother, Doug, and I offered to build the plant and dock. We took the truck Doug had given the corporation for stock and set out for Big Pine Island to cut trees for piling. We sought and found trees of about ten to twelve inches in diameter and at least eight to ten feet long. When the dock extended outward to deeper water, the pilings would have to be longer.

We sank the pilings by using a plumb and pumped the sand from under each piling and then piled the pumped sand back around the pilings when they were secure. This made for a very strong dock and building foundation for our oil rendering plant.

After about a month or two we were at last ready to bring down the *Ocean Queen*, the boiler, pressure cooker, the meat grinder, and the other stored items. Each were swung off the deck by using the winch, and moved into our new building. Now, we had only to bring in electricity and water for our business. That was soon accomplished and we felt like celebrating! Eureka!

The members of our crew included Captain Nick Armeda, stationed in the pilothouse; my brother, Doug, engineer, and in charge of running and taking care of the engine; Dick Hendry, a cousin, was our cook, hired to be in charge of buying rations and cooking for a crew of four; and I made up the fourth crew member. I did all the general work that needed to be done on the boat.

We were lucky to have a large icebox in the forward hold that held 5,000 pounds of ice.

Our boat was well stocked with all the things we needed for our trip out into the sea. Among some these things were gasoline, diesel fuel, batteries, and tools of all kinds and sizes.

We were getting impatient to leave, but we needed to have the fish line ready and operational before we departed. There were about three and a half miles of 3/16" galvanized chain that would become the shark line. Every fifteen feet we snapped a drop chain onto the main chain. These drop lines were about two feet long and they had a snap and a swivel on each end. On the one end was a hook where we planned to place a two-pound chunk of meat.

After all of our long preparation, we finally were ready to go out on our first shark expedition into the Gulf of Mexico. Our plans were to leave from Bokeelia and go through the Boca Grande channel and from there out into the deep water.

The weather was clear with a slight breeze. We could smell the salt air stirring. We had run about four hours out, which placed us about thirty-five to forty miles out in the Gulf of Mexico. The water was blue and deep. Hardly any wind was blowing and the sea was calm.

Ocean Queen *tied up at Bokeelia home port, at northern end of Pine Island. Artist, Hubert "Hugh" Hendry*

For bait I planned to harpoon porpoises as they came in to follow the bow of the boat. Little did we realize at the time what a tremendous waste of intelligent life that was and how I would regret it later on.

I began harpooning around five or six porpoises as planned. In order to harpoon a porpoise weighing about one hundred fifty pounds we used a bronzed dart about six inches long. On one end of the bronzed dart was a sharp curved arrow and on the other was something like a slightly turned up bronze tail feather. Under the tail feather was a hole, where a pole with a long rod was placed. In the center of the bronzed dart was a hole where one end of a fifteen-foot airplane cable was clamped. The other end of the cable was clamped to a ten-gallon wooden keg which we used as a float.

Since I was the one who did the harpooning, I took up my position on the port side of the bow. I am left-handed so at that position, I placed the wooden keg near my left side. I took the pole with the rod in it and placed it in the back end of the dart, then pulled the airline cable up the side of the pole as the porpoise swam along the bow about three feet down under the water. At that time I drove the pole down as hard as I could into the center of the porpoise. When the captain saw me do this, he threw the boat into neutral to stop the propeller blade from turning, so it didn't get caught up or fouled up by the mammal.

After I harpooned the porpoise, I kicked over the ten gallon keg on the other end of the cable. The porpoise sounded or went down into deep water. When he hit the end of the cable, the jolt would turn the dart crosswise inside him. He pulled the keg under water for twenty seconds and then the keg pulled him back to the surface. A porpoise has to come to the surface to breathe and as he did, I took a .22 rifle and finished him off with a well-placed bullet to his head. The float was then retrieved and the porpoise was swung up onto the deck of the boat. I thought they could lay on the deck until we reached twenty to thirty fathoms of water. To determine our depth, we took a sounding of the bottom by throwing over a six-pound cylinder of lead on a long cord with a shallow cup on the heavy end. In this cup, clay was pressed. Whatever was on bottom stuck to the clay as we pulled it back up. We were looking for rocks. Fish and sharks like to live in the areas we call "salt and pepper bottom.

After about five or six of these mammals were on the deck, we thought we had enough bait for our three-mile shark fishing line.

Before butchering the porpoises strewn about the deck, Captain Nick moved the boat several hundred yards away from the rocky bottom. We cut them all into two-pound chunks and hooked each chunk onto separate drop chains. After the porpoises were butchered, the crew washed all of the blood over the side of the boat to attract the sharks.

When all the hooks were baited, we dropped one of the two anchors that was on one end of the three-mile chain. The captain set a straight course at about two miles an hour. We ran out about a hundred feet of chain and snapped on a fifty-five gallon steel barrel for a buoy. A white flag was placed on top of it so that we could find it the next morning when taking up the line. The main chain went over a roller on the side of the boat and a crewman snapped on a drop chain with a large hook and a two-pound chunk of meat.

It took us about an hour to snap on the drop chains. After that we snapped on a second steel drum for a surface buoy. Then we released another hundred feet and snapped on another large anchor. Finally all three miles of chain was out and most of it was sitting on the bottom of the Gulf of Mexico.

Once the line was out, the captain started the engine and we headed back toward the rock bottom that we had found a few hours before.

We dropped anchor and then began fishing with long hand lines for grouper and red snapper. The hand lines were about one hundred fifty feet long and made of heavy brown cord. On the end was a six-pound lead weight. Above that were two drop lines about one and a half feet long attached to the main line. We baited each hook. Sometimes we pulled in two fish at a time, one on each hook. The average weight of the grouper or red snapper was ten to fifteen pounds.

When fish are pulled up from such depths, they swell up and their eyes pop out.

After only a few hours of fishing, we caught at least 500 pounds. All of these were put in our large icebox and iced down.

We planned to stay out in the Gulf for an entire week each time and hoped to fill the icebox before we returned. As we fished, Dick Hendry, our cook, prepared our meals. When it was time to chow down, we stopped fishing and ate after cleaning up.

One of seventy-five sharks caught each day by crew of the Ocean Queen. *Pen-and-ink drawing by Hubert "Hugh" Hendry*

Sometimes we had fish chowder or red snapper to eat. The food always tasted wonderful out on the boat, with the water lapping along the sides. At five or thereabout in the afternoon, we took up anchor and headed back to the far buoy on our shark line. Upon reaching the buoy, we tied up until the next morning.

After working all day, we looked forward for evening to come. We talked and told stories until around eight o'clock. By this time, everyone was tired and wanted to turn in early.

The ship had sleeping accommodations for only four people. There were three bunks, one in the pilothouse for the captain and two in the engine room on each side of the engine. Doug and I slept there. Dick preferred to sleep on a sleeping bag on deck out under the stars. Stars are always more brilliant when fifty miles away from the city lights. The fresh smell of salt in the air and the gentle rock of the boat put everyone in a restful mood in a few minutes.

There was much excitement and anticipation that first night! All wondered what we might catch the next day on our shark line.

Morning came almost too soon and too early. It was a little after daybreak when we heard the cook rattling pans and soon we smelled coffee boiling, followed by bacon and eggs.

We all began to stir, washed our faces, got dressed, and did our morning chores. After breakfast and coffee, the time had finally come to take up the shark line. Just what would we catch? It's hard to describe our excitement, but we couldn't have been more excited had we been children!

The captain entered the pilothouse and started up the engine. My brother, Doug, assisted. In front of the pilothouse, there was a large winch with levers on it. There was one lever to start it turning and another lever to use as a brake. Each served a purpose, one to stop the turning and the other to lock it in position. Two more levers were near the winch. They operated the boom from the front mast pole. This enabled the operator to pick up a large load from one side of the boat and swing it on board the boat or to the other side as might be needed.

Doug operated the winch while I went up on port side of the bow to see what was coming up from the depths. I took up my position on the port bow and signaled Doug to start pulling up the anchor on the shark line. After the anchor was up and the large buoy was on board, the end of our main chain was placed over the roller on the port front of the *Ocean Queen.* The other end was placed over the chain puller on the end of the winch.

At my signal, with the boat running, the winch engaged and pulling on the links of chain, the boat started to slowly move forward. As the drop chains came up, the brake was set on the winch as each drop chain was unsnapped and laid to one side.

After about four or five empty hooks had passed, I could at last see a large white object down about thirty feet down coming to the surface. It was our first shark—a tiger shark around eight feet long. When its head came out of the water, I signaled to Doug to set the brake on the winch while a deckhand swung the large boom over to my side. The boom had a cable from the winch that ran through a series of pulleys from the mast to the boom. On the boom, we had a large gap hook made from a crow bar. This was placed in the open mouth of the shark. Then the drop chain was unsnapped. When signaled, Doug engaged the winch to lift the shark and swing it over to the starboard side of our boat and down on the deck.

Many of the sharks were dead from drowning when we pulled them up, but some were alive. In size they varied from six feet up to fourteen feet depending upon the type of shark they were. We saw dusky sharks, blacktip sharks, hammerheads, and tiger sharks to name a few.

After the first shark was aboard, we kept pulling them in until we reached the buoy on the other end of our three-mile long chain. We caught seventy-five sharks that first day, and usually averaged seventy-five each day thereafter. They covered the entire deck of the boat.

After taking up buoy and chain, we started cutting off the shark fins. We placed them in a salt brine solution to remain overnight, to remove the fishy smell. When morning came we removed them from the brine and hung them up on a line to dry in the sun. They were allowed to dry for a couple of days before we packed them down in burlap bags. They were then stored in the hold until they were sold for Chinese soup.

After the shark fins were cut off, the crew split the sharks open and took out their livers. They were placed in fifty-five gallon steel barrels. As each liver was placed in the barrel, a couple of handfuls of rock salt were thrown in to preserve it. When a barrel was full, a lid and ring latch was snapped into place, sealing it up tight before they were dropped into the hold of the *Ocean Queen.*

All of the rest of the shark meat, hides, and everything else was thrown overboard. Nowadays, the meat is sold all over the world to restaurants. We never did get around to marketing it for cat and dog food.

After the day's catch was taken care of, we sat down to lunch and talked about how things went. When lunch was over, Captain Nick plotted a new course on his charts and we were under way soon looking for more porpoises for bait.

This procedure was repeated every day for one week at a time or until the vessel was loaded down. Then we headed for Bokeelia to unload the cargo of shark livers, shark fins, and fish.

While in port, the shark livers were processed for their vitamin A oil. The first thing in preparing shark livers, after firing up the boiler, was to cut the shark liver into small pieces and run them through the grinder. We also added about six pounds of caustic soda to the livers to help break them down during the cooking process. Our pressure cooker would stir the mixture for about an hour under a slow boil. We had designed into it a reduction gear to slow down the agitation in order to accelerate and to assist in the oil separation. When an hour of heated agitation and mixing was completed, the mixture was pumped into settling tanks and allowed to cool. It was cooled overnight to allow the oil to rise to the surface. The oil could then be drawn off the top and stored in fifty-five-gallon drums for shipment.

When all the oil was extracted, it was shipped to our Chicago customers in the fifty-five-gallon drums. The Chinese buyers came to pick up their dried shark fins. We could now relax.

During this time, new supplies and provisions were being obtained for our next trip out.

While we were waiting to make our second trip, an exciting event happened. We spotted a large two-hundred-pound jewfish underneath two of the dock pilings. I hurried to the boat and took out the harpoon and tied the airplane cable to the dock. Then I removed one of the top boards on the dock and harpooned him. He wrapped the cable around the piling and shook the entire pier. Finally, we borrowed a small boat and went under the pier after him with ice tongs. This enabled us to pull him into the boat.

We threw him in the icebox, iced him down, and cut him up for shark bait a couple of days later.

Our next trip out was pretty routine, but we did have one eventful night that I remember well. We had just baited our hooks and let out the long line. Doug noted that I had harpooned two porpoises that we hadn't used. Rather than throw them overboard along with the bloody parts that we usually disposed of, we decided to put hooks alongside their carcasses every foot of their length. These hooks were all snapped to a main chain which dropped down about a hundred feet and the other end of the chain we tied to the main railing. Had we thought about it, we would have put a buoy on the surface of the water and tied it to the boat, rather than tying chain to the main railing. We then went about our usual business, and went on to bed.

About 1:00 A.M. we were awakened by a sawing noise; it came from the main railing. We all jumped out of bed and ran to the railing and looked down into the water. We could see two large sharks, each around ten feet long. They were connected to individual hooks and to the main chain which was secured to the main railing. We could see them in the dark because of the phosphorus content in the water. Whenever there is phosphorous in the water in the tropics every moving thing gives off a sparkling effect. It really was quite beautiful! After churning about and around for twenty minutes the two sharks pulled together and broke the chain. If we had used a buoy, there would have been more give, acting like a shock absorber.

Our next trip out was again routine, but before we could even put out our line, the barometer started falling fast and the wind began to blow around thirty to forty miles an hour. Captain Nick had us batten down the hatches and tie down all the loose barrels on deck. He slowed down the *Ocean Queen* and headed it into the wind. This is the way we rode out the storm. All the waves were blown down flat during the height of the storm and there were only streaks of foam on the surface.

When the storm died down, so did our engine. The battery went dead and we couldn't get it started. We were about fifty miles out in the Gulf of Mexico. Doug tried and tried to get it going. In desperation, he had an idea. He decided to take off the clutch plate which was on the back side of the engine, then asked me to get him a long iron bar. He was trying to reach back inside the engine, bypass the solenoid, and rotate the wheel by hand. It started turning and then began to spin. Once going, the battery would recharge and the engine was revived. It worked and soon we were on our way.

Usually our trips out had varying degrees of excitement, but I can say that each trip in itself was a different story. Sometimes we found weird things inside the stomachs of sharks like parts of chickens and their crates, heads of large sharks that had been bitten off and swallowed by another shark, and once we even found a white surgical glove.

On one of our last trips out, when our long line was out, Captain Nick rose early. He wanted to have red snapper for breakfast. He baited the two hooks above the six-pound lead weight at the lower end of a hundred-foot cord. Taking hold of the cord above the hooks, he swung it around his head before throwing it in the water. When he turned it loose, the top hook swung around and hooked him in the back of his right hand. His reflex action pulled him back, and propelled the six-pound lead weight to strike him on the head. One of the crew rushed over to him. Captain Nick was conscious, but stunned. He held up his injured hand. Dick paused for a minute or two trying to figure out what to do. I arrived at that time and made the decision. It seemed to me that it would be best to cut the skin with a razor blade and pull out the hook from the top of his hand. I did this after disinfecting it with iodine.

Because of Captain Nick's advanced age, somewhere in the upper eighties, I decided we should cut the trip short and get him to a doctor. This was to be his last trip out. He retired after this incident, but he had served the Eureka Products Company very well as long as he was able.

After a short search we located a forty-five-year-old replacement named King Gomaz. He was familiar with larger boats like ours and was also an experienced fisherman. He did a good job and everything went well for quite a while.

After five or six years, the company and our attitude toward it changed. It was hard work and we, the stockholders, were tired of the steady grind; so we decided to take a vacation. We hired a crew to do the work so the operation would continue as usual. As the crew was leaving Fort Myers and were heading toward the mouth of the Caloosahatchee River, bad weather hit. The captain decided to lay over and come to anchor until the weather was better. As near as we could determine, some of the crew went ashore and came back with liquor and beer. This was against all of our rules and the captain should not have allowed them to have alcohol on board.

What happened next, we don't know. We later heard that there was a fight. Then the boat caught fire and burned to the water's edge. All of the crew abandoned the ship and swam ashore. We first heard about it when reading the *Fort Myers News-Press* the following day.

That was the end of the Eureka Products Company. Even though we hadn't made much money, we were all enriched by our experience.

Harold Hudson—Marine Scientist

Written by Charles Hudson, and edited by his cousin, Ella Kathryn Hendry.

Ella Kathryn Hendry's note: The later generations of the Hendry family included a nationally recognized marine scientist, Harold Hudson. Because of his connections to Southwest Florida and research in the Florida Keys, this story about Harold, by his brother, Charles, is included.

I remember when I first heard about the birth of Harold. Captiva Island, where we were vacationing in June of 1935, was hot and steamy. The mail boat slowly docked while my father waited, sweating profusely, under an open shed for our daily mail delivery and grocery order. In the mail was a letter from our aunt in Washington D.C., informing us that we had a new cousin named James Harold Hudson, who was to become known by his middle name.

It wasn't until several years later that we had our first meeting. I looked at the little fellow whose hair was a deep auburn brown and whose head seemed to be too big for his little body. I thought that he had to be very smart to have such a big head. Surely such a big head had to be full of brains! As it turned out, he had more than his share of gray matter and used it to good advantage.

* * *

My earliest and most lasting memory dates back to the summer of 1936 when we lived in Washington, D.C. At that time, Daddy was working at the Ambassador Hotel. The family lived in a second-story apartment. It had a set of concrete steps leading up from the ground level in the front to a small landing at the apartment entrance.

One afternoon as I was playing with my wagon in the front yard, Mama called me to come up for supper. When I came inside, she asked me where my wagon was. I told her it was still down in the front yard. She said, "Go bring it up and put it away."

I immediately went out the door, hurrying down the steps. Harold, who had been crawling on the floor, followed me out the door and on to the landing. I pulled my wagon up the steps and at the same time, Harold fell through the railing to the concrete walk below.

Mama dashed out the door, picked him up, and rushed him to the hospital. He suffered a fractured skull and had severe bruises, but thankfully he survived a near fatal fall. As a result of the fall, he stuttered until he was in his late teens.

As I look back on this traumatic event, I can now see why he was pampered. It wasn't until I was much older that I was able to realize why he had been so favored and why I had to do a disproportional share of the chores. Eventually we returned to Fort Myers where we grew up in a subtropical country setting.

We both liked to fish and we often stalked Demps Branch, which joined Yellowfever Creek just below our old home place on Barrett Road in North Fort Myers. Harold would cast his Dalton Special lure for lunker bass. Somewhere there is a picture of him, barefoot in old jeans holding his black line rod and reel, showing off the three big bass he caught in Demps Branch. The largest fish was just over eight pounds and by far the largest bass any of us had ever caught or seen.

During these early years, Harold joined the Boy Scouts and excelled in the program. He sought and earned nearly every merit badge in the book, and soon rose in rank to Eagle Scout in record time. He went on to become assistant scoutmaster. In this position, he turned his talents to teaching the troop. I'm sure that if Troop No. 18 is still in existence and old records are intact, Harold's achievements would fill a significant section.

In the late forties, the face mask for swimmers came into vogue. The masks that we could afford worked but leaked around the rim. They also left a red ring around our faces. Harold spent more time under water than most and as a consequence he always had a red ring around his face.

He was fascinated by the beauty of the underwater scenes in the creeks and the Caloosahatchee River. He would spend hours searching the bottom of the river for never-ending revelations of the world below the surface. Needless to say, I don't think he ever picked up a fishing pole again from the first day he put on his mask. That didn't mean he didn't fish, he just changed his method of catching the big ones.

Being as creative as he was, he cut some rubber bands from an old tire tube and bound them to the end of a twelve-inch bamboo section. It had a welding rod inside it a quarter of an inch thick tied in a .45 cal. pistol casing. The casing formed a socket for the rod to rest in when it was inserted through the bamboo. The end of the rod was pounded to form a sharp-pointed spear head. Harold didn't know it at the time, but he had reinvented the Hawaiian sling!

Armed with his simple but effective underwater slingshot, Harold speared snook, red fish, mullet, and sheephead. They all fell prey to his deadly aim. Well, not all, for he took only what the family could use. He never speared any that were too small to eat.

Whenever we went on a family cookout on Pine Island and the fish were biting, Harold geared up and dove into the water with his mask and harpoon. He swam under the dock around the pilings until he found a big red fish or snook for Mama to fry. At times this created a problem, though, because when we were ready to leave, Harold was nowhere to be seen. So there we sat, with everything packed up and ready to go home. Someone would either have to go in after him or we would just have to wait for him to surface!

I know some airplane pilots who have logged 20,000 hours in the air. I am sure that Harold has logged double that under the surface of waters around the world in the nearly fifty years he has spent at it. He has enjoyed every minute of his professional life doing what gave him the most pleasure in the world.

One of his achievements came during his Navy days at Swimmers School in Key West during the early fifties. The Key West Navy base had a swim meet of which one event was an underwater swim for maximum distance in a pool, while wearing only a mask and no flippers.

Harold remained under water for so long the instructors became worried and dove in and made him surface. They feared he was in danger of lapsing into unconsciousness. He swam eighty-five yards. The record still stands. I dare say that the record might have been even higher had he been allowed to remain under water for a longer period of time!

After attending and graduating from the Fort Myers High School, Harold enlisted in the Navy. When his hitch in the Navy was over, he attended the University of Miami where he graduated with a bachelor of science degree. He then went on to distinguish himself in the field of coral reef research, pioneering the transplanting of coral in Florida and restoring many reef areas in the Florida Keys. His work on coral growth rates has taken him to reefs around the world.

Harold's picture illustrated the April 1978 *National Geographic* magazine article, "Man's New Frontier—The Continental Shelf," subtitled "Core Sampling for Clues to Climate."

> Unlocking the planet's archives, long cores drilled by the U.S. Geological Survey on the shelf off Florida . . . reveal Ice Age records in the underlying rocks. When the massive glaciation lowered the level of the sea, the limestone bottom was laid bare to weathering that testifies to such long-ago events.

> Cores taken from coral heads in the Florida Keys show growth bands . . . similar to tree rings. These reflect the reef-building polyps' reactions to seasonal variations.

> A ten-foot sample from the heart of a living coral head alongside a broader X-ray photograph of the core ... shows weather variations in the keys from 1620 to the mid-1970s. Colder-than-average winters appear as darker bands on the photograph. They prove that intensive reef deaths in 1969-70 were caused by severe cold—not, as had been suspected, by pollution.

Harold pioneered the technique of core drilling as a tool to study coral growth rates. As a consequence, Harold's work has also been the subject of national TV shows, most notably ABC news and the program "Reading Rainbow," to name a few.

Even though Harold's work has been highly recognized, he is a very modest person, who tells little about himself. I found out about his achievements as follows: Mama had the *National Geographic* article framed and placed on the wall alongside of the underwater scenes he had painted for her. By luck, I saw parts of two television shows about him, and managed to tape half of one.

In the August 1993 issue of *Power and Motoryacht* magazine, there appeared this article titled "The Reef Doctor," written by Amy Rapaport. The subtitle was "Underwater housecalls are just a day in the life of Harold Hudson."

> Harold Hudson is not one of those stereotypical mad scientists with horn-rimmed glasses and a pocket projector who spends hour after hour in his lab mixing combustible solutions, scrambling DNA coding, or dissecting infinitesimally small organisms under an electron microscope. Nor is he a glory-seeking public figure who traverses the country giving interviews and accepting awards. He's just an ordinary guy—except that he's had an ongoing love affair with coral reefs for more than 20 years.

> Hudson is a regional biologist for the Florida Keys Natural Marine Sanctuary in Key Largo, Florida, where he conducts reef restoration projects and makes damage assessments of injured reefs. So instead of the usual lab coat and safety glasses, Hudson's normal attire is a mask, a snorkel, and SCUBA gear.

Hudson began his career as a fishery biologist in 1964 in Florida where he studied young pink shrimp and calico scallops in Florida Bay. In 1977, he moved on to the U.S. Geological Survey (an organization within the Department of the Interior), where he studied the growth rates of reef corals and sediment-producing marine algae and examined the geologic history of coral reef growth.

While working with the Geologic Survey, Hudson did his first damage-and-restoration work on Molasses Reef in Key Largo, which had been injured in a major ship grounding. He transplanted a good portion of the damaged coral, and fortunately most of the reef survived. This, Hudson says, prepared him for his present work with the National Marine Sanctuary.

Hudson mostly works solo, and likes it that way. "Everything I do is out in the field where the corals grow. I'd much rather spend the day snorkeling over a reef, surveying its progress, than examining a dead chunk of it in my lab." Even so, he needs someone to help him with day-to-day functions; that's where Darlene Finch, a program specialist in Washington D. C., comes in. "Because of Darlene," Hudson says, "I am able to do all the work I do."

Reef Resuscitation

These days, coral reefs are a hot topic, and for good reason—they're disappearing. That's of concern since reefs are not only beautiful, they provide food and shelter to thousands of marine creatures that are crucial to the food chain.

Reef-building corals inhabit a limited range worldwide. In fact, the Florida Keys are blessed with the only true reefs in the continental waters of the United States, stretching from the Dry Tortugas to North Key Largo. This reef tract contains more than 50 species of corals and more than 150 species of tropical fish. And Hudson is trying to keep it that way.

There are two types of coral: hard coral, like staghorn and head coral (round) coral; and soft coral, like sea fans and sea whips. Regardless of the type, you should never touch, stand on, or take living coral, since even human contact can mean disaster. Nor should you anchor on a coral reef. Instead, tie up to a mooring buoy.

What you may not know, however, is that oil and bilge discharges damage reefs as do fertilizers, pesticides, and, other wastes, which introduce nutrients that erode coral. Even though people have become more aware of the damage they can inflict on a reef, destruction continues.

Two major threats plague coral: breakage and natural disease. Hudson treats both.

Man, storms, and nutrients cause coral to fracture. A fractured piece of coral is like a severed limb; it eventually dies. Yet it is possible to upright overturned or broken coral, re-cement it to the reef, and have it survive—Hudson calls this process "transplanting." In theory, the procedure is simple: Take the piece of broken coral, swathe it in cement, and attach it to the reef. "You've got to know precisely what you are doing," Hudson warns, "or you could do more damage than good. Especially since all this is taking place underwater." You can't just leave the coral and assume it will heal. Just as a physician does with his patient, Hudson must watch the coral, examine it, and make sure it has stabilized so it will survive.

The cement is a special mixture of lime-based Portland Type II cement (like the type used in sea walls and docks) and molding plaster, combined with just enough water to make a putty-like consistency. The cement must be applied to the coral fractures immediately, as it hardens in three to six minutes after mixing. Hudson says that the survival rate for this coral-equivalent of a skin-graft is 90 percent for hard corals and 60 percent for the more fragile soft corals.

The Black Band

One natural malady that affects coral is Black Band disease. It only affects head coral, which ironically suffers the least from all other threats. The organism that causes the disease enters the coral at preexisting blemishes, like those caused by feather-duster worms. The organism eats away at this blemish in a ring pattern — hence the name "Black Band." Since the organism eats from the center out, it leaves a stark white skeleton of decomposed coral tissue in its wake, eventually killing the entire coral. The result is often massive damage to coral.

If caught in its early stages, Black Band disease is treatable. Hudson developed a technique using a "natural aspirator" that literally vacuums up the disease. Once the process is finished, Hudson uses modeling clay to seal up the lesions the organism left in the raw tissue. "The modeling clay acts like a Band Aid," he says. "It seals up the wound and prevents reinfection from the disease." Treatment is 70 percent effective—a rate not as high as Hudson would like. Since the disease filaments are microscopic it's impossible for the aspirator to always get every speck of it.

All the restoration costs money, and you'd think Hudson and his fellow biologists need a great deal of it. Not so. According to Hudson, there's enough money from fines against boatmen who have damaged the reefs to finance the entire restoration project. "We do have adequate resources to fund this program, which is both good and bad. On the one hand we have the money, but on the other, it's from those who damage the reefs." For Hudson, all his efforts to heal the reefs are well worth it. He has saved a lot of coral in the four years he's been with the Sanctuary, but the war is far from over. Damage is being done to coral reefs every day, and much of it is irreversible. Yet as long as Harold Hudson—a.k.a. The Reef Doctor—is on call, there's hope.

["The Reef Doctor" is quoted by permission.]

Appendix A: Indians
Billy Cornapatchee

Historian Sara Nell Gran provided the information below in a brochure titled *1975 Captain Francis Asbury Hendry Reunion*. It is reproduced with her permission.

In 1878 several Indian canoes stopped at the residence of Capt. F. A. Hendry on the banks of the Caloosahatchee in Fort Myers, located approximately at the site of the present municipal yacht basin. The party of Indians remained for several days. Among the party was a very bright, young Indian lad named Billy Cornapatchee (or Billy Corn Patch).

Captain Hendry had long been skeptical of the commonly held theory of the day that an Indian did not have the capacity to read and write. Captain Hendry was a firm believer in education.

He had recently employed a tutor from Virginia to live in the settlement, and conduct classes for his children and other children in the small settlement. In 1878 the "academy" was scheduled to open.

The thought intrigued Captain Hendry that here was an Indian lad who could be educated, and bring to his people the benefits of a formal education.

He discussed the matter with the Indians, and they, at that time agreed to permit Billy to remain in Fort Myers with Captain Hendry and attend classes.

Billy Cornapatchee remained in Fort Myers as a guest in the Hendry home for three years, and attended classes with great diligence.

In 1879 this experiment in Seminole education reached the attention of Captain Richard Henry Pratt, founder of the Carlisle Indian Industrial School, Carlisle, Pennsylvania, and one of the significant figures in the history of Indian education.

In August 1879, Captain Hendry wrote to Pratt informing him of the first breakthrough in getting a Seminole into school, as follows:

Fort Myers, August 10, 1879

Dear Capt. Pratt:

Your esteemed favor of 22 July to hand, glad to hear of your safe arrival home.

I am pleased to acknowledge the receipt of the Indian Comm. report. I read it with interest. I am happy to state that little Billy Conapacho [sic] is now stopping with me and going to school, our school having commenced since your departure.

Mrs. Hendry having surrendered the point and is quite willing to have him as her guest. He has clothed himself in a decent suit of civilized clothing and looks nicely. I hope to keep him, although I am sure he must take his wild Indian Rambles, he learns fast and attends promptly, not missing an hour.

There are no records of his schoolwork, these having been lost when the school burned in 1886.

An article in the *Fort Myers Press*, however, relates:

He is an exceptional Indian, having, through the benevolent action of Captain Hendry, received a fair common school education in Fort Myers. (See Educating the Seminole Indians of Florida, 1879-1970 by Harry A. Kersey, Jr. of Florida Atlantic University.)

Following is the story of Billy Corn Patch as reported by D. B. McKay in the *Tampa Tribune*, August 30, 1959, which quotes from an article by Albert DeVane of Lake Placid, Florida:

Billy Corn Patch (Co-nip-ha-chee Hadjo) was born on the headwaters of Fisheating Creek about 1856. He was of the Wind Clan, the son of Allapatta Hadjo (Alligator Clan); his mother was of the Wind Clan.

The Wind Clan among the Seminoles and Creeks has had the distinction of being the police clan (or family of firsts or aristocrats) of the nations for the last 200 years.

Corn Patch had two brothers, Billy Fewell (Hadjo) and Miami Billy (Co-nip-yaa-hali Hadjo). The three brothers were great leaders among their people, also friends of the white man. He had one sister who married Cypress Tom Tiger, the last overall chief of the Seminoles, who was killed at Bluefield in 1890. Through her descendants, the Wind Clan is perpetuated to this day among the Seminoles, [reported McKay].

While Corn Patch was attending school with the Hendry children, his education came very near causing very serious trouble between the Indians and Captain Hendry. The Indians did not want him to go to school and learn the white man's ways. A council was held among them about 1878, and a messenger was delegated to go to Captain Hendry, telling him the Seminoles wanted him to go home to his people; also if he did not let the boy go, or send him home, that they would take him by force; also as a threat to him, stated that they had rather see him dead than educated in the white man's ways.

Captain Hendry told the messenger that it was entirely up to the boy, that if he wanted to go home with them it would be okay with him but if the boy wished to stay in his home and go to school with his children he could do that.

The boy was asked and he stated that he wanted to stay with Captain Hendry and go to school. The messenger stated, "We are going to take him anyway." Captain Hendry stated, "When you come to take him against his will, that means another war. Me and my friends will kill the first Indian that lays a hand on him to take him away."

Things rocked along for two or three years. Chief Chipco and Tiger Tail went to the lighthouse keeper, telling him they wanted to write a paper to Tallahassee, that they wanted the boy home. He wrote Secretary Bloxham, his reply is in the State Archives at Tallahassee.

Billy Corn Patch went back to his people in the Big Cypress to plead his case before the Council. Some wanted to ban him from the Nation; some wanted to kill him. One of the oldest counselors pled his defense stating "some day we may need him and his education."

At the end of the Council, they decided to let him live among them, on the condition he would not teach his children or anyone else to read and write. This he agreed to do.

DeVane said that through arrangements made by Capt. F. A. Hendry, Corn Patch was the interpreter for Dr. Clay McCaulay when he made his report on the Seminoles to the Secretary of Indian Affairs in 1880.

* * *

Billy Corn Patch returned to his people and married Nancy Osceola (Ell-A-Pat-ee), no relation to the war chief Osceola. She was called "Little Nancy" by the whites. They had three boys and three girls; a son Ingraham Billy who took his name from J. E. Ingraham and is now chief medicine man of the Cypress Trail Indians; another son Josie Billy, a former medicine man, now a very prominent Baptist preacher and medicine doctor; another son Charlie who died a young man. The daughters were Camella, Effie, and Mollie.

He was devoted to Captain Hendry and when he heard that the Captain was dying, he and his brother, Billy Fewell, walked sixty miles from deep in the Glades to see him.

Billy Corn Patch died at the old government road corduroy pole crossing of the Ok-Hol-Ou-Coo-chee, or Col-laway-choo-chee slough (meaning boggy water) east of Immokalee, while on his return home from Fort Myers with his cousin, Dr. John.

He was buried in a log pen about one-half mile south of the crossing in a hammock. He was 70 years of age.

McKay's article quotes DeVane as the source of the following:

Josie Billy (Cocha-No-Gof-Dee) was born in 1885, in Big Cypress, a few miles from the present Big Cypress Reservation.

Josie grew up, and, like his father, he wanted to learn to read and write, but his father had told him to not learn to read and write, as the Indians would kill him and "me, too."

Bill Brown established a trading post at the old boat landing on the edge of the Everglades, exchanging alligator, deer and otter hides for merchandise. Josie became a firm friend of Mr. Brown. Once, Mr. Brown gave him a piece of a lead pencil. He carried it home and was printing figures and letters from an old newspaper. Josie's father saw him, taking the pencil away from him, again telling him he must not learn to read and write, as the Indians will kill both of us.

Josie began to figure out some other way. It is said, Necessity is the mother of inventions so Josie had to figure out a new invention. While strolling along the Everglades, whittling on a stick, he stopped by an elderberry bush in full fruit. He picked off a bunch to examine them, sticking his sharp stick into the berry, and out came the black juice. Like all boys, his pockets were filled with junk, including a piece of paper, and he began to write from his new found pen and ink. He kept his secret. The elderberry bushes became his school house and in this way he pursued his self-education.

Josie trained for four years with the old medicine man to later become a medicine man. In fact, he later became the chief medicine man of the Mikasukies which also carries with it the knowledge he learned of plants, herbs, roots, etc., used in preparation of their medicine to heal the sick. During the heyday of administering as Chief Medicine Man and Herb Doctor, he became a Christian, giving up his title as Medicine Man and going to the Green Corn Dances.

To further pursue his education, he went two years to the Moody Bible Institute in Lakeland. Josie became a great preacher and leader among his people.

He is considered one of the best herb doctors among his people, visiting the sick in all three reservations. As Robert Ripley said, "Truth is stranger than fiction." The truth is the Seminoles have had a tranquilizing medicine to treat their mental cases. How long, we do not know, but many, many years. We see no mental cases of Seminoles in our state institutions. In my own observation, I have known of complete recovery.

Josie Billy sold his tranquilizing formula of herb medicine to the Upjohn Pharmaceutical Company for testing and manufacture.

On November 17, 1964, there appeared an article in the *Fort Myers News-Press* titled "Recipe for Tranquilizer Sold by Medicine Man." It said in part:

Josie Billy is the last of generations of medicine men dating back to the beginning of remembered Seminole history. He treats and collects fees from members of the tribe for his own remedies for all kinds of illnesses.

The Upjohn people heard about his tranquilizer and bought it, flying him to laboratories at Kalamazoo, Michigan, to mix 13 herbs from which it is derived.

Upjohn scientists say years of experimentation may be necessary before a tranquilizer can be developed which can be reliable enough to offer for sale. Their objective is to determine which of the combinations of the 13 herbs can be combined for the most satisfactory nerve depressant. So far they haven't announced any conclusions as to which are most effective.

Billy has never been as optimistic as the scientists . . . although willing to go along with the experiments for cash. He warned Upjohn men that he didn't think the medicine would be effective unless accompanied by singing, incantations, and rituals.

He added that he didn't consider it proper for him to teach these songs and spells to the Upjohn men, although it was all right to sell them the herb formula, on their promise to keep it a secret.

Among the other fringe benefits of the sale of the recipe, Billy got a hearing aid and puts it on when visitors come or when he goes calling. This is a young ear for an old man . . . but sometimes better if old man not hear too much, he said.

* * *

My father often met with Josie Billy, named for Captain Hendry's granddaughter, Josephine, and for "Josie Hart" (daughter of Waddy Thompson), when they were young men at Fort Thompson visiting at Captain Hendry's home. They would go behind the barn and smoke rolled rabbit tobacco. After smoking, the two boys would climb up in the hayloft in the barn. My father let Josie read aloud to him and helped him pronounce his words. It was a secret that both young men kept.

Life among the Seminoles

In several chapters I have mentioned the Seminole Indians, whose lives were connected to the Hendry family and other settlers. I thought it important to include information about their lives and contributions before they were pushed into reservations. One of my favorite sources is James Lafayette Glenn's, *My Work Among The Florida Seminoles*. He describes an Indian village in this way:

> Since these people have no saw mills and therefore no lumber they do as our fathers did. They hew their houses out of the forest. The trees here are not oak or pine, but cabbage palms. The circle of huts has been called a village, but in reality it is a single house with eight or more rooms. The walls of the house are six posts which support a palm *thatched* roof, and a floor that is made of half logs. The floor is about two and a half feet above the ground. They do not go into their houses, but either sit about the sides of this floor or lay down upon it. But each hut has its special use in "housing the family."[1]

> [One hut is the pantry.] Although the Seminoles are hunters, they have always relied, in part, on garden and grain products for food. In this hut the family keeps its seed for the next year's planting, its lard, its dried meat, and other household supplies.

> [Another hut] is a sewing room. The women are genuinely feminine in their love of pretty clothes. They design and make the most gorgeous of all human costumes.[2]

It was thought that the design for their unique costumes comes from the Spanish gowns worn by the early Spanish female settlers.

Glenn comments further:

> The dress or shirt is made of many color patterns, each of which is sewed to others in the same manner that our mothers worked out the color schemes of a quilt. In one of their skirts, which I own are eight different colors of cloth, and twelve hundred different pieces. From twelve to eighteen yards of cloth are used in making it. Some of the patterns are no more than one-half inch square. . . .

These garments are made with a small hand-driven sewing machine. The seamstress sits cross-legged on the floor of this hut, with her machine and cloth in front of her, and turns the crank on the heel of the machine with one hand, and guides and feeds the cloth into the machine with the other hand.[3]

The third hut . . . is the dining room. Strangely enough, the dining room floor and the dining room table are one and the same platform. The food in the pots and pans in which it is cooked is placed in the center of the platform and the family members sit on the outer edge of the platform with their feet hanging over the sides to the ground while they eat.

They have a pot of grits at hand, which they call Sofkee, and from which all at the table use a common dipper to drink the semiliquid.[4]

The grits itself is made from corn that is grown in a nearby garden, either by pounding it with mortar and pestle made of cypress, or a white man's hand-powered grist mill, or it may have been bought at the store of some white trader. They also buy flour, corn meal, or loaf bread. They serve biscuits, sweet potatoes, honey, fish, pork, venison, wild turkey, pumpkin, comptee, which is made of a starch-packed root, gopher or land terrapin, turtle, heron, and other water fowl or "swamp cabbage," which is made of the bud of the young cabbage palm.

They are fond of coffee and often times sweeten a single cup with some four teaspoons full of sugar. For all the above mentioned foods, they are poverty stricken and often do not find enough to eat. When any people are really hungry they do not stop to ask if the food meets government regulations for sanitation. The Seminoles may, and often do, eat semi-decayed meat, or other unwholesome food.[5]

In the center of this circle of huts is a thatched roof supported by posts. It has no floor in it. It is the kitchen. Here is the campfire upon which is cooked the food and about which the many cooks in the house gather. . . .

The men in the household often help in cooking the meal. They get water, or put on the coffee, or fry the meat, or adjust the logs of the fire. Of course, there is the same kindly interest between the husband and his wife, or wives, that we know in our own homes.

Besides the rooms already described . . . there are four or five bedrooms . . . In general the family is divided during its sleeping hours as our own are divided, since they sleep with their clothes on, they are less conscious about their bed fellows. . . . It is the law and custom of these people that the bride shall bring home her bridegroom to live in her father's household, or perhaps, we ought to say her mother's household, for it is the mother's name that is not changed in marriage. . . . A new bedroom is built for each new bride and groom. . . .[6]

[Harvey A. Kersey, Jr. notes, "Moreover, children were not stigmatized by illegitimacy or by divorce of the parents, because they stayed within the matrimonial kinship group.

Among the Seminoles this took the form of, camp, comprising several generations' households related in a matrilineal clan.] [7]

It is also a "catchall" house much like our own . . . pots and pans may be piled on it to bask in the sunlight, or products from the garden or field may be thrown here, or a saddle from a horse may rest here.

Back of these huts is the farm plot which the family cultivates. It contains eight or nine acres, and since it is hammock [According to Webster, is a fertile area in the southern U.S. and especially Florida, that is usually higher than its surrounding and that is characterized by hardwood vegetation and deep humus-rich soil] land it will grow corn, sugar cane, sweet potatoes, pumpkins, or other such products. No fertilizer is needed. [8]

Glenn also states that muck, humus-rich soil is twenty feet deep in some parts of the Everglades and that if it catches fire it will burn down until it reaches muck that is wet. When this happens, a heavy covering of smoke hangs over the Everglades. In the past history of the Seminoles, the farming was the task of the women of the household.

Although they work very hard, they have a respected place in the family. Often when the "Men-Folks" are drunk, the women take over the task of keeping order and at times tie up their drunken husbands or brothers with ropes. [9]

It is often thought that these primitive conditions would make living very difficult, but some years ago a man tested the theory out. His name was "Wild Bill" Belvin. He took to the woods for one year. When he returned, he had gained four pounds. In addition, he looked very well in spite of his being barefoot and wearing a homemade outfit. He had doffed his clothes and in their place made a skirt from palm fronds and cabbage leaves. He said he lived on wild food he had found and fish.

As I did research on the Seminoles, I discovered many very interesting things. One of the funniest was that Indians think that kissing—sharing saliva—is disgusting.

The courtship of an Indian maiden is well described by Glenn:

Her love of beauty is shown in this drams of color in her clothes, in the mass of beads about her neck, and in a multicolored hair net. [10] She is barefooted but her feet are clothed with her dress. She is about fifteen years old, and romance means just as much to her as it does to any girl of any other race.

When spring comes she will go with her father to the Green Corn Dance and she will meet and visit with a number of young Indian boys who live far away in other hunting grounds. Her pleasure with this one or with another will be shown by her laughter, the light in her eyes, the swift motion of her body, and her interest in her conversation with him. The two will find the place and the time to talk to each other, or to be together in the group games at the festival, or to eat at the same table. She will play the marvelous drama of "sweetheart" with the same beauty and appeal that young womanhood has known everywhere and at all time. But that drama will never be climaxed with a kiss, for she and her sweetheart shudder at the thought of a saliva-coated lip. They will show their love for one another more by deeds and less by words or expression. The implacable law of human conventions may turn the Romeo-Juliet of their lives into tragedy.

The old family clans mark off certain young men from her list of possible companions. A few Seminoles cannot marry at all, for tribal law forbids it.[11]

As with other races the parents are to be consulted, and respect for the father or the mother is a very strong force in this social set-up. If there are no conventions that stand in the way, after the two sets of parents discover that these two young people are in love, they make up their minds about the matter and discuss these options with each other. If they disapprove, they try to break up the romance, but if there is no objection the young man courts her as any other young man. He gives her his things, and she is as happy to eat a deer that he killed as a white high-school girl is delighted to wear the sweater that her sweetheart won on the gridiron.

If she and her sweetheart continue to love each other and to find happiness together, the parents of each family make up their minds that they want them to marry. A day is appointed. To the white man, of all the possible disappointments, this romance is climaxed with just that. (That's all there is to it.)

No tribe in all the world loves pageantry more than the Indian, and the Seminole has created the most colorful of any of the Indian tribes. But this marriage—this crowning hour of the greatest of all human drama—this wedding day is without pageantry. All day she watches the trails that lead to her home, and all day she hopes for sundown, and is eager lest he might not come. But he does at sundown, and do they run and kiss or does the medicine man invoke an undying pledge from one another? Nothing like that at all. She must tell him she is happy he has come, but he just comes to her camp and begins to live there afterward. His entrance into camp at sundown on the appointed day concludes the contract.[12]

The marriage over, now comes the daily living. The bride will soon be doing all the same things as the other women. She could help in making bread from the coontie root, which is a member of the cycad family. When the roots are gathered they are cleaned and are pounded in water so that they release a starch-like substance that can be used as a thickener or it can be made into flour. The flour will come from the sediment that settles in the water. It will be dried and then made into flour, then flour can be made into bread.

The bride will work in the fields and prepare food for the communal pot. I have been told that at meal time, when all are seated around the cookpot, one spoon will serve all the family. The spoon will be dipped into the pot, raised to a family member's mouth, and eaten. When empty, the spoon will be passed to the next family member waiting his turn.

When the women prepare for the "Green Corn Dance," large branches of the Florida holly tree are gathered for their red berries. This is not the regular type holly. It is a special plant: its Latin name is *Ilex vomitera* or *Yaupon cassina*. It contains caffeine. From these berries a drink is brewed for the men.

Author's sketch of Seminole chickees. Each chickee was considered a room in the house. Four to six cabbage palm trees support a thatched roof with a platform. Seminoles eat, sleep and work on these platforms.

At the Green Corn Dance, which is celebrated in the late spring, this brew is served to the men as part of spiritual renewal. The purposes of these dances are for spiritual renewal, fasting, dancing, naming of adolescents, and the administration of justice.

When the brew is hot enough, it is passed from man to man. Each drinks from the same bowl. When he begins to sweat, the drug is taking effect, he is no longer hungry or thirsty. The drink can be useful for cleaning out one's system as its name implies, Ilex Vomitera (vomit).

The central figure in this gathering is the Medicine Man who is supported by a council of elders for each band of the Seminole and Mikasuki people.[13]

Florida: A Guide to the Southernmost State says:

To appease Yo-He-Wah, the Seminoles make sin offerings twice a year, and hold the "Shot Cay Taw" (Green Corn Dance) on the first day after the appearance of the first new moon of the vernal equinox, the beginning of their New Year. The sin offering of the hunt is the rite of burning the first deer killed in a new season in the woods where it fell, an act which is believed will bring health to any ailing member of the hunter's family, as well as forgiveness for his sins. Another sacrifice is the custom of burning a small portion of every deer slain on or near the campgrounds, before the meat is prepared for a stew. When the stew is made, the Indians dip their middle fingers into the broth and sprinkle it over the graves of the women and children in the burial ground to ward off evil spirits. All the adult males are interred in the depths of the jungle.[14]

The husband will join the men of the family in providing for, caring for, and protecting his village. They can work jointly in making a dugout, or other activities that call for helping one another.

The making of a dugout canoe is still attended by great ceremony. After a powwow in camp, the leader guides his tribe into the swamp to select a cypress tree that is to be converted into a "pich-li," a craft often thirty feet long. Singing and dancing take place around the tree; then the men selected for the task, fell the tree, remove the branches and bark, and bury the "ash-a-vee" (cypress log) in a wet mud bank where it is left for eighteen months to age. The unearthing of the log involves more ceremony and feasting. After about a week of drying, work begins on shaping and hollowing out with a (pit-a-chen-a-1-gee) which resembles a hand ax. As the work progresses, the children join in, squatting around the canoe and beating on it with sticks. From the sound of this tattoo the cutters can tell when the desired thinness has been obtained.[15]

Returning to Glenn's *My Work Among the Florida Indians*, we discover:

When a child is born in an Indian home, the mother must leave her home and her bedroom and hide somewhere in the palmetto or brush, and there with a bed of palmetto leaves on the ground give her baby into the arms of a midwife. The father cannot see his child for a period of several days, and the mother and child must not come back into the Seminole house until the danger of death has passed. For if an Indian dies in one of these bedrooms, the whole establishment must be burned.[16]

Glenn continues:

Motherhood in our own race is compelled to carry on when it seems that the task is beyond all human strength.

The wastelands of the Everglades is very destructive to life. Vast stretches of rock and water interspersed with all but impossible sloughs, almost devoid of any food-producing plants, but covered with saw grass, and growing an abundance of water moccasins, with no roads and few sign posts, or even so much as land marks, with the grocery or drygoods store many, many miles away; a region which is largely nontillable and at times is flooded with water, wherein the game supply grows less and less each passing year, where there is frost at times, and frequently an all but devastating hurricane. In such a region, she sings her lullaby over her baby "Sleep my baby, sleep," or carries him on her own strong back and shoulders. She not only defends him from the blasts of storms, the ravage of disease, and the pain of famine, but she is the only grammar school, high school, and college he will ever have. Without books or newsprint, she must learn from nature and from folklore wisdom the "ages may have for her offspring." And strangely enough what was true and wise for her, in her childhood, is no longer *wise and true* today. Like the old south her old world has gone with the wind, and she, herself, is a stranger in the new world about her. On several occasions, when I have been lost, I have found her in her travel through the Everglades and she has guided me to my destination. Anyone who comes to know her and her work comes to honor and respect her.[17]

Kersey provides an excellent prognosis of the status of the Seminoles:

> Transcending all else was the Seminoles' sense of self, an awareness of belonging to a unique group whose cosmology began beyond the memory of the older wise ones. Their belief system was still firmly rooted in the land, in natural phenomena, and in the spirit world. Their time orientation, sense of fatalism, and code of appropriate behavior were generally at variance with the conventions of white society. Thus, there existed an inherent cultural chasm that could never be totally bridged. Indians might take on the material trappings of the white society that engulfed their land practice, scientific herding and marketing techniques, attend school, and even revise the way they governed themselves, but beneath it all they remained fundamentally Indian. Even the infusion of Christianity initially took place within a context that was essentially Indian, not like the Native American Church, which was a distinct religion, but in much the same manner that Mayan and Catholic beliefs were blended in the Mesoamerican church.

> From this point onward the Seminoles would constantly be seeking to achieve and maintain both personal and social stasis—an equilibrium that would allow them to survive the overwhelming changes of the late twentieth century. With greater mobility Florida Indians were inevitably drawn into prolonged contact with the dominant culture, and it became increasingly difficult to practice the old folkways or retain traditional values. Interpersonal conflict increased and the classic "caught-between-cultures" syndrome emerged to plague successive generations. Ultimately each Seminole would have to find the camp, light the fire, and sing the song— and be Indian in his or her own way.[18]

Endnotes to Appendix A

1. Glenn, James LaFayette, *My Work Among the Florida Seminoles*, p. 2
2. Ibid., p. 2
3. Ibid. p. 2
4. Ibid., p. 2
5. Ibid., p. 4
6. Ibid., p. 4
7. Glenn, p. 4
8. Glenn, p. 5
9. Glenn, p. 8
10. Ibid., p. 83
11. Ibid., p. 84
12. Ibid., p. 84
13. Ibid. p. 80
14. *Florida: A Guide to the Southernmost State*, p. 45
15. Ibid., 130-131
16. Glenn., p. 85
17. Ibid., p. 10
18. Kersey, Harry A., Jr., *The Florida Seminoles and the New Deal*, p. 179

Appendix B: The Koreshan Settlement

The Hendrys and other settlers were aware of the strange utopian settlement just south of Fort Myers, but most had little contact with Dr. Cyrus Teed and the Koreshans. I've included the following because the settlement was a curiosity to my father's generation.

According to historian Grismer in *The Story of Fort Myers*:

> In 1870 Dr. Teed "discovered" what he called "cellular cosmogony"—to most people an incomprehensible jumble of scientific, sociological and philosophical balderdash. Among other things, the learned doctor preached that the earth is a hollow sphere, 7,000 miles in diameter, and that the sun and moon and stars are all inside this sphere, along with all living and growing things. . . .
>
> He soon had a flock of followers who gave up their family ties and all their possessions. He named his organization the "Society Arch Triumphant" and proclaimed himself "Cyrus, the Messenger," a composite of Christ, Buddha and all other Messiahs.
>
> Deciding that the name "Cyrus" was not impressive enough, Dr. Teed later adopted the Hebrew equivalent of Cyrus—"Koresh." And he called his organization The Koreshan Unity.
>
> *The Chicago Herald* reported that in April, 1894, Koresh had 4,000 followers and had collected $60,000 in California alone.

Grismer noted:

> The *Fort Myers Press* condemned Koresh unmercifully and so did newspapers throughout the country. For instance, the *Tallahassee Sun* said March 16, 1907:
>
> Teed is not the first rascal who has made religion a cloak for his designs against the property and personal liberty of others. But he is the only one to do business in the state.

Teed began to complain that he was being crucified. The newspapers continued their assault and suddenly, on Tuesday, December 22, 1908, he died. Grismer continues:

> All activities at New Jerusalem were halted. No one talked above a whisper. He had told his followers that he was immortal; that after his "physical" death he would rise again, and ascend to Heaven, and that all the faithful would go with him. Everyone prayed. A constant watch was kept over his body. After two days his followers began having horrible suspicions. The body of their beloved messiah was beginning to decay and give forth noisome odors. And then, after four days, Dr. William Hanson, acting health officer of Lee County, appeared in New Jerusalem and issued orders that Koresh be buried forthwith.

> Reluctantly and sorrowfully, the Koreshans heeded the demand. They secured a bathtub, put the body of Koresh into it and placed it in a brick reinforced concrete tomb at the end of Estero Island. There it remained, year after year, until the great hurricane of October 25, 1921. Waves swept over the island and when the storm died down, the tomb of Koresh was gone. Not a trace of his remains was ever found.

Visiting the Settlement

I remember being taken to the Koreshan settlement when I was a child. In many respects it was nothing fabulous, just many large wooden two- and three-story buildings, in a state of disrepair. The lawns were dry from lack of water and plants and shrubs seemed uncared for or abandoned. Their days of glory had long passed. I did look for the little graves that I had heard were there and found none. Evidently that was just another bit of unfounded gossip. Men and women were to have lived in different buildings and they were supposed to be celibate. I later found out that the graves found were of children who had come to Koreshan with their parents.

Glossary

Definitions of Seminole terms come from James Lafayette's, *My Work Among The Florida Seminoles,* except where noted:

The Green Corn Dance: "The primary religious observance of most Southeastern Tribes is celebrated in the late spring by those observing traditional ways. Originally it was a series of ceremonies lasting several days. It was a time for fasting, spiritual renewal, ceremonial dancing, the naming of adolescents, and the administration of justice. In Florida, the central figure in this ritual was the medicine man, supported by a council of elders for each band of Seminole and Mikasuki people."[1]

Swamp Angels: mosquitoes

Fire Water: liquor

Satan's Angels: drunkards

Sofkee: grits

Devil's Angels: bootleggers

Cassina-Cacina Vomitera: holly tree

Ilex Vomitera Yaupon Cassina: A very hot brewed drink containing caffeine was served as part of spiritual rites. All drink from the same bowl. After drinking, sweat begins to form, the Indians are no longer hungry or thirsty. Helps clean out their systems.

Chickees: palm-thatched roof house, made with four to six cabbage palm trees and a platform under roof for shelter.

Inclemas Cha: good

Cochena: pork

Tuggilaggi: bread

Coontie Plant: an arrowroot starch plant that was used for food, soupy like grits. Also used to make cornstarch.

Macana Stick: A stick twenty-eight inches long with stones or pebbles encrusted in it.

Red Ochre Paint: war paint

Bohio: oyster shells, mud, and cemented lime

Sarsaparilla Tea: Indians taught the French how to use it, Spaniards boiled it and drank its tea to stay healthy.

Tabby: A construction material made of equal parts of lime, sand, oyster shells, and water. It was mixed and poured into forms.

Lacrosse: ball game, with twenty players on each side. Pine trees made the goal posts. One who carries the ball is confronted by the others. He carries the ball between his feet or propels the ball directly to the goal. His team mates assist him by fighting off the opposing team. The prize for winning is some small fish bones.

Dates of Interest:

First Seminole War over in 1818.

Second Seminole Indian War, 1835–1842.

1845 Florida became a state.

Third Seminole Indian War ended in 1855. Lt. George Hartsfeld destroyed Billy Bowlegs' garden. Some call it Billy Bowlegs' War. He surrendered thirty-eight warriors, eighty-five women and children and they were shipped to Oklahoma. In 1842, Billy Bowlegs became chief. When he surrendered in 1855 he settled for $1,000 for each warrior, each sub-chief, $500, and $100 for each woman and child.

Interesting Tidbits

In 1892, egret scalps sold for $1.25 (feathers were collected during mating season).

1901 it became against the law to kill egrets.

Glossary Endnotes

1. Surtevant, William C., "The Medicine Bundles and Busks of the Florida Seminoles," *Florida Anthropologist* (May 1954), pp. 31-70

Bibliography

A *Golden Guide to Orchids*. New York: Golden Field Guides, Western Publishing Company.

Allyn, Rube. *Salt and Freshwater Fishes*. St. Petersburg: Great Outdoor Publishing Co., 1969.

Anderson, Robert. *Guide to Florida Wild Flowers*. Winner Enterprises, 1989.

Baldwin, Neil. *Inventing the Century*. New York: Hyperion, 1995.

Beater, Jack. *Tales of South Florida Pioneers*. St. Petersburg: Great Outdoors Publishing Company, 1965.

Beater, Jack. *True Tales of the Florida West Coast*. St. Petersburg: Wordshop House, 1959.

Bell, Ritchie, and Taylor, Bryan J. and Florida Federation of Garden Clubs. *Florida Wild Flowers*. Chapel Hill: Laurel Hill Press.

Bell, Ritchie, and Taylor, Bryan J. *Florida Wild Flowers and Roadside Plants*. Bynum, N.C.: Joyce Kacherigs Book Design and Production, 1992.

Brown, Canter. Florida's *Peace River Frontier*. Orlando: University of Florida Press, 1991.

Brown, Robin C. *Florida's First People*. Sarasota: Pineapple Press, 1994.

Bullen, Adelaide K. *Florida Indian of Past and Present*. Gainesville: University of Florida Press, Gainesville.

Burnelli, Vincent. *Thomas Alva Edison Pioneers in Change*. Englewood Clifts, N.J.: Silver Burdett Press, 1989.

Clark, Ronald W. *Edison. The Man Who Made the Future*. New York: G. P. Putnam Sons, 1977.

Carr, Archie. *The Everglades*. Time-Life Books.

George, Jean Craihead. *Everglades*. Wild Guide Natural History Series. National Park Service, 1972.

Conot, Robert. *Thomas A. Edison, A Streak of Luck*. Da Da Capo Paperback Press, A Subsidiary of Plenum Publishing Corporation, New York, 1979.

Coon, Nelson. *The Dictionary of Useful Plants*. Emmaus, Pa.: Rodale Press, 1974.

Creary, Rosilans. *Edible Landscaping with Food Bearing Plants and Resources*. A Sierra Club Book, 1952.

DeVane, Albert. *Devane's Early History*. Volume I, Sebring Historical Society, Sebring, Fla., 1979

DeVane, Albert. *Devane's Early History*. Volume II, Sebring, Fla.: Sebring Historical Society, 1979

Duncan, Wilbur Howard. *Trees of the Southeastern U.S.* Athens, Ga.: University of Georgia Press, 1988.

Duncan, William H., and Foote, Leonard E. *Wild Flowers of Southeastern United States*. University of Georgia Press, Athens, 1975.

Ellis, Keith. *Pioneers of Science and Discovery, Genius of Electricity*. Wayland Publishers, Ltd. 49, Landowns Place, Hove, East Sussex BN 3 lHF

Fleming, Glenn, Pierre, Genelle, and Long, Robert W. *Wild Florida Flowers*. Banyon Books, Inc., Miami, Fla., 1976

Fernald, Merritt Lyndon, and Kinsey, Alfred Charles. *Edible Wild Plants of Eastern North America*. Idlewild Press, 1943.

Fernald, Merritt Lyndon. *Gray's Manual of Botany*. American Book Company. New York 1958.

Florida, A Guide to the Southernmost State. American Guide

Fritz, Florence. *Unknown Florida*. University of Miami Press, Coral Gables, Fla., 1963

Garrard, Jeanne, and Hannau, Hans W., Joint Authors. *Tropical Flowers of Florida*. Miami: Argos.

George, Jean Craighead, *Everglades, Wild Guide*, Department of the Interior, 1972.

George, Jean Craighead. *The Wild, Wild, Cookbook*. Thomas Crowell, 1982.

Gibbons, Euell. *Stalking The Wild Asparagus*. New York: David McKay Company, Inc., 1962

Glenn, James Lafayette. *My Work Among the Florida Seminoles*. Orlando: University Press of Florida, 1982

Godown, Marian, and Rauchuck, Alberts. *Yesterday's Fort Myers*. E. A. Seeman Publishing Company, Inc., 1975.

Gonzalez, Thomas A. *The Caloosahatchee, A History of the Caloosahatchee River and the City of Fort Myers*. Fort Myers Beach, Fla.: The Island Press Publishers, 1982.

Grismer, Karl H. *The Story of Fort Myers*. Fort Myes Beach, Fla.: The Island Press Publishers, 1949

Hanna, Alfred Jackson, and Hanna, Kathryn Abby. *Lake Okeechobee*. Indianopolis: The Bobbs-Merrill Company, 1948.

Hargreaves, Dorothy, and Hargreaves, Bob. *Tropical Trees Found in the Caribbean*. Portland: Hargreaves Industrial, 1965.

Harrar and Harrar. *Guide to Southern Trees*. New York: Dover Publishers, 1962.

Kersey, Harry A., Jr. *Educating the Seminole Indians*. 1897-1970, Florida Historical Quarterly, 49.

Kersey, Harry A., Jr. *The Florida Seminoles and the New Deal*. Boca Raton: Florida Atlantic University Press, 1989.

Jewel, Susan. *Exploring Wild South Florida*. Sarasota: Pineapple Press., 1993.

Luer, Carlyle A. *The Native Orchids of Florida*. New York: New York Botanical Garden, W. S. Cowell, Ltd., 1972.

McCay, D. B. *Pioneer Florida*. Tampa: Southern Publishing Company, 1918.

Moore, Minnie Wilson. *The Seminoles of Florida*. New York: Moffat Yard, 1920.

Morton, Julia Frances. *500 Plants of South Florida*. Miami: E. A. Seaman Publishing House, 1974.

Morton, Julia Frances. *Wild Plants for Survival In South Florida*. Miami: Miami Hurricane House, 1968.

Neil, Wilfred T. *The Story of Florida's Seminole Indians*. St. Petersburg: Great Outdoors Publishing Company, 1956.

Newton, James. *Uncommon Friends*. Orlando: Harcourt Brace Jovanovich Publishers, 1987.

Nicholas, Barbara, Wallis, M., Harrison, S. G., and Nicholson, B. E. *The Oxford Book of Food Plants*. London: Oxford University Press, Ely House, 1969.

Packard, Winthrop. *Florida Trails*. Pineapple Press.

Pearse, Eleanore H. D. *Florida's Vanishing Era* (From the journals of a young girl and her father). 1887-1910. Winnetta, Ill., 1947.

Peithmann, Irvin M. *The Unconquered Seminole Indians*. St. Petersburg: Great Outdoors, 1957.

Pritchard, Peter C. H. *Plants*. Vol. 5, Rare and Endangered Biota of Florida., Gainesville: University Presses of Florida

Richett, Harold Wilson, Editor. *Wild Flowers of America*. New York: Crown Publishers, Inc., 1953.

Ripple, Jeff. *Big Cypress Swamp and the Thousand Islands*. Colombia University of South Carolina Press, 1992.

Schell, Rolfe. *1000 Years on Mound Key* (revised edition). The Island Press, 1968.

Shounatoff, Alex. *Florida Ramble*. New York: Harper and Rowe, 1974.

Stone, Calvin R., *Forty Years in the Everglades*. Tabor City, N.C.: Horace Carter, Atlantic Publications, 1979.

Stone, Spessard, compiler, Jean Allin, editor, *John and William, Sons of Robert Hendry*. Bradenton, Fla.: Genie Plus, Inc., 1984.

Stone, Spessard, compiler, Jean Allin, editor, *John and William, Sons of Robert Hendry*. Revised 2nd ed. Bradenton, Fla: Genie Plus, Inc., 1989.

Tatum, Billy Joe. *Wild Foods Cookbook and Field Guide.* New York: Workman Publishing Company, 1976.

Vaegelin, Byron D. *Florida's Vanished People.* Fort Myers Beach, Fla.: The Island Press, 1969.

Watkins, John V. *Florida Landscape Plants.* Gainesville: University of Florida Press, 1969.

Will, Lawrence E. *A Cracker History of Okeechobee*. St. Petersburg, Fla.: Great Outdoors Press, 1964.

About the Author

Ella Kathryn Hendry is a former public school teacher and reading specialist who taught in Florida, Arizona and California.

She was graduated from the Florida State University and received her master's degree from Arizona State University. She is also a graduate of the Institute of children's Literature, and studied writing for children at the University of Alabama. She's a veteran of World War II and served in the WAACS as a War Room librarian.

She has been published in numerous magazines and newspapers through the country. She is also an artist, and has published *Honeycomb*, a children's book. Her art work has been shown in Phoenix, Tempe University and the University of Alabama.

A native of Fort Myers, she lives in Charlotte County, Florida, where she continues to collect Hendry family history.